James Pumpelly

Twice Melvin

James Pumpelly

Print ISBN: 978-1-54393-869-2

In memory of
Millie Pumpelly
and the marvel of second chances

Excerpt from Mary Pumpelly, New York, Charles Scribner, 1852
(on the beheading of John the Baptist)

There no funeral wailings loud,
No obsequies, that mourn the proud,
No hearse, nor hatchments, pall, nor shroud,
    Betoken mourner's gloom;

But glorious, more than regal halls,
That night, those narrow dungeon walls,
And honer'd were those mortal thralls,
    The prison, and the tomb.

That cell had been a place of prayer,
And holy angels waited there.
Upon a golden charger laid -
    At Herod's high behest -

The head was brought unto the maid,
In presence of the guests.
Receiving it, Salome spake,
    Impassionate and wild:

"Oh why, proud Mother! doest thou make
A pander of thy child!
Enough sure that a daughter's name
      Were sullied by her mother's shame.

"At last the hunted blood is shed -
The curse be doubly thine! -
Take, take this long devoted head,
      Oh would that it were mine!

"For he hath gained a martyr's crown,
And I! - the Homicide's renown!"

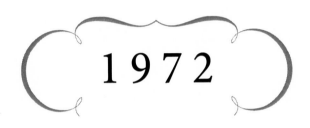

1972

To regret deeply is to live afresh.
(Thoreau)

I

MY STORY BEGINS WITH MY FUNERAL. BORN - AND soon to be buried - in Plainfield, Vermont, my quaint little village is about as close to monastic life as one can imagine short of taking the vow. More so when it's raining, which it is on this April afternoon, the valley's Winooski River chanting its way round barrier rocks like so many white-hooded monks, the overreaching elm and maple trees dripping penitent tears from the dampening breath of the mountains. At ease by a patchwork of houses, the rain-laden nods of native perennials acknowledge the wend-ing procession, not a few of their number in pious repose along the chancel of the Church of the Good Shepherd, its glistening steeple enshrouded by the morning mist. In the village church, stifled sobs accompany the rustle of rain across the skeletal stained glass, lancets of amber and rose casting gloom on my casket thrust up through the nestling blossoms.

But if anyone present is immune to the communal melancholy, it's my long-dead and recently reappearing Aunt Martha:

"Take a gander at this blubbering bunch of hypocrites, will you, Melvin?" Aunt Martha jabbing my ribs like Eve coming home to roost, our secretive stance, peering through vertical cracks in the vestry door, forcing the two of us closer than we've been in years. "Take Thelma, for instance, sniffling as if she were stretched out in that box, instead of you-"

"But Thelma has always been a good crier," I interject, "a necessary talent for her profession, I suppose."

"A Sunday-school teacher?" Aunt Martha derides, "give me some credit, Melvin. There's no call for tears in a kindergarten class. Not unless you happen to be on the wrong end of Thelma's 'board of education.'"

"Right," I whimper, recalling the board's familiarity with my behind. "Then again, she's championed some causes that could make anyone cry," I add, moving aside to give her the benefit of my view.

"Why, nephew, are-are you suggesting?" Aunt Martha halting in mid thought, "... no, I suppose you're not," she finishes, offering me her curiosity.

"Not what?" my attention now solely hers.

"Suggesting she had anything to do with your death," Aunt Martha emphasizing 'death' as though the very word is anathema.

"Foolish, indeed," I agree, chuckling at the thought of a Thelma Peabody harangue initiating some unfortunate's demise. "But if there's anyone out there who might have such ability ..." I edge back for another look, "it would have to be the reverend, his expertise in the supernatural more likely than Thelma Peabody's."

"Look at you!" she snips, "the pot calling the kettle black! I don't know which is worse: a lawyer or a preacher!"

"A minister, for sure," pride in my law firm serving me well. "An attorney has a legal right to charge for his services."

"And who wrote the law that makes it legal?" she cavils, "and who, but an attorney, can legally inflict a heart attack with the aid of the post office?" Aunt Martha puncturing my argument with yet another indefensible probe. "Between you and your law partner - that, that, that what's-his-face sitting a little too close to your wife - there's probably few folks this side of the Montpelier Statehouse who haven't opened a mailbox to the wallop of one of your bills."

"You mean George," I correct; Aunt Martha like a yammering coyote on my trail, "George is my law partner's name, Auntie, not 'what's-his-face'; and as to his proximity to Melody, George is merely acting the gentleman he is," I argue. "Should my wife feel the need of a compassionate shoulder, there's no bigger one out there than his."

Aunt Martha ignoring my rebuttal, motioning me to listen to the reverend, her interest in his every word not unlike her attention to hearsay.

"'Only that day dawns to which we are awake,'" the reverend quotes, "and for our departed friend, that dawn is a spiritual one, the kind of dawn Henry Thoreau may well have been referencing when he penned those words in *Walden*. We take comfort in the assurance our dearly departed is now awake to the glory of that new and spectacular dawn. He lives, our Melvin does. He lives afresh! Any regrets he may have suffered left behind, abandoned abruptly, even gladly, in that paltry portmanteau one drops at the crossing."

"Not bad ... not bad at all," Aunt Martha opines, patting my boney hand sympathetically, "but entirely too tame, this service of yours. Too tame, indeed. And I'm going to do something to liven it up. After all, you are my nephew, Melvin, and that makes you special! Makes you deserving of a better send-off than the old reverend's managing," her decision to tamper with the powers-that-be marking my death as nothing more than the inception of a new round of troubles.

For five days, Aunt Martha has been enlightening me on the superior skills of disembodied spirits (her passing, a decade before mine), our impromptu meeting occasioned by my sudden arrival. But it's onerously apparent she's kept up with the times, her postmortem antics in step with the latest events, the Right Reverend Rolundo (his big basso profundo waxing eloquent in my eulogy) hardly more surprised than I am as Aunt Martha begins demonstrating her savvy.

Falling rose-petal soft on listening ears, the reverend's pleasing elocution brings me back to my wife, her blue eyes misting with tears - then suddenly widening, as Aunt Martha's magical "thought imposition" finds a voice in the reverend; old Mother Eve's fascination with the unknown as nothing compared to the stark fear of knowledge in my beloved's eyes.

"Now as paradoxical as it may seem," the reverend's sonorous bass climbing to a decidedly stressful pitch, "profound thoughts can be more easily entertained in a comfortable setting. Why, even Thomas a Kempis could have improved his philosophy had he allowed himself a few luxuries ... yes ... and suspecting this, our Melvin ... aaah! our Melvin," his unnatural falsetto squeaks, "our Melvin worked feverishly for success. True, we may have thought of Melvin as an aspiring young attorney; but he was much more than that ... more, even, than all his sudden wealth and ill-purchased fame would have us know. He was a philosopher ... a thinker ... a bender of facts. Ah! and a bender of backs, I should add; a veritable genius in legal crimes!"

With this sudden and unexpected turn down tribute's trail, I can almost hear my mourners' heartbeats, the excitement of some bizarre or bawdy discovery perversely refreshing amidst the sickening sweet of funeral sprays, the one exception being Vincent Tenklei, an English Poetry student at Plainfield's Godhard College, his dark face glistening with a patina of sweat.

Vince had been my only charity case, his unique situation alerting my greed. Hailing from Rhodesia, Vince, I had schemed, could open a few international doors if I handled his case gratuitously, one involving a small fortune in some New York tenements bequeathed by his uncle. The simple matter of paying off a few tax liens acquainted me with his seemingly limitless offshore accounts - and his bankers, their shadowy world of hidden wealth a realm I hoped to explore. But now exploration is at my expense, Reverend Rolundo blundering on with his invisible, soprano guide.

"He had a painter's talent for color," the minister shrieks, his eloquence lost, his keen blue eyes growing spasm large, his labored breath, for all the world, portending angina pectoris. "Melvin knew the power of a pliant sentence; a well-placed word, peony brilliant; the charisma of listening. And how do I know this?" he whines, as though quizzing himself, "be-because ... because confiding in him was like dropping pebbles to the bottom of a well ... little secrets kept to be drawn when lust demanded."

By now, even Thelma Peabody is squirming to the edge of her pew. Perched scandalously close to Vincent, Thelma appears to be everything she taught me not to be as my Sunday-school teacher. The busiest old maid in Plainfield, Thelma manages to profit from her organic vegetable farm while organizing protest marches in nearby Montpelier - marches in accord with her Sunday-school interpretations of the King James Version, her rendition of Joseph's coat a Bible story I've never forgotten. Thelma's graphic, animated discourse on the metaphysical meaning of said coat's colors ("sacrificial red" among them) was more than an adolescent imagination should ponder in the winter-dark of a wind-swept, window-rattling night. The glowing embers of my bedroom hearth frequently birthed bloodthirsty fiends; the current rattling more the closet skeleton type, though the blood is my remembered own.

"Now full of distrust, now of angry courage," the Reverend's piercing pitch frightening the congregation, "Melvin Morrison never lacked for motivation. Prodded by pain ... drawn by delight ... he knew if he did what was in his lustful heart he mustered within him a loyal troupe, a deceptive effrontery, a bit of show that always kept us guessing, kept us ignorant of his sins: an ignorance allowing him a secret life at the expense of our blind admiration."

Vincent's nervous, choking coughs allow my entrance: "Surely you aren't going to tell them that, Aunt Martha," I plead. "Think of my Melody, my grieving wife, Melody. How could you?"

"No, how could you?" she breaks in churlishly.

"I-I was mortal then, remember?" I stammer, "unlearned in the scheme of things. It was my legal assistant, Charlene, who led me astray - the seductive way she retrieved a file, or served my coffee."

"But you never drank coffee, Melvin," Aunt Martha reminds me, "so don't be pulling that innocence ploy on me. I happen to know what that buxom little assistant of yours served up."

"I didn't know ... I-I mean, yes, of course I knew," I admit awkwardly, aware now that lies are as useless as pricked balloons in the ethereal realm of spirits, "but that's still no reason for you to meddle in Melody's memories."

"Right. It's you that should be doing the meddling," Aunt Martha rejoins, tugging me like a string of linguini through a crack in the door. "And if I were you, I'd get started right away, because it's hotter than old Nebuchadnezzar's furnace where you're apt to be going. Fact is, you'd better start doing some meddling now, and fast; start negotiating for another chance – which is what I'm trying to give Melody. Focus on Rolundo and you'll see what I have in mind."

But I can't, my thirsty eyes returning to my sweet wife's face like awestruck tourists to Trevi Fountain, Melody's innocence a patch of color on a somber day. For having slipped so unsubstantially through her youth, my wastrel years are now a haunting, a specter ever mocking morrow's call. Unlike the faithless who, when alarms pass, forget the saints, my memories unveil a conscience, the sacred spark illuming wistful might-have-beens - the Reverend interrupting my reverie:

"For all his father's stern admonishments, Melvin fared no better than Balaam's ass, the very angel's sword but scant restraint when pleasure called. Endowed with a prurient eye for the ladies, our Melvin became a man of easy virtue, an aficionado of feminine wiles, his backstairs reputation even now a thing of awe."

"Enough!" I implore, my inamorata fainting dead away, her nymphlike figure folding all too easily across the experienced lap of my law partner, George (brutish bachelor he really is). "Look what you've done, Aunt Martha! My funeral's not half over and you already have Melody in the lap of another man! Have you any idea what that scoundrel's like?" I ask testily. "In the game of romance, George O'Malley acknowledges no limits whatsoever. He has, as it were, an instinct for infinity, forever temporizing, regarding his randy blunders as inconveniences wrought by what he deems as the weaker sex."

Instantly, I recall Aunt Martha's own reputation, her former talents including an ability to discompose, the sum of my protests seeming to her as illogical as borrowing money to settle one's debts - as making further trial of my discretion, the Reverend's fulmination continues:

"In the game of carrot waving," he squeals, "Melvin Morrison was the consummate player. Though reared in the sanctity of a good parson's home, his scheming heart fairly rejoiced in the affairs of greed, his knack of rooting advantage from the pigsty of litigation evidenced by his recent victory in the *Rogue vs. Way* case. You must all be familiar with that one," he gasps, startled by his own observation. "The media was so unrelenting, so biased, the newspapers portraying the Rogue Sperm Bank's board of directors as venerable saints; the Boston bank's suit as heaven ordained; the bank's effort, to keep its depositors anonymous, as a public act of mercy; the poor Way's claim that their Rogue child had gone every which way but right, doing just that, passing on before a verdict could be rendered. And why? Because of Melvin's expertise in the chambers, that's why. One has to wonder just what sort of account Melvin kept with that bank."

This time, the protests come from the mourners, my partner, George, standing up with a contemptuous "Damn!" his martial manner pleasing me despite the fondling way he stretches my swooning wife on the pew. Too long have baited breaths been made to wait, too harsh their marked astonishment, George's Munchausen flair for the incredible redeeming my beleaguered reputation with precipitous effect.

"Objection!" George O'Malley booms. "Objection! What accounts my clie--, my partner may have had are not on trial here, Your Honor."

"Agreed," spits Rolundo, his skill as a religious raconteur lost in histrionics. "It's his second set of books we're interested in, his double-crossing entries that don't add up."

"Rev-er-end Ri-bald," George rumbles, stepping threateningly into the aisle, "may I approach the bench?"

"As you like!" Rolundo thunders, Aunt Martha's sudden withdrawal, before the menace of George, reducing the man of God to a state of dementia, his wrinkled face woeful, doom gathering about his shaming eyes and quivering lips as though he doubts the eternal verities.

"Now see here, Judge," my partner reasons, leaning across a cornucopia of carnations to within a whispering nearness of the pulpit, "I remember reading somewhere that compassion finds another's faults like sunlight after a shower; and if this be true, it accounts for our present pall of gloom; for nowhere in your callous ravings have you shown us a single ray of light. Now, I ask you, Judge, what kind of message are you trying to send here?"

"I-I don't know," mutters the befuddled minister, "b-but what I do know is what the good book tells us, 'In fire gold is tested, and worthy men in the crucible of humiliation', to which I humbly add Shakespeare's line, 'O, how poor are they who have not patience.'"

"Quoting Othello is not germane," George counters, "unless you're referencing the 'hell' in Othello's name. Is that it? For that's what you've been giving us for the last five minutes! I believe I speak for both sides, Your Honor, by requesting an immediate ruling."

"Acquitted!" Rolundo spewing the word like a wine-taster, as eager to feed, my mourners, led en masse by Thelma Peabody, rush the bewildered parson promiscuously - all save Vincent, who is sweating profusely; my wife, still lying peacefully on her pew; and Charlene Mally, my legal assistant, who, by taking advantage of the confusion, is bending over my casket to plant a kiss on my two-timing lips.

Now, I must explain that my funeral is in the early seventies, an era in which Vermont ladies are inclined to bedeck themselves with beehives, my native state forever behind the times - a.k.a. "backwards" - including Charlene Mally; which is why she is leaning over my casket from my top side down, her stiff-sprayed beehive fastening to the Vietnam War medals

Melody inappropriately pinned to my Brooks Brothers suit. And it's not until George, in his inimitable, commanding way, begins ushering my grieving friends back to their pews that anyone notices the provocative posture of a voluptuous female glued to my cold, dead face. As raucous as Rolundo was but a moment before, and as clamorous the crowd, not a sound can be heard save the swishing of wood-handled fans - as though the air is at fault for the view. Even George doesn't makes a move – a rare sight to behold – Charlene's undulating posterior rising and falling like Beethoven's *Eroica* in an eagerness to disown her score. And Aunt Martha? She's nowhere to be seen, or felt, or tuned-in, or however two spirits get in touch, leaving me alone with my body. My corpse, with Charlene attached.

The solution comes to me with the same dispatch with which Reverend Rolundo, decrepit as he is, sprints for the vestry door. Recalling what Aunt Martha has taught me in the five short days since, as she puts it, I "vacated the premises", I manage a permit to "reenter". Charlene may never kiss again, for the one I give her evokes such a shriek that it leaves her hairpiece affixed to my chest like a mohair vestment in sacramental brown. Literally tearing herself from my chest, she rears and whirls as though fending off attack, jumping astride George's back as my wife lets go a piercing scream at the phantoms deserting my casket - the sight of a headless horseman, galloping for the vestibule with the stolen soul of her man, enough to bring her round.

A revelation comes to me - and Aunt Martha, as well. Here I am, reposing innocently, my body lying, as it were, on a sacrificial altar, a catafalque of all the miseries I've left behind. And my peers? They're all, with one accord, rubbernecking: watching the spectacle of George and his wigless rider make for the exit. It's like I'm safe at the back of the world. No one sees me. No one, at the moment, even remembers me. I'm free. Unencumbered. Uninhibited. Free as a baby.

"That's a good idea, my dear," Aunt Martha chortles, startling me anew. "It's your second chance. One wrapped in an infant's blanket and placed under your own family tree. A tree planted right here in Plainfield. What more could you ask for? Being born again in your own hometown – which, come to think of it, is something your dear parents were praying you'd experience the last time around."

"What are you talking about?" I ask, surprised by her reappearance. "And aren't you ashamed of the mess you've made of my final respects?"

"Not 'talking,' Melvin, 'thinking,'" she parries. "Thought is our mode of communication now, not speech," she corrects, ignoring my question of shame. "Where once you thought one thing, felt another, said a third, and did a fourth, here your thought is clarion, the tongue's artifice of no account. Antiquated. And the sooner you concede that the gauze of speech can no longer hide old emotional wounds, the quicker you'll find you heal. The truth shall set you free, taught our dear Lord. Remember that one? No, I suppose you don't," she thinks rhetorically, giving my casket a piteous look, "but I know you remember the Rogue case ... the Boston sperm bank ... your deposits there, and how Melody yearned for a child. It's still possible, you know. The baby could be you!"

My eyes are on Melody again, the grieving villagers smothering her in ill-timed condolences. "Sorry about that woman," the Reverend's wife declaims; and, "Sorry about that crazy eulogy," Charlene's mother adds. A baby might be just what Melody needs, I decide. And pregnancy would be a good defense against George, too. (I recall several recent plights where George cried fowl when a lady cried wolf.)

"There you go again," Aunt Martha chides, "conniving will get you nowhere, Melvin. Truth. It's truth we deal in here. And I don't mean the kind you were paid to defend in court. Here, the truth shall set you free, not incarcerate you. Think about it: set-you-free ... rhymes with Mel-o-dy. Set-you-free. Mel-o—"

"I get it, Auntie, I get it."

"Failing to plan is planning to fail," she scolds. "Gotta make use of what you have ... or had."

"You reduce life's hurdles to croquet wickets," I argue. "You can't imagine how many purse-packets of tissues Melody cried into wads and shreds. If a baby were possible, we would have five by now."

A bone-rattling chill overtakes me as I recall that, while Aunt Martha was among the living, her strength was often derived from the weakness of others - my aunt's fingers doing a paradiddle on my casket. Suddenly, I find myself complicit in her Delphic implication. Maybe Thoreau was right: To regret deeply is to live afresh!

There is nothing more improbable than life,
its war of loss and gain so never-ending.

II

THE UNTIMELY DEATH OF MELVIN MORRISON HAS
become George O'Malley's Damascus. Transcending grief, his own life
comes back like curtain calls, his every indulgence a play on memory's
stage. Only three months have elapsed since Melvin's demise, but they
seem more like years; for George is thinking deeply, thinking himself into
depths he's never plumbed.

Maundering along the blue-iris banks of his late-summer pond,
George's morning is alive with promise, its color, its sound, all astir in the
Green Mountain breeze: the gently sloping meadows laughing with lupine;
foxglove bells dipping to the buzz of bees; bobolinks and purple finches
warbling their answering calls; even an army of ants appearing friendly, old
soldiers filing quickly out as though intent on following his lead.

But where is he going? At forty-three he is more than ten years
Melvin's senior, a disturbing fact nipping at his nonchalance like a rabid
dog. He's reached that ripeness of age when one should just sit back and
enjoy a kind of virtuous fondness for women, a time when imagination
should prevail over action, when desire should be sweeter than satisfaction. If he's known anything intimately, it's selfishness, its accusing finger
marring the walls of his solitude. With Melvin's death has come an awakening, a vision of life, of love – the promise of life in love - a season for

sharing, a quest for that happiness known only by two. A quest Melody Morrison personifies.

Melody is not easy to forget, her very name like the song within; her delicate beauty, her porcelain blue eyes, a comforting tune playing down the halls of George's mind - halls that should remain empty for a time, the smack of impropriety barring the doors; impropriety reminding him painfully of his flight from Boston, his attempt to start anew in Vermont. One tryst too many it had been - the wife of his Boston law partner. But Melody is different: a wife, yes, but a wife with promise, one who will eventually be coming out like a debutant at some merry widows' ball. Time is all that matters now: time to bury the dead; time to amend his ways; time to court the future, that ever beckoning part of one's life Melvin has proven dubious.

Circling his pond, his steps strike under him awkwardly, unsteadily, much unlike the purposed man he's always been; his array of courtroom triumphs having lent him a strut, a conquistador's grace, a way of exiting boardrooms and bedrooms as though danger were his sole pursuit. But now he finds himself mincing, cautious, fearful his pleasant rearrangement might fall apart, might crumble like his recent expectations: those randy desires he harbored when engaging a local commune to landscape his rolling grounds, to border his pond, to make his new estate as beautiful and wild as the hippie girls he thought his employment would buy. But they ignored his advances, going about their work like Pavlov's dogs, planting their flowers in a practiced routine allowing no notice of strangers.

And a stranger he is. A stranger in Vermont, and estranged from Boston, his escapades precluding his appearance in court – which is why Melvin had handled the Rogue case; another notch on the bailiwick that could have been his had he not forfeited it by a notch on his bedpost. Young Melvin had been his hand, his greedy finger from a safe but manipulative distance in the Back Bay pie - as well as a front to Vermont's nobility. For so these Vermonters seem to be, four generations the minimum tenure before one has right to the title. And now Melvin has abandoned him, leaving him a peasant in a princely realm. It's not as though these knights of the farm will do him harm; but neither will they take him in, their cold-shouldering silence shrugging him off with a kind of righteous, indifferent impunity.

What manner of man can flourish in such guarded soil? From dung he's sprouted, and by dung he's profited; though the stench drove him out

- his own stench, he admits, allowing a chuckle. He's pressed the grape of life to its last drop and still come away with a thirst; a deficit he blames more on the vineyard than any care he failed to give it. A logical conclusion, too, when one senses the pollen of life astir in the Green Mountain air. Even his old farmhouse seems more alive, more alert than the Charles River brownstone he abandoned, its chiseled facade, under a century of soot, but a stone-shuttered shadow from a lamp-lighted past. Still proud is the old house he bought in Vermont, proud as the brawny men who hewed it from the wilds, bequeathing it a kind of primitive grace outlasting the decay of years – years following each other like beads on a rosary till the house has become like a prayer, a chant in the praise of life, of living, of everything vital he's missed; coming, as he has, from a city where men spread their nets to catch the wind and only go home to die.

To die? Death is a certainty. Life is not. Life is a challenge echoing from Melvin's grave. A challenge for Melody. A challenge for him. A challenge best met by two - as from his rambling back porch he turns to survey his pond, the enveloping meadow, the distant copse of silver maples disturbed by the mountain breeze, their waving leaves like so many hands in a fluttering farewell from the past - a past he's pleased to quit.

The breeze comes down to play, to rattle the wind-chimes the hippies hung from the Boston fern, the music like that of a bell, a telephone summoning him through his house and into the front entry hall to press the black crescent piece to his ear, muttering, quizzically, as though questioning the source of the rings:

"H-hello ... hello?"

"George?" a sultry voice queries, "... George, is that you?"

"It's me, Charlene," George gasps, trying to sound composed, collected. "Just a little winded from a jog round the farm, that's all. Part of my new, holistic workout," he fibs, reaching for a horsehair chair he'd found in the barn and placed in his hall for some husband he might wish uncomfortable, "my spiritual regeneration. But what's up? Why'd you call?"

"Well ... I called," Charlene hesitant, selecting words as though avoiding a contretemps, "I called because I have an idea. A suggestion ...something to aid your regeneration."

"You do?" the old carnal man coming alive within, "and what makes you think I need help? Maybe it's me that'll regenerate you!" he blurts, suddenly thrilled at the prospect of conquest.

"Now George ... Mr. O'Malley," she parries coldly, "you know I'm not that kind of ... well, never mind what you do or don't know. What I meant was I have an idea for your practice. A suggestion that might bring you a client. You'll have to agree: it's been dead around here since .... ." Trailing off, she leaves the impression of tears.

"Now, now, my dear," George croons, his reformed persona doing battle with the inner imp, "I was just pulling your pretty little leg, that's all," he charms, wishing he could do just that – and more. "Now, tell me what you've got on ... on your mind!" he finishes with a start, stumbling over a recalcitrant imagination.

"Clients, Mr. O'Malley. Clients," she redirects.

"Call me George, dear. Save your Mr. O'Malley for the clients – if, or when, we land any."

"But that's just it, Mr. O'Mal-- George, that's why I phoned; because if you have no clients, I have no job - though I do have a solution," Charlene topping mundanities with an afterthought.

"Talk on, darling, I'm listening."

"All right ... George ... it's like this. I figure the locals don't need a stranger butting into their affairs when there are native attorneys who know whose skeleton is in which closet; and, more importantly, who has the keys. The way I see it, you're a sure loser in their view, a distinct disadvantage ... like some yokel trying to get sugar from an elm. You don't know where to tap," Charlene's red lacquered nails tapping her handset indicatively.

"And you do, I suppose?"

"Sure, I do; but I'm not a lawyer. All I can do is lead you to the right tree."

"And then what? Leave me out on a limb?"

"No, it's not that simple. For just because I point out a sugar maple is no guarantee it'll give up its sap. And even if it does, there's still the secret of turning the sap into sugar, you know. I reckon the Boston Irish don't know squat about that."

"You'd be surprised by what I know, sweetheart; especially when it comes to getting sugar from a sap," he chortles. But having learned that to admit error is to acknowledge wisdom, he thinks better of calling her down, presuming the merit of her intentions. "Forgive me, Charlene," he continues with delicate regret. "I should be thanking you for your concern, not arguing your point. But you've been painting the problem, my dear, not the solution; and I've been aware of the problem since the day I convinced Melvin he was the solution ... since the day we became partners. But Melvin's gone, and the solution with him."

"But it's not gone!" Charlene exclaims. "The 'solution', as you call it, is very much extant. It lives. It thrives in the memory of Melvin. And what better connection is there to that than his wife? Don't you see? If Melody Morrison were to let it be known she intends to complete her law degree and join the firm-"

"What?" George interjects, bouncing up from hard coil springs of the horsehair chair, "join the firm? Now, that would be a coup, a real sympathy grabber ... and a boon to my bank account, as well. But she's said nothing to me-"

"And she probably won't unless you go to her with the proposition ... you know, like she owes it to Melvin to complete his dream, to see Morrison & O'Malley into its second generation: Morrison, Morrison & O'Malley – the O'Malley moniker if you live long enough, the plurality of Morrison representing Melody and her son."

"Son?" George gasps, ignoring her disparaging reference to his age, "what son? They-they never had a son, Charlene. What are you-?"

"Melody's pregnant, George. Thinks it's a boy. And she's planning to complete her degree. Thelma Peabody told me all about it."

"Pregnant?" he echoes, "p-pregnant by-?

"By Melvin, of course," she quips peevishly. "Who else would it be?"

"But-but-"

"A Rogue baby, George. Melvin left ... well ... Melody was able to conceive after the fact, so to speak."

"The fact of what? ... Oh! the Rogue Bank! I get it!"

"Get it, or forget it, George," Charlene snips. "All that matters now is what we do with what Melvin left behind. His memory. A memory Melody can turn into dollars. Dollars, George. Dollars for all. The locals will back her. It's their civic duty, their Christian duty, their selfish duty, even, to keep the keys in trusted hands."

"... Keys?"

"The closets? The skeletons?"

"Oh, that! Yes ... well, if what you're telling me is true, it appears Melvin just let one out."

"What do you mean?"

"I mean that between the two of us - between Melvin and me - we slipped one over on the Ways. Turns out it was Melvin's last case – that *Rogue vs. Way* debacle – and since he's not here to suffer the consequences, I'll share a secret. There were two reasons Melvin represented the Rogue Bank in its suit to suppress the Ways. The first was because I got him retained. The second was because neither the bank nor Melvin had a choice in the matter. The suit had to prevail. Otherwise, the Ways would have learned who the donor was ... may have made it public; and that would have been the ruin of both the bank and its donor alike."

"And who was the donor?"

"Well, let's just say that after the way the Way kid turned out - lacking so many essential parts it gave up trying inside a year - there was no way the Way party could ever know the truth, which is why the Rogue Board and I operated sub rosa. We were the only ones who knew the donor's identity."

"Then, you ... you were the donor?"

"Now, I didn't say that, Charlene. I said I knew the donor."

"No, you didn't, George. You said you knew who he was; which is not necessarily the same as knowing him."

"All right, I knew him. But he didn't know-"

"He didn't know what? That you knew him? Come on, George. How can you know a man and he not know you?"

"No. I meant he didn't know he was the Way donor. Otherwise, there was no way he would've handled the Ways the way he did."

"... Melvin? It was Melvin?"

"You guessed it. But I swear he never knew. You see, Melvin was a regular donor while a student at Harvard - which is how I met him. Not then, but later ... after the Rogue Board called me in on the case. As a coincidence, I soon deduced that Melvin could be my way out. My way out of Boston, that is. I came up here to find him, prepared to tell him the perturbing facts ... especially, if it made me his partner. But disclosure wasn't necessary – telling him, I mean. Melvin was delighted to take me on. And

I was just as delighted to hand him his first Boston case. It worked out well for all concerned."

"But it didn't, George! It didn't!" Charlene squawks.

"How so?" George wondering if he should have kept his secret.

"Melody's pregnant ... and-"

"Not by Melvin, she isn't."

"But-"

"I know. You said she's carrying a Rogue child ... thinks it's a boy. Even thinks it's Melvin's. Well, believe me, Miss Mally, the Rogue Bank would never make the Melvin mistake twice! You can trust me on that one!"

"Oh! God have mercy!" Charlene wails, "first, Melody looses her husband ... and now her son's father. And I ... I ... Melody's been deceived, George. Deceived!"

"Said deception being in her best interest, Charlene; a kind of pre-conceived, deceptive conception."

"But I still can't believe it ... I-"

"What can't you believe, my dear?"

"That Melvin could-could've done this to me!"

"To you? What has he done to you, for heaven's sake?"

"Pregnant, George. I'm pregnant! The big PG!"

Woe unto you, lawyers! for ye have taken
away the key of knowledge.
(Luke 11:52)

III

SHADOWING GEORGE AND CHARLENE, AUNT MARTHA
feigns contrition, chiseling at my attention; but to no avail, the inscrutable
distractions of the Great Beyond leaving me so jittery the angels in our
neck-of-the-worlds are installing grid shields over their wings. According
to Aunt Martha (or "A.M.", as our winged friends refer to her), my night
flight over was erratic, my struggles like that of a drowning man, my frantic
grasping at arms and wings resulting in the fall of two angels. I don't recall
the episode, although A.M. assures me it was terrifying for my escorts.
Whether this is true or not, I don't know; but the sight of these delightful
creatures flying about with what looks like fan cages attached to their backs
is enough to make me wonder.

On the other hand, this second realm is no different from the first
when it comes to stories, much of Aunt Martha's lore reminding me of my
childhood nights, on my mother's lap, enthralled by the Brothers Grimm.
But there's one angel-tale A.M. recites that deals an "ace" to the end of
"grim". It has to do with Aunt Martha's thought imposition, or the reverse
thereof. She calls it thought deprivation. I call it theft.

As the angel-tale goes, there are roving bands of thought thieves up
here, flighty gangs stealing the past-ports of newcomers who led immacu-
late mortal lives. A.M. claims there's a thriving overgound, a kind of white
market where thieves sell their purloined past-ports to conniving souls live

19

set on returning to Earth – and making the journey, I should add, with far less karmic baggage than the freight train load they rode in on. But like my childhood myths, I have to assume angel-tales are the stuff of make-believe. I'm certain the Almighty keeps Her own set of books. I figure there's no one boarding a galactic train unless the ticket's been purchased, processed, and punched till the darn thing's holy. (And yes, according to Aunt Martha, the Almighty is a "Her", a theory I find comforting; rational, even, when remembering how impetuously my prayers were received: some answered, some ignored, some thrown back like a slap in my face. Or a black eye - like the night Sally Thurston's dad stomped up the stairs as I tried to raise Sally's bedroom window, cursing and praying in the same breath.)

Of course, the fact that these trains go out in all directions doesn't lesson the likelihood of the past-port tale. And I don't mean just east and west. Some of these sleek beauties fairly fly, shooting straight up into the wild black yonder, their stardust sparks reminiscent of the great iron wheels grinding America's transcontinental tracks. The lumbering giant A.M. calls the Soul Train reminds me of the coal burning locomotives I saw in the westerns as a child. "It's the beast of the breed," says old Jesse, a fallen angel who lost his wings in an attempt to hold up the train.

A one of a kind marvel, the Soul Train's means of propulsion is what some people on Earth would barter their eternal souls for if the trade secured them the patent. Perpetual motion, it is, a clever balancing of sinners and grief. An up and down, piston-like action reminding me of a skyscraper's elevator; only the Soul Train doesn't stop at in-between floors. Instead, it loads to capacity at Star View Station, with passengers and sins to bear, then descends, by the weight of the doomed and their cargo, to its deep and dark destination. Upon arrival, the passengers are ejected and their baggage thrown off; whereupon, the grief of sinners queued up at Star View Station acts as a counterweight to pull up the emptied train.

Trains and commerce go hand in hand, Star View Station a major going concern. Coming from Earth (and in particular, from a capitalist country; and more specifically, from the legal profession), I'm surprised to find money is not a medium here. Promises are the coin of the realm. The only similarity is the bank on which these promises are drawn, "In God We Trust" the golden inscription across all its precious scrip. And that's why I hold suspect the aforementioned angel-tale. Promises made on the white market, if there were such a thing, would by nature be worthless, such trading counter to what backs our scrip. Trust.

Another major adjustment for me is the absence of time; for, whereas – sorry, words like "whereas" and "wherefore" are difficult to relinquish, their pointing finger attitude still useful in my discourse with A.M. – for, whereas time was once my most valuable asset, my income escalating commensurate with my fraudulent over-billing for same, it's nonexistent up here. And with time out of the picture - I mean its practical application, the recognition of time as a dimension; for I still appreciate its limitations in Realm One - I'm impelled by new patterns of thought. It's confusing, too; like finding yourself standing alone in the middle of an infinite desert ("middle" a term you can understand since Realm One inhabitants think everything revolves around them). Another way to portray this phenomenon is to accept that the highflying space trains may not be "fast", my perception of their travel being what my prism allows me to see. But I haven't explained our prisms.

Upon arrival, prisms are among the most marvelous accessories we're issued. Despite the fact light is no longer blinding, we wear them like sunshades. I can see things in the distance as clearly as things up close. And what's more, I can look "in" as well as "out". I can review, for example, my nature, my uniqueness, my possibilities, my fate, as it were, should I choose to empower it.

Another accessory is the pack of filters accompanying the prism. One learns quickly to use them, their miraculous ability to block certain truths about all that protects one's sanity. Just imagine reviewing the missed opportunities in your life – and all at once! For me, it would be torture. A second death. But our filters have a compassionate quality, their blocks fading out, one by one, until at last all things are known. By then (the "time" of "then" irrelevant), one is ready to see all, to know all, to be all; that is, to be all one can be – which brings me back to A.M., back to her persistent blocks, her fascination with eavesdropping on the mortals we left behind.

"Two choices you have, Melvin," she's saying, or rather, "imposing" on my nervous, galactic thoughts. "You have a body developing rapidly in that other woman of yours, and you have a body in the womb of your wife. You need to choose before one of them goes on the white market ... before some stowaway ends up the captain of one of your vessels."

"Now wait just a-a-a damn minute, or whatever the equivalent is up here," I sputter, "you're confusing me. I can't sail more than one vessel at a time, can I? So how is it I have two ships in the harbor?"

"'Blessed eternity' is the expletive you were looking for," she corrects, "and regarding multiple vessels, pirate ships don't count. Besides, you already know which one is Captain Hook's; and if you don't, you need only check the manifests. One of them's hot, what's in the hold stolen from another's berth."

"To the point, A.M.," I interject, "it's truth we deal in here. Remember?"

"And promises," she appends, "'I do' counting high among them."

"If I've learned anything from you so far, auntie, it's that whatever it is you do is darn sure not what I do," I parry.

"Check your past-port, nephew," she chortles. "'I do' is what you did, not what I do."

"If I did what you do, or if I do what you did, I'd be on the Soul Train for sure by now. It's just you women who get off with those lame excuses: blaming the snake for provoking desire, the man for providing the snake; the snake for starting the fire, the man for failing to quench it."

"Ha!" she laughs, "you wish! I wouldn't be flattering myself if I were you, touting a mere worm as a snake. Worms are fine for bait, I suppose; but they're not what a woman wants to catch. She wants the big one, Melvin; the fighter, the pulls and tugs on her high-test line ... the veritable pole that wears her out."

"So ... are you telling me I should be Polish?"

"Earth no! To go back through Poland, you'd first have to check with Chopin. Rumor has it he's been handpicking all the male returnees of late - wants to be sure they know his *Minute Waltz* has nothing to do with baby making."

"Well, excuse me!" I think, pretending injury, "I fly corrected!"

"About your flying, Melvin, we've got to work on that, too. Somehow, you've managed to log a negative on your frequent flier account; and you know what that means."

"No, I don't," I ponder, "... unless it means I fly backwards."

"Close, but no dice," she rattles. "But never mind the problem, it's solutions we're up here for, and I've got one."

"You seem to have a monopoly on solutions," I throw out, thinking I'm on a roll, "... at least when they pertain to me."

"That's because you're all I have, nephew," she mumbles, "my last chance."

Although "thinking" is our ordinary means of conversing, we can energize thoughts, set sound waves in motion. But as energized as Aunt Martha is, she appears subdued, despondent, a pall of silence darkening her luminous face - like one of those gloomy ghosts huddling in line for the Soul Train.

"Me?" I ask foolishly, finding a space in her misery, "and what happened to my grandparents? Your mom and dad? I've posed the question repeatedly, but you never answer. So, I'll ask again: why aren't you looking after them?"

"But I am ... or did," she mutters, "... they'd taken off before I arrived."

So I have grasped her meaning. Grandma and Grandpa arrived with prepaid tickets, ready for a seat on the space train; which could only mean she hadn't, else why would she still be here?

"I know what you're thinking," A.M. protests, "but look at yourself. What are you doing here?"

"Mercy killing?" I offer sheepishly, hoping to lend her some cheer, "perhaps a sacrifice to atone for your sins?"

"There's no such thing as sacrifice here," she avers, regaining her verve. "Sacrifice implies denial, a doing without, a giving up of something you desire. You'll learn we don't do that here. We exchange, that's all. Its simple, effective, and infinitely more rewarding."

"But exchange can be a sacrifice, too," I reason, recalling how I'd overcharged my clients.

"Not here, Melvin," her gimlet-eyes reading my thoughts. "What we are in this realm is much nearer to what Plato described as the 'essence'. On Earth, we may have called a painting 'beautiful', or a child 'happy', but what we meant was the painting suggested beauty, the child suggested happiness; for neither was the essence of beauty nor happiness. Here, we learn to recognize this difference; as well as why the difference exists: to teach us to strive for betterment. We learn imperfection suggests perfection; imperfection defines perfection. Imperfection is the absence of perfection, as is sadness the absence of happiness."

"But," I argue, "not everything has an opposite. Take, for example, light. To say light is the absence of darkness is to deny light its power, its energy. It would be ludicrous to define light as non-darkness. To do so would imply a negative, suggesting light to be the absence of something else instead of the energy it is."

"Very good," A.M. complimenting me with an approbatory smile, "and what about truth? Would you define truth as the opposite of fallacy? Or perhaps the absence of fallacy?"

"No," I reply, some of my Harvard electives rushing to my aid. "Truth is pure. Truth exists alone. Truth is not the embodiment of good at some certain point, or some specific place, but that which never changes, never alters; whereas, fallacy exists only insofar as we enable it. Without our support, it ceases to exist. Truth, on the other hand, exists whether we support it or not."

Aunt Martha is duly impressed. "With such a philosophy, Melvin, your chances of being sent back are greatly enhanced."

"And what if I don't want to go back?" I conjecture. "What if I want to stay here? Or, what if I want to move up a realm or two?"

"Oh, nobody wants to stay here," she asserts. "One of my teachers explained it this way:

The goal ever recedes from us. The greater the progress, the greater the recognition of our unworthiness. Satisfaction lies in the effort, not in the attainment - joy lies in the fight, in the attempt, in the suffering involved; not in the victory itself.

"I know this to be true, because my classes are filled with people studying to improve, to move on."

"Classes?" I query, fearing some correctional curriculum for which I'll have need of patience, or worse yet, humility. "What kind of classes?"

"The subjects are unlimited, infinite in variety."

"As well they should be," I banter. "Any university domiciled here is the ultimate institute of 'higher' learning."

"Not so, nephew," A.M. thinks bumptiously. "There are others infinitely higher. And I know whereof I speak, too, because I was told this by a most reliable source."

"Who?" I ask, at a loss as to what she means.

"Why, Gandhi himself!" she vocalizes emphatically, a bit of pretense in her tone.

"The Gandhi?" I cry, even the thought of Aunt Martha conversing with the great Mahatma giving me chills where my spine used to be. "That's impossible!"

"Hardly," she challenges. "Gandhi was the little fellow teaching our class – History 1001 - his preface to our studies unforgettable:

The first thing you have to learn about history is that because something has not taken place in the past, that does not mean it cannot take place in the future.

"There!" I shout, assuming I've trapped her in specious swagger. "Gandhi would have never said that – at least, not up here; for to speak of the past is one thing, what with all of us coming from Earth; but to reference the future is quite another, since time is not a dimension here."

"Think of 'future' as 'forward' on a movie projector dial, and 'past' as 'reverse'," she demurs. "In this way, you can turn the dial in either direction to view some scene or another, all the while remaining in the 'present'. That's what Gandhi's teaching means: just because we've never achieved perfection in the 'past' doesn't mean perfection is unattainable. You see, Melvin, Gandhi is still like he was on Earth, living for others rather than himself; his great love for his fellow beings allowing him to pass through many realms to teach whatever is needed; though, by rights, he could be residing in the highest heaven."

"Ah!" I sigh, considering what she's implied. "Then, some of us can go wherever we choose. Is that it?"

"That's it," she answers flatly, her ready agreement lacking the spark of participation. "And once comprehending this, we discover a delightful prospect: we can be transformed, then translated; 'translated' the term used when one moves to another realm. We can exchange any lack for the fullness of its opposite being. In fact, that's what I'm doing with you, Melvin: exchanging all my misspent Earth years for the value of yours yet to be."

I am dumbstruck.

"Thoughtless, are you?" she asks, reading me like a blank page. "Oh well, don't let it bother you. It's just part of being male."

"Paid me back, didn't you?" I tease, thankful to see her returning glow – thankful, even, for her unfailing memory, the episode reminding me of an epigram I pandered to witnesses:

> For if the power of mind has been so changed
> That all remembrance of the past has fled,
> That is not far, methinks, from being dead.

But even as I toy with my recollection, musing on the merit of sharing it, A.M. snatches my plaything away.

"Lucretius, Melvin?" she bothers to vocalize, "you are quick to learn ... and that's good. Good for me, as well."

"And so it is," I rejoin, amazed she recognizes the author of my little courtroom ploy, "and your knowledge of Lucretius ... I just never took you for a scholar, Aunt Martha, notwithstanding your acquaintance with Gandhi."

"And I wasn't ... I mean, not when I was your aunt," she admits, "but I was there - on the scene, so to speak - when my Roman contemporary was spouting his stuff, his *De Rerum Natura* all the rage among my radical friends; his attempt to explain the universe in scientific terms, to free people from superstition and fear – especially fear of the unknown - something needed even now"

"My goodness!" I think with a shudder, "that would be sixty, seventy years before Christ! Surely you're not that-"

"Old?" she finishes for me, her defense fully summoned. "'Old' is a spurious adjective, Melvin, as is 'experienced'. No. Such words are besmirching. They leave a woman feeling tarnished. 'Aware' is a much better choice. Or 'learned'. 'learned' and 'sensitive'. Yes, 'sensitive'... now that's one that'll open doors."

"Bedroom doors?" I crack.

"And just who am I to be suggesting that to you!" she charges. "But since you brought the subject down, allow me to quote your Roman poet, my enlightened contemporary:

> ... it seems absurd that souls should stand
> Beside the marriage bed, ready at hand,
> And at the birth of beasts; that without end

For mortal husks immortals should contend,
As in a race, to beat the others in!

"You're casting pearls before swine," I venture, amused by her sem-
blance and show; wondering if it's obstinacy more than constancy that
keeps her with me. "Of the two little gifts being wrapped down below, neither was found in a marriage bed. And as to beasts, I have to believe you're
referencing yourself, Aunt Martha, going back, as you claim, to Rome's
seven hills and the suckling wolves."

But try as I might to engage her, she's gone, tugging me along to
attend her favorite sport. Spying. It's about as near to Eden as I'll ever be –
what with me playing Adam and Evesdropping.

Put all your eggs in one basket and watch that basket.
(Andrew Carnegie)

IV

CHARLENE'S PREGNANCY IS THE BEST KNOWN SECRET in Plainfield. Between the chicken and the egg, there's no doubting who has the egg, making George the suspect chicken. When your number's up, it's up, and guilty or not, George is taking heat for Melvin. If the truth be known, Plainfield's gossips would take the same pleasure imagining Melvin taking heat down below. But they don't know, making George their man.

George is in an ecstasy of pity. With Melody's heart in a sling, he yearns to woo her: widow, gorgeous, graceful; even a fool not missing her rhythm. But there's Charlene, as well: single, seductive, pregnant; her rhythm long missed by a fool. And after Charlene's visit with a Boston specialists regarding her baby's prospects with Melvin as father, George is uncharacteristically focused, the specialist supporting Charlene's belief that Melvin may or may not have been responsible for the way things turned out for the Ways. Her delusion allows George to try another man's shoes. "One step at a time," he counsels himself, "one step and you're halfway there" - "there" growing so large in his mind that imagination moves out (as well it should, it having dirtied the place for too long), leaving Charlene in charge, his chatelaine. And not only of his dream-castle, but of his law practice, too, her intuitive vision of Morrison, Morrison & O'Malley trans-muting into real agreement. For Charlene, there remains only the dilemma of moving O'Malley to the head of the moniker, things changing so, since

Melody committed to the firm (and George to the baby) that she rues her intervention.

Her secrets are public now, *The Plainfield Press*, like a tardy town crier, announcing what is quietly known, redeeming the gossips by the glare of two cryptic calls: Morrison to Harvard, then Home to Hang Shingle & Diapers; and, O'Malley to share "O" with Miss Mally – the latter reducing George, in the smoke of tavern jokes, to just what it might be he's sharing: whether the "O" stands for Obscene or Obstetrics.

Despite all the butts and rebuttals, when the smoke clears, the press has measurable effect. Clients. Clients compelled by their wives' curiosity. Clients compelled by their own curiosity. Clients clamoring for George's time, inventing disputes a big city lawyer might settle, and congratulating him - if not sincerely, at least salubriously - on winning the pearl of great price. It's as though he's found the philosopher's stone for all the handshakes his sore arm is suffering; an irony bringing a smile when he considers what might have happened had Melvin not died. It isn't that Vermonters lack a worldview - one James Wilson, of Cabot, Vermont, fashioning America's first globe way back in 1810. No. It's what this view purports: no matter how slowly the world turns, Plainfield consistently places second.

Plainfield natives work diligently for their moniker, "plain" a euphemism for most of the village women, while "field" describes the flat stretch of valley shared with the Winooski River - "Winooski" yet another euphemism: the Indian word for "onion"; though it's probably the "plain" more than the "field" that has the onion's effect on tourists.

Melody and Charlene are patent exceptions. The prettiest, so far as George can tell, their beauty like the pall of death on their peers. But do we call it dying when the bud bursts into bloom? George reasons. Maybe so, if Melvin had been discovered in crime. And it was a crime, George conjectures, imagining himself a local; for it was audacious of Melvin to enjoy more than his share - nay, double what is culturally allowed!

Then again, maybe Melvin's affair - even Charlene's pregnancy - would've passed unnoticed had he lived. After all, the natives take pride in their Godhard College, an institution renowned for Liberal Arts - an enigmatic fame translating to "anything goes." The college has not let them down. In fact, about the only thing Godhard has let down is the jeans of its student body, the liberal art of tattoos on butts and bellies everywhere – Vincent's unblemished derriere notwithstanding.

Vincent Tenklei has renewed his bond with the firm, retaining George for his latest dilemma: Thelma Peabody. Upon Vincent's overt display of grief at Melvin's funeral (his profuse perspiration mistaken by some as "buckets of tears"), Thelma appointed herself his grief counselor. "Organic vegetable patch be damned!" she railed, "and protest marches to boot! I'm going to see you through this emotional trial if it kills me!" which it almost did: Thelma collapsing, in the dead of night, on the young man's dormitory bed. Not to be outdone by calamity, Thelma let it slip - so to speak - that while her attacker was trying to escape, she espied her name tattooed on a cheeky part of his body.

"Such a rumor is more than I can turn the other cheek to," Vincent confides to George, "in as much as the other cheek may be the one in question – if you see my point."

And "see it" George does; or rather, "not see it", the Polaroid he shares with Judge Nancy Whittaker providing the judge's first peek at a dark moon, a tongue-in-cheek chuckle, and a hasty cease and desist.

With marriage approaching, George is determined to shoot straight, the incident he dispatches for Vince about as close as he comes, post engagement, to unseemly action. But with George, even the lack of a problem can become one, his new resolve a matter of mind more than heart. Commensurate with his resolve plays the chatter of success, his new clientele tending toward the distaff side, wives who find it prudent to seek council from elsewhere. Coupled with this growing temptation is the restraint Charlene blames on her condition, refusing the innocence of a kiss, detouring the whole of his natural urges to a distant and unfeeling future. Even Judge Nancy Whittaker plays the temptress of late, inviting him into her chambers on the pretext of tea for two, dropping hints, along with her robe, about his expertise with a camera. But despite such judicial buttonholes and juridical loopholes, his resolve is winning the day - if not the night - until Thelma makes her move.

Not to be outmaneuvered, Thelma takes Judge Whittaker's cease and desist as a call to action: contriving the Melvin Morrison Memorial March. Though George can't publicly oppose the scheme (any tribute to Melvin benefiting the firm), he can well oppose the schemer. There is just no telling what might appear on Thelma's placards. The more he ponders the possibilities, the larger her specter grows, until, with apprehension outweighing judgment, he prays advice from Judge Whittaker.

"What to do? What to do?" he moans, "any action I take will be amiss."

"Why not manhandle the issue? Or, if you like, I'll handle it for you," the judge coos, switching off the lamp by her sofa. "I'm only too delighted to help."

George is not solely to blame for his indiscretions. Hidden deep in his tragic gray eyes is something that makes women melt, something that arouses their nurturing instinct. Tall and muscular, with just enough Irish ruddiness to boyishly blush his cheeks, his shock of curly, chestnut hair is the finishing touch, ladies sooner thinking him just down from Olympus than starved off the Emerald Isle. It's this god-like aspect that leads him perilously close to the altar; only his scandalous escapes reducing him to mortal.

What George lacks is a need to love - a need fatal to liberty - George skirting the nuptial sacrament with increasing aplomb. Skirting, until now; Charlene blinding him to the snare, what good there is in his self-filled heart playing hero to a damsel in distress – perhaps, because for once he's not the villain.

Charlene, that pert little vixen, minds not the least his rescue, her condition taking no account of facts. With a charm that's cereal-crisp and just as thin, she woos George to submission, his resolve expressed in commitment. "Your child - our child - will not be fatherless," he wheedles, unaware she provokes his cajolery - Charlene thinking: as fathers go, George has a reputation for leaving; a tragic possibility that might rank me up there with Melody.

Melody is more than a wife; more than an obstacle to be challenged. With Melvin gone, she's an icon, a virtual virgin to worshiping men; a fact abrading Charlene's patience – not so much the virgin image as the worshiping thereof – Charlene's desire to be desired eroding propriety; which is why she conspires with Thelma.

Wiry as the beans in her vegetable patch and gray as the line she crosses, Thelma has lost nothing to her years, her snapping black eyes still as virulent as her long-remembered wedding day. Ever mindful of that fateful winter's day, of a hope grown cavern cold, it has become the pain fueling her beacon, her guiding light for "women's rights" - Thelma standing statue-still atop the church house steps, bleached fear-white as she waits, despairing, staring out across the sleet-marbled lawn with diminishing hope he will come, a hope strangling on rage until her blistering oration before the holy dais wilts the very flowers.

"If a man can't make it to his own wedding," she advises Charlene, "he can't make it anywhere." Admitting, nevertheless, that love is the one thing a man can make. "If George O'Malley marries you, he will at least be there for that!"

"Having been there once, to return lacks the appeal of discovery," Charlene retorts.

Their difference of opinion poses no threat to conspiracy, reason being a slave to revenge: for Thelma, Melvin to be a de facto defamer; for Charlene, Melvin to be in fact defamed – a slight to tarnish Melody.

Melody, however, is anything but tarnished. Glowing from having lived so deliciously, her love for Melvin remains fever hot, her candle-scented evenings sweet windows of mind, the past wafting by like bright colored leaves to collect in soft, rustling heaps. And though her studies are ill-timed for childbearing, Harvard gives life to her memories, a symphony of scenes ever playing: the old horse chestnut tree on the Common, witness to their misty engagement; their ethereal plans for the future, dream-built in the stillness of Walden; their moon-kissed midnights on blankets, serenaded by the river Charles; their all-night, coffeed-out crams for exams before ecstatic release in lovemaking; Melvin beside her - then, as now - only now she carries in her, about her, a dream; a hope; an expectancy growing larger than life.

Returning home for an October weekend only amplifies the dream, the nearness of Melvin: lovers strolling through her father's orchard to the scent of apples-turned-cider under trees; hiking hand-in-hand over trail-crossed hills all ablaze under maple and birch; a table for two against a firewood wall in the old Montpelier tavern (a table shared, on a winter's night, with chattering legislators bringing disputes from the Statehouse next door, their farm-spun philosophies, their family names, all older than the flag they serve); the snuggling drive home, their hearts all aglow, their hopes Eiffel high - their love, eternal and warm in the feathery breath of dreams.

Yes. It's good to be going home – if only to remember.

From the heart it has sprung, and to the
heart it shall penetrate.
(Beethoven)

V

CLOSE AS HILLBILLY COUSINS TO OUR EARTHBOUND
friends and family, Aunt Martha is making literal one of my mother's
expressions, "moving heaven and earth" to get what she wants. And what
she wants is making me frantic in a realm with no frenzy; which, along
with flying backwards, is making me an anachronism in a realm with no
time. I am out of it, in to it, kept from it, led to it, blamed for it; in short,
fit to be tied to it, if guarding it can spare it from Martha. But as the novice
under Martha the master, my aunt calls all the shots (something I would
gladly do if I knew how to aim one at her).

"It", of course, is the Melvin Morrison Memorial March, the pending
triumph of Thelma Peabody in unholy alliance with my "other woman."
And not just my "other woman", but with scores of this branded class,
Thelma organizing a new women's cause under "miscellaneous"; a cause
with immediate and catastrophic effect, if the marchers live up to her slogan: "Miss Cellaneous is opening her files". Even old Reverend Rolundo,
as Aunt Martha irreverently reveals, is keeping Helen the organist in tune.
And George? Now that he lost, or rather, misplaced his resolve, he's setting a pace even Aunt Martha has trouble matching, his troupe of pending
divorcees approaching SRO in the old Montpelier tavern. I'm concerned
for George; though not for the same reason as Aunt Martha. I've never
known him to drink, his vice relating more to a wolf than a wagon; but

now he's wolfing them down, quaffing such quantities of Guinness Stout his exit requires a lady on each arm to see him to bed – a staggering sight that steams Aunt Martha. (Or a steamy sight that staggers Aunt Martha? Either way leaving her as drained as George.)

Unlike A.M., my concern is not for the pleasure of his tavern-going clients, but for the incessant pleasure of his tavern-going. For the more chances he takes malting his parch, the less are his chances of halting my march. So, while Aunt Martha remains absorbed in bedtime affairs, I have to create a distraction, something to keep her from Thelma's debacle.

In all my excitement with everything new, I've yet to visit my parents, their crossing occasioned by an accident a few years before my demise. It's a reunion I genuinely desire - the more so if it saves A.M. from her madness. Setting my distraction to work, I think decisively:

"M-y f-a-t-h-e-r."

Getting no response, I try again, straining to surpass what is capturing Aunt Martha's interest:

"My father!" I shout aloud, "my father, and my dear, praying mother. Where might we find them now, auntie?"

With a piqued look intended to make me seem the guilty one, she answers at last, "I'm surprised, Melvin, that you haven't inquired before. And after all you put them through, too ... sewing your wild oats. No wonder your dear mother spent her nights on her knees – probably praying for a crop failure, if you ask me-"

"Which I am not," I break in. "But I do want to see them ... to apologize for the worry I caused them; and," I admit, succumbing to a tinge of triumph, "I'd like to see how they've adjusted to a place so different from the heaven they expected."

"Oh, that didn't take long," she cracks sardonically, "their contrition for preaching the 'don'ts' without the 'dos' was so sincere they were put on an express back to earth."

"You mean, I-"

"I mean, Melvin, you can't visit them when they aren't here anymore. Your mom and dad are down there again," she thinks convincingly, my gaze following hers to a little Appalachian town appearing to rise out of the midnight mist. "They're six years old now – your mother a boy and your father a girl - but they've already met at a summer camp meeting, making eyes at each other during prayer."

"Camp meeting?" I echo, recalling the sawdust floors of my youth. "Are they going to tread the same path as before?"

"All paths lead to truth, my dear boy, if only we go far enough. The last time, your parents got stuck on the first page of rules ... never looked up to enjoy the game."

"The rules?" I ask, wondering if A.M. really has all the answers. "Might those be the rules we were following tonight while peeping in on George's game? You know, 'rule of the roost', and that sort of thing?"

"Get too cocky, nephew, and you might end up like this youngster." Zooming in on my mother - his little bed but a pile of rags by a potbellied stove - she rattles the coals for his warmth.

"Better to be loved than lost," I reply, referencing my current condition, "besides, poverty has fathered many a great man."

"Don't give me that bunk," she snips, whisking me off to my father. "In a universe replete with supply, demand has no cause to lack. Just look at this poor little girl," A.M. adjusting my father's ragged coverlet, "shivering in a coal-dusted shack while there's coal aplenty to warm mansions."

"I suppose you're going to say the folks in those mansions should be supplying the coal needed here," I remark rhetorically.

"Not the point," she ponders with annoyance, "it's the choice we make that allows that to be."

"So, am I to understand-"

"You're to understand if men would refuse to toil in the mines until their wages were commensurate with the price of mansions, then-"

"Then mansions would be nonexistent," I finish for her, "or coal in over-supply."

"Oh, enough of this," she cries, flitting over Boston Harbor before I can argue the point. "I've done what I can - shown you haste makes waste."

"I don't follow-"

"Your parents' eagerness to return to earth, their continuing lack of patience, earned them births next available instead of selection by merit. Take, for example, your Melody," she continues, closing in on a Back Bay brownstone with a view of Longfellow's Bridge and a distant, hazy Harvard. "Before entering her present life, she waited patiently for parents most suited to teach her the lessons she needed. And though she came to them late in their life, it only made them love her the more. And now? Well, now she's practicing one of her lessons learned: giving birth by choice – a commendable start for any contemplating soul to consider."

"I suppose you're referring to me," I think meekly, just the nearness of Melody humbling me after all I'd done to dishonor her.

"Regarding a commendable start, yes; but as to contemplation?" she appends, rocking from side to side, convulsed in an agony of merriment, "I don't think so, Melvin. No. I wouldn't call coming home drunk after winning that Boston case-"

"Not the contemplative type, am I?" I interject, the while contemplating the sleeping beauty before us, her pictures of me on the bureau, on the wall, and on the nightstand near the crucifix I'd bought her in Rome. "Then contemplate this!" I snap, removing my prism and fixing my gaze on the cross:

> Twenty centuries past a star
> And still the moment lives
> When love came gently down;
> The healing hand sent from afar
> To pained and hopeless gives
> A peace on earth unfound.

"Very nice, but unpolished," she remarks, "a diamond in the rough."

"A diamond, to be sure!" I retort. "Melody inscribed those lines to me on our first night in Rome. We were-"

"I know," A.M. cutting me off, "... I was there."

"You-you were?" I gasp stupidly, her curt admission leaving me colder than I already am; for I had not, until now, considered what private moments she may have invaded.

"Yes, and Melody was expressing her love for Christ, not-"

"Hush!" I fume, not wishing my memories altered, "what's done is done. What's needed now is a plan for the future."

"What's done is done," she mimes, "a plan for the future. Why, Melvin, you speak as though time were real."

"I'll tell you what's real," I say, through tears where no tears should flow, "Melody's love, that's what. And to the extent it's confined to the body beautiful there is how much I believe in time. And what's more," I add sorrowfully, "it's being wasted."

"How quickly you learn," she murmurs, her customary quibbling subdued, "if ... if only you had listened before."

"Listened?" I ask, her murmurs not as audible as her thoughts.

"Yes ... listened to the voice within. That still, small voice ever there if we listen."

War-daubed, her patchwork face seems yet in battle, her fire-blue eyes still keen for quarrel, there being not one among our relatives whom she hasn't bested in her time. But as I observe her in the peace of Melody's sleep, the truth of what she has said begins spreading as light across her scarred and wizened mien, her cloistered spirit unfolding like some gold and bejeweled chrysalis, her velvet rays of forgiving love reaching out to touch my tears. And I love her in return, understanding who she really is - how alike we tortured souls must be within our pride-erected walls.

"You've got to go back to her, Melvin," she affirms sweetly, her very words a heart's caress. "Her faith requires it ... her love demands it ... and your love, dear ... your love can do no less."

"So be it," I whisper worshipfully, placing Melody's crucifix, with a photo of us together in Rome, atop the empty pillow on the double bed, "... so be it."

Not every man that saith unto me, "Lord, Lord," shall
enter into the kingdom of heaven…
(Matthew 7:21)

VI

PASSING OVER NOT LONG AFTER GIVING HIS DAUGH-
ter's hand, Melody's father left his wife Thankful to look after their only
child. "Happiness is a clear conscience, a kind heart, and a worthy aim,"
Thankful's husband had been wont to espouse; and with Thankful in cheerful accord, her worthy aim - indeed, her only aim – is the happiness and
well-being of Melody. And now with Melody coming home for the weekend - home from Harvard to stay with her mother instead of going back
to the house Melvin had purchased in the village - she wants the old farm
to be as it was, the familiarity of things to have that indescribable sense of
welcoming, that peculiar amiability with a placid past.

Hobbling happily through her chores, Thankful abandons her
kitchen routines for the memories in Melody's room, adjusting the lambre-
quin over the mullioned window to better invite the sun; shaking a throw -
passed down from her own dear mother - to drape over the rush-bottomed
chair; dusting the silvered glass in a birch-bark frame her grandfather had
made as a boy; smoothing imaginary wrinkles from the patch-work quilt
laid out across the old rope bed; filling a bulbous, porcelain, blue jardinière
with the best she can find in her hothouse; all the while letting slip an occasional sigh belying her inner delight, her round-shouldered stoop seeming
out of place, out of character with the spark in her eyes - her face like unto
one who has seen an angel, as she answers a backdoor knock.

Far from an angel, the caller is Simon Farley, out on one of his bike rides, requesting a dip from her deep-water well. As Plainfield's would-be poet and needs-be bicycle repairman, Simon's most talked about line is his own name, his comic insistence on being addressed as "See-*MOAN* Far-*LAY*" outshining his most ardent verse.

"And to what do I owe the pleasure?" Thankful's face losing some of its shine. "What brings you by on this fine October morning?"

"Same thing as always, Thankful," See-*MOAN* par-*LAYS*, gambling on her hospitality, "seems I've worked up a powerful thirst."

A three-season fixture along the Winooski trails, Simon is ever on some idyllic pedal in search of new inspiration. Frequently, his quest tires more than inspires, returning him panting and gaunt to his hay barn-turned-studio, repair shop and bed loft, in hopes of a better day.

"I've taken to leaving a dipper for you," a suddenly inhospitable Thankful replies, "so you can help yourself as the need arises." Barring the door, it's obvious she's "involved", betwixt and between some secret endeavor Simon is determined to discover.

Fidgeting, her bandy-legged visitor will not be put off, drawling, "W-e-l-l, I'm athirst, Thankful ... but it isn't water alone that will quench it."

"What have you in mind, See-*MOAN*?" Thankful quibbles, unflinching in the defense of her doorway. "Be ye a'hungered, too?"

"Aaaah! Blessed are they which do who hunger and thirst after righteousness," he oozes, running a hand through his thinning gray hair, "if only you had that to fetch me, Thankful, I'd-"

"Out with it, SI-mon!" Thankful's patience run dry. "What be it you're after?"

"It's See-*MOAN*," he frowns, lips drawn tight as a deacon's, "and it's about our Melvin. I think I might know why he ... what made him keel over out there on the trail."

"Blessed are they that mourn: for they shall be comforted," she mutters ponderously, standing aside for his entry, "but what, pray heavens, do you mean?" she asks, closing the door behind him. "What's there to know about heart attacks? I thought when you found him out there he was already ... well .... ."

"Departed?" he helps her, helping himself to a fresh lemon cake, still warm on the sideboard for Melody. "The coroner said he'd been ... said I found him at least an hour after he'd -"

"Departed?" Thankful hanging his jacket on a Shaker peg, then pouring him a glass of cream-thick milk. "You needn't mince words with me, See-*MOAN*; not after that fiasco of a funeral we had."

"And I'm glad you put it that way," he sighs, taking the fresh morning milk as an offer to join her at table, "the 'needn't mince words' part, I mean; for:

Today, amidst the beauty of fresh fallen leaves;
Along crisp-scented paths under river-edge trees;
I recalled there a tryst, a young lad and his lass;
Their matutinal mattress of dew-freshened grass.

And how, me bethinks, I passed slowly unnoticed;
The lad too intent on his sweet lassie's bodice.
Twas Melvin I tell you, and young Melody;
The morning too-"

"Are you going to eat that piece of cake?" Thankful interrupts, "or blow it stale with your breeze?"

"I was just trying, Thankful, to lead you somewhere," See-*MOAN* moans, "trying to take you there gently."

"Lead?" she echoes, pretending alarm.

"Yes," he mouths, his face in the frosting:

Take you back to a scene,
Where love was implicit;
To contrast the obscene,
Where love was illicit."

"What in heaven's name are you trying to say, See-*MOAN*?" she asks bewilderedly. "Skip the rhyme and give me the reason – if you know what it is."

"Oh, I know alright," he sputters, the flecks of frosting on his stubbled chin like pins in a New England ski map. "I know, Thankful; it's just the knowing how to tell you that's the problem."

"Well, trying to sing it in verse only heightens the problem," she complains.

"Heightens?" he repeats hopefully, "then-then you think my verse high-class?"

"High-country would be closer to the mark, See-*MOAN*; but we're straying from the mark in question. What do you know about Melvin? That's what I want to hear."

"Right," he mumbles, washing down the last of his cake with a gulp of milk, "if that's how you want it: straight, with no sugar. I was trying to tell you about espying them - Melvin and Melody – a few summers ago, pitching woo along the banks of the Winooski."

"You mean 'spying', don't you, See-*MOAN*?"

"Spying?" Simon playing ignorant of her implication, "no, I didn't spy on Melvin till ... well, not till I was forced to."

"The devil made you do it?" she teases, poking fun at his thin rationale.

"No, but the prince of this world must have been present considering what it was I saw," he rejoins, surprising her back to attention. "It was that pretty little assistant of Melvin's - that Aphrodite if ever I saw one – spreading out a blanket, and taking off, t-taking off her ... her... ."

"Well? Go on," she urges, a trace of agitation blushing her sunken cheeks, "she was taking off her-"

"Bonnet!" he lies, truth lacking the allure of invention, "and quite the stunning one, too. A bonnet over-sewn with brilliant, vermilion sarcenet; each ruffle, I tell you, each pleat, augmented beautifully by a colorful-"

"Come back to me, See-*MOAN*!" an unthankful Thankful implores, "your mind is astray again. Melvin, it is ... or was. Melvin and Charlene by the river. Melvin was there, wasn't he?"

"Indeed he was ... bewitched by those deep, dark eyes ... those eyes, excessively deep ... love-shaded ... secret; eyes no man dare question past-"

"Melvin, See-*MOAN*, we were talking about Melvin-"

"Yes ... and he was trying to explain, trying to tell Charlene that Melody could never know, could never be hurt ... that he worshipped her – Melody, that is – that he kept her on the pedestal of his heart ... and ... and ... ."

"And what, See-*MOAN*? And what?"

"And-and then that heart must've burst, must've gone to its temple in the woods ... must've gone there to worship, and-"

"So is that it? Is that what you've pedaled out here to tell me? That Melvin passed over in a spasm of love?"

"Well, I was going to paint it up a bit ... call it a romantic seizure, Thankful; but yes, that's what I came to say. I think Melvin may have been revisiting the sacred grove, the place where he and Melody first-first ... well, where he could repent his sins."

"And what about his partner in sin, See-*MOAN*? Your so-called Aphrodite?"

"Yes, well ... as I was telling you, he was trying not to sin anymore – since you put it that way – telling Miss Mally how he loved his wife."

"His wife?" Thankful portentous, posturing, eyes averted, a faint disdain contorting her brow, "you mean this was happening after they were married?"

"Try to understand, Thankful ... a man is just that: a man. And given the chance to consort with goddesses ... well ... what can I say? Though in the end, he made the right choice, what with him choosing your Venus over Aphrodite."

A long silence follows: Simon displacing another quarter section of cake from the sideboard; Thankful pondering how to displace Simon.

"I think," Thankful refilling his glass, "... I think we should keep this our secret, See-*MOAN*. No need to be-"

"Twas never a question, Thankful," he interjects. "My thoughts were custom-made for your ears."

"Tis good I'm not deaf, then," she quips through a restrained smile.

"So it is," he acknowledges, uncertain of her meaning.

"If I ever hear this from anyone else, See-*MOAN*, I'll know it wasn't from you shouting it out in my kitchen."

"I-I wouldn't think of it, Thankful," he mumbles, nodding thought-fully - the growl of tires on the granite-chip drive summoning them to the kitchen window.

"She's home!" Thankful erupts, "My baby's home, See-*MOAN*!" the excitement in her voice essaying joy.

"So that's why you've been so pesky this morning," Simon observes - Melody coming blithely through the rear picket gate, her mother stepping lightly down the back porch steps as though age has forgotten her feet. "So that's why," Simon repeats to himself, brushing the crumbs from his soiled flannel shirt as though Melody just might have an interest; her heart-melting smile, her dancing-blue eyes, her little-girl voice more inspiration than he's had in months. "Melvin is with me, Mama," he hears her say, "he gave me a sign last night. Put my crucifix on the pillow beside me."

"Damn that Melvin!" Simon swears. "Damn that boy!"

"Did you hear that, See-*MOAN*?" a gleeful Thankful asks, tugging her beautiful daughter into the kitchen, "Melody had a visit from Melvin last night, says he's with her now," she improvises, helping Melody out of her coat. "Felt his presence the whole way up from Boston. Now what do you make of that?"

"I think our Melvin ... our Melvin, should he be here now," Simon's eyes having a feast of Melody, "why ... he ... he would walk ... would:

Walk amidst the beauty of fresh fallen leaves;

Along crisp-scented paths under river-edge trees-"

"I do regret you have to rush off, See-*MOAN*," Thankful's insistent tone not lost on her milk-lipped, frosting-faced visitor, "and just when Melody is about to tell me of Melvin's ... of Melvin's-"

"Visitation?" Melody coos. "Melvin came to see me last night, See-*MOAN*! Put a crucifix-."

"Which is where See-*MOAN'S* going to be if he doesn't hurry back to the village," Thankful emphatic, forcing a laugh.

"Uh-right," a beaten Simon mumbles, donning his jacket and giving Thankful an expression suggesting pressure in his abdomen, "and blessed are they which are persecuted for righteousness' sake: for theirs is the kingdom of heaven."

"Yes, and blessed are the merciful," she counters, "for they shall obtain mercy - if they know what's good for 'em."

"Whoa! What's all this about?" Melody prods, as Thankful shoves Simon through the door, "a new Sermon on the Mount?"

"A new mount," Simon attempts in reply - but:

The door is shut 'fore the poet can rhyme,

As back in his rut, Simon's back-ending time.

Now peddling his Schwinn, now licking his chin;

The lemon without vies the lemon within.

The spirit must not reach for the clouds while
the belly is at the table.
(Montaigne)

VII

THANKFUL COULD NOT HAVE KNOWN, BUT I HAVE
accompanied Melody from Boston. Not that I wouldn't choose to, if given
the choice; but I haven't the choice, Aunt Martha all aglow for the jaunt.
"At the heart of our lives we hold all the cards," she lectures me, "it's just
up to us to play the game." This, to justify her eagerness to up the ante in
Melody's. And though I have good cause to distract A.M. from her aim, it
requires a hardier soul than I to suggest another game.

Notwithstanding my apprehension over Aunt Martha's return to
Vermont, my fear is vastly outweighed by the pleasure of my dear wife's
company. From Melody's alembic memory, I'm dispensed into her morning as fragrant thoughts - like the night we kissed on an ancient arched
bridge over the river Tiber, her delft-blue eyes turning hazel in the moonlight; her high cheekbones and pouting lips strikingly genteel - a mark of
nobility. I smile at the thought, for she can claim nobility, albeit native:
the kin of her blood among the noble frontiersmen who tamed the Green
Mountains. But whether because of or despite her pastoral past, there is an
inner refinement about her, an innate sense of class; her instincts, at least
socially, beau monde - a grace, a kind of courtly élan I sorely miss as the
protégé of A.M..

My aunt's past smacks more of dime store perfume, of drugstore
cigars, of too much gin and a Cin-Cin effort to hide it. It doesn't take Edgar

Cayce eyes to see where Aunt Martha has been, or where she's going; the civility of silence, the courtesy of vagueness, both averse to her clamorous nature. Nor is this nature wont to go quietly off in some stately novel, "to the manner born" not ranking among her pretensions. In fact, reading anything is too "stately" for Martha, what knowledge she professes obtained by a kind of intellectual osmosis, by a rubbing of shoulders with more fortunate minds, a rubbing of bellies in more fortunate times - which is why I'm against her getting involved with Arthur Steinberg again.

Arthur has been a Plainfield fixture for as long as I can remember; though I'm aware – as is every old midwife in the county – that Arthur hails from New York (Brooklyn, to be exact). But Artie has a way about him that makes you forget he's foreign. Maybe it's the cockeyed felt cap he wears everywhere, or maybe his disarming humor – or perhaps his business.

Billed as Vermont's most extensive collection, Poor Art's Book Mart is a pleasure for any rummaging antiquarian to visit. Ignoring his hand-lettered sign: "Poor Art's – where bookends don't meet nor hat trees leave, and friends can be found under cover", and continuing past sagging shelves over-burdened with dog-eared, coffee-stained textbooks of outmoded theories, the trained and patient eye can usually find, among apple-crated novels from the cellars and attics of souls long departed, a rare first edition or two; finds which, in Boston or New York, bring more than the price of the relaxing vacation that discovers them. But the irony – or sadness, depending on your point of reference – is that Artie can't read very well. (Artie unabashedly telling any who will listen about the time a tourist - a southern Baptist - asked him if he were illiterate. Seems this Baptist deacon's discovery of *Fanny Hill* in the Topography section aroused his dig – if not his desire.) Like Aunt Martha, Artie's education is empirical: his interest, his raison d'être being his neighbors, his customers, the startled tourists he challenges with greetings. Artie loves his fellow man. That's why we became friends, just my entering his shop endearing me to him.

Frequenting his "emporium of knowledge", as he calls it, throughout my high-school years, I depended on his collection more than the Montpelier library; a dependency Artie regarded as a bond. A blood-brother bond. An inseparable bond, I suppose; for Artie didn't allow my stint in Vietnam to affect his loyalty; his regular shipments of requested books always gratis. After my discharge and subsequent scholarship award to Harvard, his excitement seemed centered in friendship, his ebullience more on the vital, the visual, the victuals of a little New Hampshire diner I would have to pass on my drive down to Cambridge. "The best damn lox and bagels this side of Brooklyn," he informed me - though that's not what I had when I stopped there. Not the first time, nor any of the dozens of times afterward. Maple-cured ham, it was. Maple-cured ham and blueberry pancakes. Simple, but oh what a treat when you're hungry! And where this little diner is in New Hampshire seemed always to be square in the middle of our hunger when Melody and I drove home.

These are the memories prompting Melody to pull in for breakfast - with Aunt Martha and me along Dutch treat. I can tell she's thinking of me - missing me, to be honest. Eating at the diner was a habit with us. In fact, I'm almost positive she's stopping in remembrance of us - of me. No, I'm sure of it; for Melody has never been car crazy like I was; never took notice of sports cars, hot rods or vans. So, I'm certain she takes no notice of Artie's old primer-patched book van parked at the front entrance.

It's Aunt Martha who espies the van, squealing, "Look who's here, Melvin! It's Arthur Steinberg; the Art of my old gin rummy!"

"More like the old rummy, art of your gin, if I remember correctly," I rib her. "The way I figure, you used that gin bottle of yours to siphon money from a poor drunkard's wallet."

"Calling me a cheat, are you?" she pouts, tugging me along the counter to Artie and leaving Melody to find a table alone. "Well, let me tell you how it really was," A.M. pretending injury. "Two drinks and I was the better player. It didn't matter if he had 'em, or I had 'em. Just two drinks and I'd be off on a winning streak."

"Must be my prism, Auntie," I joke, "making me see things that aren't real."

But there is no mistaking what is real in the diner, Artie Steinberg noticing it, too: a beautiful woman, Venus pale, feinting like a shadow by the door, a plaintive look in her misty blue eyes as though only a knight can rescue her.

Appearing like he just stepped out of the comics, Artie tips his soiled felt cap politely and waddles his bemused corpulence to her rescue - her recognition, her relief, her immediate bonhomie affording him confidence; the agony of her bereavement unnoticed by his boisterous greeting (Artie never shaking hands with the tips of his fingers, or voicing a timid "Hello"), the spell-binding, slow-motion sequence that follows leaving the diners agape and Aunt Martha and me in the gallery.

"Well, would you look at us," Aunt Martha thinks, her countenance having the sweep of expression that begs no reply, "... two gawkers agog in Magog."

"Show-stopping gorgeous, isn't she?" I observe, assuming my thoughts are hers.

"She's that and more, nephew," A.M. sighs, "but it's the 'more' that makes her beautiful."

"And that is?" I mumble, watching Artie escort Melody to the comfort of a booth; feeling jealous, suddenly - and foolish for feeling it, too; still, wishing it were me sliding in to enjoy her, to reach for her hand, to be the twinkle in the laugh of her eyes.

"Why, didn't you see it?" Aunt Martha asks with surprise, "she's got that glow about her, Melvin. I thought that's what you were taken by ... that kind of 'holy mother aura' the first baby sometimes brings."

"And that's what everyone is gawking at?" I gasp, believing her, but still not seeing it myself. "They're staring at some kind of glow?"

"Oh, mercy, mercy me," A.M. laments, "I forgot. You can't see your own aura, sweetheart."

"Aura?" I repeat, completely flummoxed, "and what ... and what's with the 'sweetheart', Aunt Martha? It's not like you to use endearments."

She seems not to hear me - whether by thought or energy voiced – her attention all on the sacred booth, the Madonna and Magus deep in some beatific colloquium, the subject of which is me.

"That's wonderful news," a beaming Arthur booms, his difficulties with reading having deprived him of the 'Shingle & Diapers' review, "another little Melvin to bless our lives."

"And a blessing I'm sure he'll be, Artie, if he's anything like his father," Melody agrees, swelling my spirit chest. "Melvin was never overtly religious," she adds, fingering the crucifix on her gold rope-chain and bringing it to her lips for a kiss, "... but he was spiritual, nevertheless."

"Oh, and how I agree," my raucous friend replies, "what spirits I managed to keep in my war chest never quite enough to quench his thirst on a fire-lit winter's night – almost always a Sunday night, as I recall. The boy was in the habit of skipping church right up till his daddy died. It was only after the other reverend came along that he would attend at all."

Smiling at his picaresque blunder, Melody thinks better to leave it unaddressed, returning him to 'church'. "Yes, Melvin did have an aversion to the Holy Rite; though not to the Holy Rote, that being something he worked very hard to practice. And perhaps - now that we can all look back - perhaps he suspected the church; thought it responsible for some of the very ills it warned against; thought it incapable of Christ-like compassion-"

"You mean like his funeral?" my friend Artie interjects, "that Rolundo and-and-"

"His puritanical panegyrics?" Melody suggests. "Yes, I've thought of that. I've even wondered if Melvin knew somehow that his funeral would be ... well ... if maybe he avoided church because of some presentiment of how it would eventually dishonor him."

"Maybe so," Artie concurs, "but if you ask me, a body doesn't need to look too hard these days to find an excuse not to attend The Church of the Good Shepherd. Even Thelma Peabody's been criticizing her minister of late - editing her Sunday-school lessons, she claims - which reminds me: the Melvin Morrison Memorial March. You do know about that, don't you?"

"The what?" Melody putting down a dainty bite of maple-cured ham, her few words metered, rhythmic, a kind of intellectual shorthand: "Did-you-say-?"

"Yes," Arthur interrupts, pleased as a child to know something she doesn't. "Thelma's been organizing a march for Thanksgiving; says more folks will be in town then. And that pretty young thing that works at your husband's law office - what's her name? Cheryl? Sugar?"

"Charlene," Melody pleased that he still refers to the firm as "your husband's".

"Charlene. That's the one. Anyway, she's helping with Thelma's scouting."

"What do you mean, 'scouting'?" Melody asks, Arthur's hobbyhorse caparisoned in vagueness.

"You know, getting questionnaires filled out by as many women as they can ... and not letting any of the men know what the answers are."

At this bit of news, both Melody and Martha are aghast: the former with amazement, the latter with amusement - Melody shoving her pancakes away, Aunt Martha shoving me with unrestrained elation. "Did you hear that?" she babbles, "they're actually going to pull it off, those two; Thelma and your 'other woman'. Going to redefine 'memorial', pay you more tribute than you're owed – if you know what I mean," the last little jibe under the guise of a wink.

"And I suppose you want this to happen?" I snarl, assuming my most confrontational tone. "Am I to understand you wish my Melody publicly ridiculed?"

"Melody?" A.M. gasps in revulsion. "Why would Melody be ridiculed? It's the damn men folk those two are after, not the dames. And there's one or two of those critters I'd like to get hooks in myself."

This last comment confirming my fear: Aunt Martha will be front and center at the march. That daymare now virtually settled, I think it prudent to ask, "And who might those unlucky gentlemen be?"

"Simon Farley, for one," she growls, "and the other one's that sanctimonious, parsimonious, mealy-mouthed minister of Melody's; that two-timing, double-talking, triple-tonguing, organ-grinding, Presbyterian, sexagenarian, libertarian-"

"Hold it there Hoss, you're headed for the pea patch," I bark, "for who is to say which is worse? What you hold against Reverend Rolundo? Or what he holds against Helen the organist? I believe either offense is cardinal."

"And how so for me, Melvin?" A.M. for once responding to reason. "How is telling the truth a cardinal sin? And you know it's the truth, because you saw for yourself what he was doing with-"

"Stop! Aunt Martha, stop!" I shout, just the thought of what I'd seen making me ill – or rather, making me recall the unpleasantness of being ill. "Besides," I argue, "we can continue this discussion some other (here, I almost say 'time'), some other, some ... oh, for St. Pete's sake! In some other life for all I care! Right now all I want to do is follow what's happening with Melody."

"You mean you're not a wee bit curious of my grief with Simon Farley?" she poses ingenuously.

"No. Well ... yes; but after we've heard these two out," I reply, nodding my perfectly clear head in the direction of Melody and her felt-headed auditor, "after we've learned all the latest."

The latest turning out to be old news to Aunt Martha and me: Melody relating, with an excitement approaching religious fervor, how her "sign of the cross" proves the eternality of our oneness; how our undying love is unaffected by physical death; and Artie divulging, with the amusing deviance of a child, what rumors are afoot on George, his clumsy effort to soften hard-core rumors more effacing than effective, his references to George's cunning in the language of law as "cunnilingus", and his good rapport with the local police as "copulatory", leaving Melody choking in mirth. But what Artie reveals next is indeed news:

"I'm on my way to Boston," he says, tugging nervously at his cap, "yep, gotta do some sleuthing there for a friend."

"You? A gumshoe?" Melody genuinely taken aback, and relieved to be off the subject of George.

"Yep, and a sticky business it is, too; what with the culprit I'll be secretly investigating none other than Simon Farley."

"Surely you jest!" Melody rejoins, the idea of Simon being the subject of anyone's inquest seeming as funny as it is foolish. "Who would want to dig into Simon's past? And for that matter, what's there to learn in Boston since Simon never goes more than a half-day's bike ride from Plainfield?"

"Well, the whole thing's secret, you know," a blushing Artie tugging his stained felt cap to within a hair of his bushy eyebrows, "but I don't see the harm in telling you. And besides, what with you a soon-to-be lawyer and all, maybe you can advise me on how I should go about my mission. This doggone sleuthhound business is something I've never done before."

"Maybe so," Melody comforts, "but first you must tell me who wants this information, and why this information might be in Boston."

"Oh, that's easy," a guileless Artie gushes, "'cause who wants it is Thelma Peabody; and as to why what she wants is in Boston, well ... she thinks that maybe Simon once ... maybe he was seeing more of a young lady from there than decency allows, if you get my meaning."

"I do," Melody says hurriedly, cutting off a more graphic explanation. "But what right does Thelma Peabody claim to be delving into somebody's past?" she asks, accepting a warm-up of coffee. "She wouldn't want some-one looking into her past, would she?"

"Well, that's just it," my artless Artie articulates, "'cause she thinks that's exactly what's happening – thinks Simon's the one behind it, too."

"No! I can't believe that," Melody arching one perfect eyebrow, "not Simon. The only thing Simon Farley would have an interest in digging through would be the poetry in your book store."

"Confound it, Mrs. Morrison!" Artie exclaims, "you are good! Damn conceptive of ya to know that!"

"To know what?" Melody smiling at his misuse of words.

"To know that Thelma was in my store the day Simon was looking around, knocking books out the backs of my shelves about as fast as I could pick 'em up – Thelma coming back later to tell me why."

"Why what?"

"Why Simon was making such a mess of my store."

"And why was he?" she prods, impatient to hear the end of this lunacy.

"To distract us from what he was really doing - planting a bug."

"A bug? W-what kind of bug?" Melody stammers, the image of some creepy-crawly giving her a shiver, "an insect he found on the trails?"

"Would to God!" Artie's patronizing smile bristling his wiry whis-kers, "would to God that's all it was! No, my dear lady, it was one of those spy things. You know, like those electronic deviants the Russians use; only Thelma told me he probably got it from a mail order spy catalog; a post office address in Boston. She wants me to look it up. Wants to know if he's on their mailing list."

"Mailing list? Spy catalog?" Melody mouths, stirring a quarter tea-spoon of sugar in her coffee. "And did you find one? one of those things Thelma said he was there for?"

"Well ... no. No, I didn't," a long silence follows the admission.

"Artie," she says at last, "I believe you're right. I believe I can help you."

"I thought as much," he booms, pounding a fat fist on the table, Melody reaching for her coffee before he spills more than enthusiasm. "So, where do we begin?"

"We begin by you continuing your trip to Boston," she says evenly, her dulcet voice gaining an edge of authority, "only there's no sleuthing to be done for Thelma. Instead, I want you to locate that mail order place she told you about, then purchase a goodly assortment of those electric insects for me – the while keeping our new partnership secret, of course."

"You mean 'bugs', Mrs. Morrison," he corrects politely, "but why do we need them?"

"It's not that we need them at all, Artie," Melody whispers with a wink, "it's just the having them that will do the trick."

If Artie understands where she's going with all this, it's more than Aunt Martha or I can comprehend; for no sooner has she finished speaking than the thoughts that inspired her are gone, vanished, her mind on another matter.

"What do you make of it?" I ask, my unflappable aunt always ready with reply. "Do you think she actually has a plan?"

"In as much as she's female … ." She doesn't fail me.

"And what about Simon?" I continue, "or Thelma Peabody? I tend to agree with Melody on those two. Do you?"

"Regarding Thelma, who can tell?" she answers, the two of us following Melody back to the car, "but that See-*MOAN*, he's something else altogether."

Remembering her earlier allusion to a grief she had with Mr. Farley, I bring it up. "Is there something personal between the two of you?"

"Not really," her reply not what I expect, "not unless 'personal' and 'relative' are one and the same. For you see, the reason that rascal didn't come to your funeral was out of spite for not being allowed to spout his poetry at your eulogy. As if! Can you imagine what he may have composed, Melvin?" she conjectures, allowing a fractional pause for my knuckles-in-the-mouth contemplation. "Well, I can," she goes on. "I reviewed it before he could do you harm, adding a few lines after he finished; you know, just to be sure your mother-in-law would refuse his offer."

"You did what?" I yell with a truculent scowl. "You were out fending for your nephew's honor while preparing to dishonor him yourself?"

"But that's different," she objects stridently, "love is more resilient than the most destructive enmity - what fault-finding we do amongst family is our business. But let someone else raise a critical eye and I'm on 'em like a bad coat of paint. If you don't believe me, just wait till your march," she appends, the fire in her eyes rekindling my fondness for her - as well as my fear of what she might do. "Just wait," she repeats, "just-you-wait."

"Wait, wait, wait," I grumble, sliding into the car beside Melody before A.M. can steal my place. "If I didn't know better," I complain, "I could be led to believe the ordeal of patience is one of the lessons I'm here to learn."

Ever desireless, one can see the mystery.
Ever desiring, one can see the manifestations.
(Lao-tzu)

VIII

NO SOONER DOES ARTIE RETURN FROM BOSTON THAN
the fireworks begin; or rather, the short-circuits, frequency blips and telephone static setting Plainfield on edge. And not only Plainfield, but certain
parties with connections to Plainfield, the likes of which make decency
a synonym of secrecy, a secrecy threatened by the daily discovery of yet
another bug in some "suspect's" wall-outlet, dashboard or dial. But despite
all this unnerving evidence, no one has yet to prove Miss Peabody culpable. There is no disagreement, however, over who is suspect, the whole
of Plainfield blaming her for the plague of locusts chirp-chirping from
all things electric; such a dark cloud of suspicion making it difficult for
Thelma's "other women" to shed light on their questionnaires.

Casting of doubt is exactly what Melody intends, her willing facto-
tum enjoying a burst of creativity. Combining actual mechanical mastery
with imagined poetic proficiency, Simon Farley is timing his entries and
exits with caution; each success in the home, vehicle, or business he bugs,
but another proof of his bird-like dexterity, something Melody praises as
his "sense and sensitivity" (leaving to his pride and prejudice any comparison he draws with Jane Austin). And with Melody back in Boston before
the bugs are spread, no one suspects her involvement.

No one, that is, save Artie. After suffering one of Thelma's harangues,
he rings Melody to complain:

"Called me a 'busted garter,'" he reports solemnly, "said I let her down ... said she should have known better, should've known a man wouldn't finish anything he started except-"

"And did she mention the recent rash of bug infestations?" Melody redirects.

"Some folks think it's a commie plot, that there's a commie bugster loose among us. Maybe connected to the college ... a foreign professor. But Thelma suspects Simon," he says pityingly, a slurp from his flask betraying a nagging guilt, "thinks Simon's out to un-credit her, ambush her Thanksgiving march. But who is planting all these bugs round here, Mrs. Morrison?" he asks through a muffled burp. "I know it isn't y-you."

"Melvin's memorial march, did you say?" she responds evasively, "do you think she's canceling the march?"

"On the contr-r-rary. Says if no one shows, she'll ma-arch herself ... something 'bout your minister ... 'bout his organ recitals."

"Reverend Rolundo?" Melody incredulous, the idea as intellectually aberrant as a theosophist. "He's not a musician, Artie. No one would come to hear him."

"R-right ... same as Thelma says. Says when the rever-r-rend gives his organ r-recitals, he's the only one that-"

"Oh my god!" Melody exclaims. "To a hammer, everything's a nail. In all my effort to protect Melvin, I've opened Pandora's box; Thelma's anger, like the spark of a flint, lying asleep until the first strike of friction!"

"That's it, Mrs. Mor-r-rison," the whisky ever lower in Artie's flask, "that 'stroke of fiction' thing you said there ... that's what Thelma's holler-r-ring 'bout ... says she's gonna r-r-rewrite hysterectomy ... says there's an abortion in ever-r-y chapter."

Melody knows nothing of Charlene's intent, Charlene's refusal to consider an abortion responsible for two engagements: one to George and the other the cause de jour, the march to Melvin's remembrance. But Artie's mention of abortion prompts Melody's remembrance of George, the word vaguely connected to Melvin's ramblings about his partner - her call to the firm confirming the connection, as she's referred to the tavern:

"Just befriending a Godhard blonde," George bemoans, befuddled to be bedeviled. "What's up? I mean ... what's up with you?"

"A call of curiosity," Melody rejoins, "thought you might have the latest on Thelma's march; whether she's getting any-"

"I don't think so," George interjects, "I mean ... w-what were you asking?"

"Whether Thelma is getting any support for her march," she reiterates. "Do you think she'll succeed?"

"Not if I c-can help it," George pants, "and I'm not alone with my wish. There's a dozen or more ladies here who would sooner turn wish to reality than see Thelma turn tricks of her own."

"Well, as a matter-of-fact, it's Thelma's tricks I'm curious of, George, not yours. For unlike you, once I've passed the bar, I won't be going back every day-"

"One such trick a naughty reference to you, Melody," he interjects, "a stretch of wanton imagination if ever I encountered one. It has to do with your dinner the other night; or, as Thelma put it, 'The intimate evening Melody spent, at her mother's farm, with that lecherous South African beast, Tenklei – and, mind you, while her mother was blithely attending the ladies' missionary auxiliary at Rolundo's parsonage. Just imagine what went on out there!' she railed, 'a grief-weakened, sex-starved widow at the mercy of that ravening fiend!' I warned her that if ever I heard such depraved innuendo again, I'd sue her for defamation."

"Oh, noooo!" Melody crying the tiger-pounce of pain, "how degrading ... how humiliating. But it's true, George; I did have dinner with Vincent," she rallies defiantly, "and Mother was attending the missionary meeting; but it wasn't 'intimate', to say the least. The purpose of Vincent's call was his abiding interest in Harvard, not Mother's soup. In fact, we shared her excellent venison stew by the mere happenstance of his timing. And what's more," she goes on with the heat of anger, "I invited Vincent to pay me a visit in Boston; to come walk for himself the great old paths, advising, 'Should you aspire to admittance, you should experience the university first hand; sit-in on a few lectures; talk to some students; get a feel for the resident spirits, the ghosts of glories past.'"

"Ghosts?" George echoes, his fill of the resident spirits more akin to the glorious present, "is-has-has Melvin-?"

"He has, George; and I thank you for asking," Melody suddenly ebullient, relating her 'sign of the cross' visitation.

"Then that explains it, Melody," a sobered George replies. "That explains why every time I try to kiss Charlene, she jumps like she's seen a ghost. Maybe she's-"

"Not the same, George," Melody rebuffs, "no connection at all. But if Charlene is seeing ghosts, I suggest you take her out to the hippie commune - the one where you hired your landscaping girls. I hear the founder is a practicing spiritualist; a medium of sorts. Perhaps he can help Charlene - help her identify the phantoms."

"Maybe you're right," George sighs, "and maybe he could do me some good, too; for it's been a long, long time since I've seen a medium anything!"

The two natural ways to enter the cabinet of the gods
and there foresee the course of destinies
are madness and sleep.
(Montaigne)

IX

THELMA'S PILLORYING OF VINCENT HAS AUNT MARTHA
beside herself; a confusing feat, too, placing A.M. on both sides of me. But
among us, we've figured it out. Thelma's public pretense is a diversion, a
smoke screen to hide her anticipated indiscretions with Simon Farley, her
commitment to ruin Mr. Farley too irrational and foolishly fervent to be
unfeigned. And after A.M. recalls one of Mr. Gandhi's tenets - Achievement
requires the surrender of alternatives - we employ his key of knowledge to
unlock our puzzle.

Thelma may not admit to "surrender", but she's a master of "alternatives", attacking all of Simon's, including his alternatives from years gone
by, as demonstrated by her attempt to find his mystery girl in Boston. Her
tactic is obvious: reduce an unsuspecting Simon's alternatives to zero, then
incarnate what remains; i.e., personify his "achievement".

"If Thelma wants a man that badly," A.M. posits, hovering over the
tavern bar, "she should take a survey in here."

"The only real man here is George," I respond.

A.M. adamant. "Not my point, Melvin. If you've learned anything
from your mistakes, it should be that happiness is a shy nymph. If you
chase her, you'll never catch her."

"Thanks, Auntie, but that doesn't tell me what you mean by suggesting Thelma's presence at the bar."

"Her manhunt?" A.M. moving to keep George in view. "She would do well to note the women imbibing with George, then go check out the men they've left at home. A good list of candidates, if you ask me. Besides, now that we know what Melody wanted with those bugs, it's a good bet Thelma's going to have some time on her hands. I'm wagering your march may not happen after all."

"As if I care," I snark. "Whether the whole affair's a no-show, or the turnout's minuscule, either failure will be anticlimactic."

"Thoughts, dear nephew," she scolds, "it's thoughts we deal in here; and yours are not exactly erectile at the moment."

"So, what are we going to do about Thelma's slander?" I pose, attempting distraction from George. "What counter-measures are next? For I know darn well we're about to take some."

"Vincent Tenklei and Simon the Simple. I'll do what I can for the former, and can what I did for the latter. Our Simon is in enough trouble on his own."

"And let's not forget Melody," I append.

"Melody?" A.M. giving me one of those sometimes-I-don't-believe-you glances. "She's in no danger, Melvin. Any calculating scandalmonger can do the math on that one."

"The math?"

"Sure. She has a child on the way, conceived not long after your funeral. And your funeral was within a month of the *Rogue vs Way* win. There isn't enough lechery in Plainfield to suspect her of anything but the way of the Rogue she admits to."

"Ok." I nod, as though I follow her rambling non sequitur. "Vincent I understand, but not Mr. Farley. If memory serves me correctly, it's Simon Farley you want your hooks in, isn't it?"

"Yes," she snips, apparently annoyed with George for not rallying after his long-distance talk with my wife. "Yes, Melvin, your memory always serves you correctly here; and yes, it was See-*MOAN* I was out to spite. But seeing as how Thelma is about to do it for me, the least I can do is help."

And if ever a body needs help – excluding my own - it's Simon's. A veritable prodigy of industry on his worst days, he has the frazzled-edged appearance of one who doesn't sleep, his eyes like those of a serpent

- never-blinking, ever-watching - his tenor voice cracking at the slightest provocation. With all of his bugs in place, he's exhausting himself by listening in on the undiscovered – an improvisation of his own, Melody's instructions devoid of any reference to spying. Surveillance is now his taskmaster, a despot denying him sleep (Aunt Martha tuning in on his weakened frequency to eavesdrop with masterly ease), the sight of Simon, wobbling wearily about on his Schwinn, arousing no suspicion. Nor does his headset, the locals accustomed to Simon's eccentricities, the least of which is his spacey stare between earphones as he pumps over the river trails.

"This is so easy it's almost unfair," Aunt Martha flitting round Simon, throwing a static field over his bike for the amusement of sparks. "Reminds me of the prophet Ezekiel's wheels within wheels. And I'm going to make Simon the wheel he thinks he is!" she cries, her glowing form flashing like a pole lamp on power surges. "Simon is about to go a'courtin'!" she squeals, "about to find his elusive inspiration!"

"Thelma, I presume?" Aping Dr. Livingston's jungle encounter, I'm getting to the body of things, if only to pick up my spirit. "You mean our Thelma's about to inspire the beast within?"

"Yes," Aunt Martha's mischievous thoughts clustered like peanuts in brittle, "though the roar of a mouse will hardly intimidate a she-wolf."

"Set the traps!" My sudden elation more in Aunt Martha's diversion than any pleasure said diversion provides; my part as a spectator, in lieu of a specter, affording me needed rest.

"Not to worry, nephew," she giggles, pointing to the earphones, "Simple Simon has set his own traps. Just listen in and you'll learn what I mean."

"You did what?" an angry bass bellows, Simon almost falling off his bike as he jerks to turn down the volume, "you told Thelma about our cantata?"

"But not about your solos, darling," Helen whimpers, "only about the choruses, the recitatives, the beautiful music we attempt to make. I said nothing about your propensity to solo, sweetheart, I swear."

"Rolundo and Helen the organist?" I ask a hysterical A.M., "you have Simon tuned in to a tragedy?"

"Hey!" she protests, "I had nothing to do with it. Simon set his own traps, remember?"

"Ah, that he has; but I don't see where Simon's entrapped."

"Inspiration, nephew," she chortles, "it's what inspires him that'll nab him. As fast as he can peddle back to his barn is how fast he'll compose an elegy on the clergy, or an ode to a grievance earned," even as she speaks, the two of us reading Simon's fast rhyming thoughts to the meter of his hard-pumping legs:

No ménage a trios
Had Menelaus,
Till Helen of Troy
Bade in a Paris;

Nor Agamemnon
His Clytemnestra,
Till-

"Leave it to a virgin to romanticize sex," Aunt Martha smirking at Simon's lines.

"I beg to differ, Auntie. My experience proves otherwise. Making love with Melody was the intangible essence of romance, as near to love as mortals can soar; although, I appreciate your ignorance since you departed earth an old maid."

"Old?" she screams, the word obliterating all else I've said. "We've covered this gaffe before, Melvin. Our word of choice was sensitive, as I recall; sensitive and enchanting."

"I don't remember enchanting," I start to say; but grabbing the thought before she can bicker, I check in on Simon as we near his barn, his wheezing enough to wake up the dead. "Give it," he's panting, "give it"-

Give it to me straight
Whispers Helen,
Or don't give it at all.

Amen.

Give it to me hard
Speaks up Helen,
Make it well worth the fall.

Give it to me now
Cries out Helen,
Drive me over the wall.
Hallelujah!

But don't, oh ... nooo!
Pleads Helen,
Don't come till I call!"

"What did I tell you?" babbles A.M. "He's gone berserk, composing verse that could land him in court."

"I think not," I disagree, "for once the authorities reckon up Rolundo's damage, they won't risk Simon's inspiration at their own expense. No, they would sooner support the reverend's right to enjoy an occasional cantata than fault Simon's raffish rhyme. If this gets out, I can see the reverend taking in a few strays, a few lambs on the lam, The Church of the Good Shepherd gaining fame as a flock of black sheep."

"The more the sheep the more the fleecing," Aunt Martha allows, "but meanwhile, back at the barn .... ."

Pacing his loft, his headset a pastiche of themes, Simon is wobbling a two-step to the hi-fi sounds in his earphones. With Thelma from the left and Helen from the right, Rolundo comes front and center:

"He's out to get me!" screams Thelma; "You've yet to reach me," cries Helen; "Practice makes perfect," preaches the reverend, his persuasion having immediate effect, a "Battle me", "Straddle me" and "Rattle me" following in quick succession, their three-part harmony quickening Simon's urge, his creative surge, his dirge for the widow Melody:

A rainbow arcs across the sky;
I view its hues and wonder why.
A promise kept it seems to me,
Would in itself sufficient be.

But who am I to question God;
Or scorn His quick avenging rod;
When with His claiming of a soul,
He leaves a lamb within the fold?

Our own Madonna to adore -
Bereft of Joseph at her door -
Doth make us all the Magi be,
To gift the child of Melody.

For once, I'm moved by this unmoving man; this two-wheel-ing, word-wielding, would-be poet of Plainfield suggesting my Melody's sainthood.

"Not bad for a Plainfield pen, is it?" I ask A.M., Simon's effort at com-position spending his reserves, the little fellow collapsing across his bed.

"Better than the scalpel he wanted to wield at your funeral," she remarks gruffly, irritated by our entertainer retiring. "But about that 'lamb in the fold,'" she mumbles, looking away as though hiding a tear.

"Yes?"

"We haven't much Earth-time left, my dear; not much time to sneak you in."

Before I can collect my thoughts on the matter, or offer my sympathy for whatever has robbed her jollity, a peony express comes floating down, a perfumed message, Aunt Martha giving the petaled missive a couple of rapid, third eye scans.

"We've got to go," she says abruptly, "got an urgent meeting to attend. Melody's father wants to meet us up at Star View Station."

"Melody's dad? At Star View Station? What's this about ... his translation?"

"Hardly. He's returning, not leaving; coming down just to give us some late-breaking news."

Before I can question her more, we're off, our escort of angels like Elijah's chariot: a fiery flash through a star-studded veil.

For Gods and men and booksellers refuse
to countenance a mediocre muse.
(Horace)

X

ON A SEA OF TROUBLING SLEEP, SIMON DREAMS HIM-
self ashore - a heavenly shore – as in splendor wrought, his fancy finds
Valhalla, his Odin, his feast to manly conquest. Such high-flown inspiration is beyond what dreams can embrace, Simon's vision flinging him off
his bed to write while the spirits tarry.

But too veiled the lady, too short his stay to know her true. Still, he
comes away with a certainty, a strange awareness that to endure he must
remain where he is, to be strong he must nourish failure, to be rich he must
cherish lack – a lack of words; for more words merely count for less. And so
he writes, with soulful economy, what never has he known before:

> Beautiful words are not truthful.
> Truthful words are not beautiful.
> Yet you are both.

Struggling to remember, to envision his lady fair, he continues:

> Like the wise, you tarry –
> and are thus ahead.

> You and I are akin to the sea:
> king and queen to a thousand streams
> because we lie beyond them.

We wait for the silt to settle,
the better to learn the water;

we empty ourselves of all,
the better to see our source.

And so I wait, empty,
athirst to be filled with you.

The lines are vaguely familiar. Perhaps from an earlier rhyme, a loftier climb, a book he perused at Artie's? Ah! Yes! Thelma was there! (Thelma whispering nervously to Artie, her suspicious eyes following his movements about the store.) And to the awareness of sin that drives her to chasten others, he plays the advocate now, penning a path to redemption, a climb to his bed-yearning altar; his sacrificial loft a virginal vindication for all they've been denied:

O maiden of Sin and Sybaris,
My rhyme doth now disclose:

The night-shaded lane of Hesperus
That leads to our repose.

Pray cease the point of a finger,
And see where mercy leads;

E'en now as we go to linger
Where love funds all our needs

Fear nothing of me or my musing;
But that which would rescind,

What Venus sends down for our using
To aid our hearts' amend.

"A new world is dawning," Simon observes, it seeming the sun has risen by the flourish of his pen. "I will play Mercury today! I will deliver what the gods have written!" he cries, forgetting his earphones and climbing nimbly down from his laddered loft to the familiar seat of his Schwinn. Refreshed as the Green Mountain air, he pedals furiously to Thelma's farm.

Alas! Thelma is not so inclined, the rising sun seeming to her more a warning than a wakening, her morning meditation finding biblical agreement, her finger pointing - even as she hears Simon's knock - to a verse in the book of John, "... and men loved darkness rather than light, because their deeds were evil."

"Good morning, Thelma," Simon chimes with alarming geniality, "and a really good morning it is, too, what with the news I have to share!" the mention of "news" sufficient to make him desirable, even had she not been scheming to accomplish the same.

"News?" she repeats, dragging him through the door, "if it's a scoop you came here for, See-*MOAN*, I'll grant you won't be disappointed. Sit down while I pour you some coffee," she demands, shoving him into a newly varnished rocker perched perilously close to her own. "I was about to have some myself ... just finishing my devotions when you knocked. Take sugar?" she asks, pausing to catch his reply.

"If-if you do," Simon's entire confidence shot through, her pistol-black eyes reducing him to the remembrance of a mortal.

"I do!" she shouts, warming to the sound of the phrase, "sit back and make yourself comfortable ... be right back with your mug."

Fumbling for his poems, he almost overlooks the leather-bound Bible open on the seat of her rocker, Thelma's blue-ruled notes, protruding from gilt-edged pages, boldly inscribed with his name: "Simon: Upon this rock I will build my church; and the gates of hell shall not prevail against it."

"Your brew, See-*MOAN*," Thelma approaching gingerly with two steaming mugs. "I see you've had a look at St. John there – one of my favorite passages."

"St. John? I hadn't read that far-"

"Yep," she says deliciously, enjoying her moment of truth. "Third chapter, verse nineteen, it is; the one about men preferring darkness to light." After handing him his mug, and moving the Bible to a tattered, cowhide ottoman, she takes her place beside him as naturally as a habit. "You know the one, See-*MOAN*; the one about men's deeds being evil."

"Yes, Thelma," Simon's mug trembling ever so slightly in his upraised hand, "but I prefer the preceding verse, John 3:16: 'For God so loved the world-'"

"Oh pshaw! Everybody knows that one," Thelma glowing over her coffee, blowing a wreath of steam from her mug. "Those papers you have in your hand ... are they for me?"

"As a matter-of-fact," Simon looking desperately about for a place to set his mug, "... they are."

"Then let me have them," she directs, reaching for the crumpled sheets. "I presume these comprise the news you mentioned," Thelma waving the poetry in his face as though what she holds condemns. "Well?" Leaning closer, she appears more intent on touching him than the subject.

"I-I dreamed it," he falters, his mug shaking violently, "a kind of cosmic communication."

"You mean like those bugs everyone's finding?" she suggests - Simon spilling his coffee.

"No!" the hot coffee, soaking through his plaid flannel shirt, requiring her care. "No, not at all!" he continues, allowing, enjoying, her handkerchief daubs at his chest. "What's written there came to me in a dream last night – the free verse part, that is. The lines that don't rhyme."

Satisfied Simon boasts a hairy chest, she pokes her coffee-soiled hanky into a hole in the cowhide ottoman; then, sits back to peruse what this imagined he-man has brought her. "No need to explain," she says peremptorily, stretching to set her coffee on the hardwood floor, "I know what free verse is, See-*MOAN*."

But as she begins to read, her tone becomes butter-soft:

Beautiful words are not truthful.
Truthful words are not beautiful.

She reads aloud,

... Yet you are both.

Thelma is awestruck, his verse like golden pears from Odin's feast, her black eyes sparkling-moist with sudden tears.

Like the wise, you tarry –
and are thus ahead.

You and I are akin to the sea:
king and queen to a thousand streams

because we lie beyond them ...

she reads breathily,

We wait for the silt to settle,
the better to learn the water;
we empty ourselves of all,
the better to know our source.

And so I wait ...

she whispers, pausing to take him in,

And so I wait, empty,
athirst to be filled ... to be filled ...

She can not finish, the tears in her voice denying speech as she points, first at the words "with you", then at her heart; and finally at Simon, erupting from her rocker to surprise him with a kiss. Certain the gods have spoken, he reaches furtively for the poem unread, judging its timbre too harsh, its tone unlike its sibling. Unpracticed as a lover, he's enough of a poet to know two peaks require a valley; and with Thelma eager to mine what gems his heart may hide, he dare not risk her disappointment.

O maiden of sin ...

She begins, the three letter word pinning her back as he rips the sheet from her hand.

"S-Sin?" she asks huskily, "SIN, See-*MOAN*? Tell me more," she implores, "or let me read it for myself."

"Too risky," he mumbles, "too-"

"But risqué is nigh unto righteous when couched in love, isn't it?" Thelma shamelessly eager.

"What I meant was," Simon sloshing his coffee in hopes of distraction, "... what I meant by my reference to sin was to suggest the mercy it begs, that's all."

Abruptly stuffing the poem in his coffee-soaked pocket, he improvises:

"I've got news to tell that'll make my poetry read like one of your Sunday-school lessons."

"Well?" Thelma rising like the biscuits baking in her oven, "don't keep me waiting, See-*MOAN*."

"Its very private, you know," Simon regaining his earlier enthusiasm, the lingering memory of her kiss – and the savory smell of her biscuits - producing a Titan's confidence. "From one lonely heart to another, I invite you to share my secrets," such invitation spelling the death of what mannered decorum yet staggers between them; Thelma reaching for his hands to press them hard about her thighs, her yearning black eyes wanton pools of invitation.

"Rolundo," he whispers, "the reverend and his organist ... they-they duet in his study; though Helen complains he steals the solos."

"Our minister?" she gasps, letting go of his hands to cover her blushing cheeks, "Reverend Rolundo?"

"Not my minister," Simon quips, "but I thought you would want to know; especially since he's critical of your Sunday-school lessons. Gives you ammunition to fire back. And anyway, the reverend should know better - should know that blindness to desirable things prevents the heart's confusion."

On tiptoes, her hands seeking his, Thelma is anything but confused, her heart knowing exactly what it wants.

"It's paradoxical," she coos, "a spiritual dichotomy; for to win one must yield, to be straight one must bend, to be sated one must be empty, to be fresh one must be exhausted. These are higher truths, See-*MOAN*, which, like the higher notes we can't hear, are there whether we accept them or not. But how did you come to know this truth on Rolundo?" Thelma inching closer to his cricket knees.

"I-I heard," he stutters - Thelma directing his hands to excitement, "I-I ... let's overlook that part-"

"But See-*MOAN*," she whispers, settling seductively into his lap to bring her lips near his, "he who overlooks, like she who stands on tiptoes, is not steady."

The biscuits burn.

Happiest am I when I forget not anything but self.

XI

STAR VIEW STATION IS TUMULTUOUS, NEW ARRIVALS
milling about in the impertinent rush of a super bowl half-time. As A.M.
points out, their anxiety is short-lived, quelling palpably when they discover the trains don't run on time. But time or no time, we're having trouble connecting with Melody's dad. Aunt Martha is supposed to meet him in
the Galaxy Lounge, a fruit and nectar bar set up as a planetarium, the wait-
staff doubling as guidance counselors for travelers stunned to be in transit.

We try the usual - Aunt Martha's expertise in mind control about the
best to be found in our realm - and after missing him in the lounge, A.M.
projects a beacon of thoughts to guide him to where we are. His lack of
response, she explains, is due to interference, the crowd jostling ideas with
such frenzy they're ricocheting off the billboards; the ubiquitous, highflying crystal panels advertising everything from rose-colored glasses and
un-sin-a-man brainwash, to Prophet John's rapture insurance (a favorite
among returnees to earth). As a last resort, we're obliged to page him over
the outer-com. Following my advice, A.M. pages "Geezer" instead of his
given name "Caesar". (Melody's baby-talk name for her father.) "Geezer
will get a response if he's anywhere near the station," I assure her, my memories aplenty of family fun with Old Geezer and Old Faithful. My suggestion works, Caesar showing down just as we're ordering our nectars.

"Make that three specter nectars," Aunt Martha barks, elated to see an old friend. "So how have you been, Caesar?" A.M. telekinetically positioning a chair back stool. "How are things in ever-everland?"

"Ever better," Caesar glows, alighting on the proffered stool. "And that's why I'm here; though I didn't expect the pleasure of seeing you, Melvin."

"Let's be honest, Caesar," Aunt Martha gibes, "you didn't expect to see Melvin ever!"

"Well," the kind old gentleman obliges, "but that's not to say I didn't expect him to improve, to at least strive to make the grade."

"Thank you," I smile, shaking his hand with soul-felt respect, "and thank you for being the exemplary father and husband you were back on Earth," I add, "my frenetic, self-consumed life never allowed me time to express how I valued your example."

"Oh, you're going to have all the time you need for that," Aunt Martha quips, Old Geezer giving me a bright-eyed wink.

"Which is why I called this meeting, Martha," our illumined guest explains, "I've come to make arrangements for your trip back to Earth."

Outshining me in every way, Aunt Martha now puts me to shame, her glow approaching nuclear fission. "We did it, Melvin! We did it, my love! I'm going back for another run!"

"Not so fast, Martha," Caesar advises. "I said I'm here to arrange your trip, not insure it."

"What's the difference?" A.M. too excited to care.

"You are the difference," he states soberly. "I've come down to present the facts. It's up to you to take the case."

"This sounds like something I should be handling," I throw in, "something with more than two sides: maybe a right one, definitely a wrong one, and the obfuscated one that wins."

"It's of more gravitas than a legal case, my son," Caesar hoisting a friendly toast, "and more delicate than a whim. It's life and death ... and life-ever-after. The trouble is, the current choice can affect the life-ever-after part, too."

"I got it," A.M. calming to his gentle reminder. "I'm familiar with the way things work up here, Caesar. I was in Mr. Gandhi's history class - one of his star pupils, I might add."

"That you were," Caesar acknowledges. "I know, because Mahatma related his experiences while visiting our agronomy research center on planet Zenar. I'll never forget his comic stories about his students - about one Martha Morrison who made him see stars."

"So, what are the assignments?" Martha opting to leave her galactic report card undisputed, "or do I have a choice?"

"And what's this about research?" I break in. "Are you still tending orchards?"

"No, yes and yes," he replies. "You have only one assignment, Martha, meaning: no, you don't have a choice; or yes, you can still refuse it. And yes, Melvin, I'm back into apples and loving every eon of it."

"Let's have the facts," Martha blurts, signaling for another nectar, "... and Caesar, charge this round to your Master's Card."

"Why not?" Caesar agrees, "it qualifies as a travel expense. And concerning your facts, here they are:

"A young farm couple in Kansas lost their first child in a miscarriage. And if that weren't bad enough, they lost their farm, as well. However, as we all know, our Master doesn't allow us to suffer beyond what we can bear, providing us a way out of our difficulties, a way we may not recognize as heaven-sent until long after we've made our escape. The Kansas couple has been given such an escape, the young man receiving an inheritance from a New England uncle: a dairy farm on the outskirts of Plainfield."

"Who died?" Martha interrupts, "I must have known the uncle."

"You did. Bachelor Compton. Died of a stroke."

"And he had kin out west?" Martha incredulous. "I never thought of Fred Compton as having a family, quiet and aloof as the old codger was. But I guess we all do, don't we?"

"That we do; and that's what I'm here to offer you, Martha: you can be the first surviving child of the Compton couple in their new Vermont farmhouse."

"New?" My aunt's colorless face signaling she would choke on her nectar had she a body with which to choke. "Bachelor Compton's old place? You're asking me to start over in poverty?"

"Not asking, Martha," he corrects, "offering. Offering an opportunity, should you want it. And as to poverty, the old house will soon be rich in love ... something Melvin can tell you a little about, isn't it, son?"

"Why, yes," I reply guiltily, wondering if my father-in-law is aware of my philandering; then hastily chasing the thought away before he reads it. "Yes, Melody's love can't be measured, can't be compared to the material. If given the chance, I'd go back as the family hound just to be near her again."

"B-but I thought ... I thought I heard-" Caesar stammers, asking Martha, "doesn't he know?"

"Know what?" I interject, the idea of becoming my own wife's child an oddity of which her father may disapprove.

"He knows," Aunt Martha growls, vexed over her own impoverished prospects, "and he's committed, too; made a vow at Melody's bedside."

"Well, congratulations!" Caesar exclaims, offering another toast, "welcome back in the family! And now that we have that little enigma solved, you can help me with your aunt," Caesar giving her a censuring glance. "She seems to be overlooking the core value here, the opportunity a little apple-polishing can produce."

"Easy as apple pie for you to say," A.M. rejoins, "what with you and Faithful spending your autumn afternoons sipping applejack on your back-porch swing. I happen to have aspirations this time. I want to go places. Do things. Be somebody - not just rot on the ground I'm born to."

"The choice is yours," Old Geezer says kindly, a silent flap of his wings standing him tall. "I've accomplished my mission by giving you first bid on the babe. The stork event's up to you to attend. And you, my son," he adds, turning to me, "you will be happier than before."

"I will?" I mumble, thinking no happiness can exceed conjugal love when that love is complete and forgiving.

"You will," he affirms, reaching for the check, "for there's no love like that of a mother for her son." And so saying, he's off in a flurry of wings, leaving us both to ponder - Aunt Martha coming slowly round, warming to his offer.

"Plainfield, eh?" she muses, sipping the last of her nectar. "Well, at least I'll be able to give you some grief, nephew ... for apparently I'll have plenty to give."

"Remind me to play the stranger," I tease, "or perhaps a wealthy suitor."

"As if!" she chortles, slamming her empty glass on the bar table. "This time ... this time I'm going to be somebody!"

The latest find kills prior things and
spoils them in our mind.
(Lucretius)

POSTCARD PEACEFUL, PLAINFIELD LACKS THE STAMP,
the means to get from here to there, residents relying on nearby Montpelier
for goods and services their farms can't provide. Other than Poor Art's
Book Mart, Thelma's vegetable stand, Simon's cycle shop, two questionable taverns, a carriage house-turned-law office, a sagging general store-
cum-post office (twice the victim of ice-jams), and the occasional petal
peddlers from the hippie commune, there's nothing much to ogle save the
white-steepled Church of the Good Shepherd. A smattering of federal style
houses along the Winooski, and the colorful trails wondering up from its
banks, account for most of Plainfield's appeal; even the few stark buildings
of Godhard College covert in the forested uplifts.

Were it not for Plainfield's lone flashing light, tourist might miss the
village, its junction with the rest of the world imprudently perched on the
rim of an abrupt declivity; a peril requiring motorists to creep to a stop
and peer over the edge peradventure a climbing vehicle, farm implement,
or horse-drawn wagon is about to leap from the void. Such caution is what
discovers Plainfield, visitors often turning at the flashing light to ride their
brakes down the precipitous plunge for a unique snapshot of history.

George's near miss at the intersection (when he was new to the area)
is what prompted his discovery of the commune. To shake off the scare, he
drove aimlessly along the meandering river until attempting a turnabout at

the entrance to an abandoned deer camp - the overgrown lane long since a footpath for game of a different breed. Thus happening upon the hippie commune, George came away with a contract for flower girls to adorn his land, to cultivate his imagination; the sun-bronzed young women enjoying a minimum of cloth, a maximum of freedom, what attire they wore of the "breathing" type (heavy breathing, he fantasized), their devil-may-care élan in line with his come-what-may approach. But when his expectations were ignored, even shunned, George took compensatory action, branding the hippies a pack of scamps, a dirty, germ-ridden lot of outcasts, a part of the Winooski valley best left unremembered.

But now he's back, following Melody's suggestion, his call on "Marvin the medium" dispelling his former aversion.

Rising smoke-like from his madras cushion, Marvin is anything but enlightening. Nodding assent to George's request, Marvin chants:

"Tonight ... aummm ... tonight by the hand of my guide, to have and to hold what your soul may desire ... aummm ... but 'bring twenty,' says my guide."

"Twenty?" George glancing lustfully about for the girls.

"Green ... aummm ... backs," Marvin chants, disappearing in a wreath of cannabis vapor.

Back at Charlene's, George pleads, with jocose calumny, the merits of the pending seance:

"It's the humanitarian thing to do, sweetheart. Give the misguided a little rope, a second chance, and the next thing you know they'll be begging to come back to society," his prefatory excitement ruffling her composure.

"Come back?" she scoffs, eyeing her compact for a touch-up of strawberry gloss. "How can they come back when they were never here? Those aren't Plainfield girls, George, they're-"

"Like the ghost you've been seeing? The phantom who appears every time I try to-"

"Is that the purpose of our little social call?" Charlene accepting his help with her fox-trimmed coat, "a brush with hippies for a brush with death? I know what goes on out there, George O'Malley," she fumes, "and it's more than a roll of the grass, or-or a roll in the hay. It's a roll call up yonder, from what I hear; a kind of mystical meeting of minds."

"So," he grumbles, playing the gentleman and holding the door for her exit, "they can't be much different from us, what with me encountering the dead every time I try to-"

"It's my condition, George," Charlene swinging her hips like a runway model, swishing down the walk to his car, "... got to put the baby first, you know."

"Should've thought of that before," George thinks churlishly, revving the engine for a tire-screaming peel from her drive. "If you had, there wouldn't be a baby at all. And if no baby ... ."

But the "if" is too disturbing to postulate, his choices seeming more and more the wrong ones of late. Keeping company with the river's chill, a silent George and his sulking companion go icily on, the distance between them growing more immense with each frosty breath.

Near the end of the overgrown lane, an A-frame comes into view, the structure perched awkwardly between lean-to greenhouses. Claiming what solace he had wished for Charlene, George accepts the task of making defeat the threshold of victory. "Work," he mutters under his breath, unsure of being heard, "it's work these people need. Give them something gainful to do and their thin ideas rend by the weight of their wages."

"Is that why we're here?" Charlene's titter brittle with scorn, "to waste what gains you've amassed on more posies round your pond? Babies don't come cheap, George ... nor do weddings." Her criticism a just one, George twice postponing their nuptials in the last few weeks, claiming weddings more the bargain in the clutch of winter.

He dodges her barb. "I think we should explore a little, find what talents are masked behind the smoke."

"I'll tell you what's behind the smoke," she counters dramatically, a flippant wave of one jeweled hand venturing her entire regard for anything bohemian, "bloodshot eyes, that's what; and a hungry pack of libidos on the prowl."

"Hardly," George objects, pulling to a stop before what resembles a monster fowl with crippled wings. "At least, that wasn't my experience before." Espousing the truth - admitting a score he failed to make - he feels the better for it. "Let's see what's smokin'," he banters, opening his door as a tall, buxom redhead appears topless amidst beads hanging snake-like in the A-frame's entrance.

"Holy smoke!" George circumnavigating the car to extract his pregnant passenger. "'Hungry libidos', did you say?"

His query remedial, Charlene regarding her own breasts superior to any George might espy at the commune, her confidence a mix of competitiveness and coquetry:

"I concede, George. You're right," she assents, extending her hand for his help from the car.

"About what?" he asks indifferently, his interest fixedly elsewhere.

"About these people needing a second chance; for it looks as though chance is what they're most amenable to: the chance for a communicable disease; the chance for a puff of weed; the chance for a pill-"

"Speaking of which, I hear there's a pill now that cost less than a baby." George slamming her door in his haste to explore the evening.

"I was raped, and you know it!" she snarls, fashioning a smile for the topless girl awaiting them. "... Repeatedly!"

His smirk greets her latest distortion, a smirk broadening to a salacious grin as George passes gingerly through the beaded entry, the buxom redhead nodding at a few velveteen pillows in disarray round a large brass pot. Resembling an oily scalp with Rastafarian dreadlocks, the Medusa-like idol exhales a pungent pall as bodies bare and beautiful succumb to its serpentine pipes - George folding his long limbs nimbly across the nearest cushion, leaving Charlene in the redhead's assistance.

"Got a ticket to ride ... aummm ... got a ticket to ride?" Marvin drones.

"Twenty of 'em," George employing the excuse of passing two sawbucks to grope the redhead seated cross-legged beside him. "And there's twenty more if I choose the ride," he adds, oblivious to Charlene.

"Aummm," Marvin moans, the circle responding, "aummm ... aummm."

"Is this some kind of mantra?" Charlene whispering in his ear, her hand on his leg reminding him of her presence.

"Must be," George grunts, chagrined by the reminder. "Maybe an incantation? An invocation to spirit guides?"

"Aummm ... aummm," the circle chanting hynotically, "aummm ... aummm," Charlene joining in, "aummm ... aummm," her button blouse appearing to unfasten of its own accord, "aummm ... aummm," rousing Marvin to new intensity:

"Leander ... Leander is here!" he announces officiously, his mono-tone in eerie rhythm with the sway and bounce of encircling breasts, with the entrancing drone of 'aummms', with the psychedelic posters glowing in the lurid light–

With the beautiful woman swooning before him.

"Tonight, he swims the Hellespont – the Winooski - to unite with his Hero ... aummm ... aummm ... his goddess of legalese ... aummm ... his priestess of pleasure and love ... aummm ... ."

Charlene's blouse completely unbuttoned, her bra-restrained bust disguising her pregnancy; the while, George, unaware of her exposure, making good on his offer, his hands a busy escrow of intent.

"Tonight, Leander ... L-L-Lea-" Marvin's chanting chopped by sudden intrusion, "tonight, the Old Geezer is here ... says he has news from the Superior Court of Records," the precipitous pronouncement having no effect on the ministrations at hand, save for a general grasping for the Medusa. "Says he has news for the priestess ... no, he says. No. She's not a priestess ... aummm ... says I said that, not him. Says she's a hostess ... hosting a party ... a party unclaimed. Says that's the news, aummm ... a sub-poena ... aummm ... a writ of habeas corpus ... something about a dispute of ownership ... aummm ... a body without a soul," George paying heed to the muddled Latin, his wrested attention going solo among the group.

"Would that be the body of a woman, perchance?" he queries, peer-ing through the haze for Charlene.

"Aummm ... and oh! what a woman she is!" a weed-mad Marvin mouths, "what a ... but wait," he says out of hand, "the Old Geezer's cor-recting me ... aummm ... says the body is male ... says it's quartered in the female beside you."

"Charlene?" George incredulous, discovering her exposure, forget-ting his own prurience. "Charlene? But, of course ... why not?" he grouses, covering her as best he can, "like son, like mother."

"Like partner, like son-in-law, the Old Geezer says ... and goodbye, too ... aummm ... says he's stepping aside for another spirit to come through."

"Wait!" a riveted George demands, "I want to know who the Old Geezer claims to be."

"He's gone," Marvin drawing help from the pipes, "but in his place comes another ... aummm ... aummm ... a female vibration ... a real shaker

... man! she's more like an earthquake than a vibration!" Marvin jarred to attention. "Ma's the name ... no, Mars ... no ... no ... Martha ... that's it, Martha. Says you don't know her yet ... aummm ... but you damn sure will."

"Do I want to?" George quips, Marvin's twitching and jerking not a condition to be envied.

"You've no choice in the matter, she says ... says the subpoena from the higher court secures your acquaintance."

Charlene coming round, Marvin's mesmerizing effect wearing off - her opened blouse troubling her attention.

"The subpoena will acquaint you with Martha ... as well as reveal the identity of the soul to be assigned to that doll - ouch! - to that male vibration beside you," Marvin lurching as though pushed from behind.

"What's he rattling about?" Charlene furtively buttoning her blouse, "hermaphrodites?"

"Indeed not!" Marvin answers for him, his blank-eyed stare suggesting a trance, "and no Salmacis are you, woman ... aummm ... nor is that Hermaphroditus beside you. No indeed. That gorgeous mortal you so despise would never consent to that! He's too intent on multiplicity to ever unite as one!"

"Greek mythology," George explains. Salmacis was a nymph who fell in love with Hermaphroditus and became united with him in one body."

"Well said ... and so says your partner," Marvin rails. "Says your partner is sorry for causing the babe's - ouch! Stop that! - the bitch's condition ... aummm ... wants to apologize to both of you."

"My partner?" George flummoxed. "I-I haven't a part-"

"Melvin?" Charlene interjects, "is he referring to Melvin?"

"The letter 'M' she's showing me ... two of 'em ... two 'M's ... except the last one is ... aummm ... squared ... aummm ... has a little numeral 2 behind it."

"Melody?" Charlene gasps, "could-could it be his wife? that bane of my-"

"Or his son, perhaps?" George obtrudes, his suggestion no less disturbing. "Or maybe there's no one there at all," he amends, dismissing her misgiving. "Maybe it's just the weed blowing in the wind."

"Ouch!" cries Marvin, flinching from an invisible slap, "Martha says that damn woman there beside you knows ... says she's the one who was always serving coffee to the innocent man who never drank it ... says she's the one responsible for the unclaimed freight in her hold, not the victim who died ... aummm ... died with grief on his heart ... aummm ... and sin on his hands."

"Victim!" Charlene shrieks, the circle of boobs bouncing en masse for the pipes, "I am the victim here, not that ... not him ... not that lying bastard who ran out on me before I could-"

"Ran out on you?" Marvin interposes, his trance apparently allowing emotion, "Did you say he ran out on you? Wrong, wrong ... aummm ... wrong you are!" he repeats emphatically. "He didn't run out; he dropped out! But he's coming back! Back into your life! Back into your law office, even! Back ... aummm ... back ... aummm ... back to slobber a kiss on your two-timing lips!"

"Noooo!" Charlene wails, fainting dead away.

"Oh hell yes!" Marvin insists, unaware of his guest's collapse, "and what's more, that gorgeous hunk beside you ... aummm ... will not be trapped. He ... aummm ... he won't be at your wedding."

Caught between Charlene's collapse and Marvin's maledictions, George is anything but amorous, the redhead taking advantage of his distraction to escape, to play the hostess, returning to offer a recovering Charlene a paper cup of something dark - something with the sharp aroma of Chianti - and a thin slice of what could pass for pizza, Marvin continuing his chanting, his ranting, his topless devotees aummm-aummming him on:

"The woman's going to have a baby," he raves, "a boy ... aummm ... but just who that son might be is still up in the air."

"This is making no sense. No sense at all," George fumes, "and the more he goes on, the more confused I become."

"Well, don't say I didn't warn you," Charlene caustic, exasperation in the flash of her eyes, "the only chance being taken here is our own!"

"And I'm in no mood for gambling," he agrees, helping her to her feet. "Let's go while that chance lingers."

"You just wait!" threatens Marvin, the redhead guiding them to the entrance, "Earthquake says you just wait ... aummm ... says you'll know her by the thrill of a touch ... by the memory of some old tavern night ... by the familiarity of a moan ... by the-"

"Sex!" Charlene spits, hurrying George to the car, "you would think that with all their hallucinogens these people could find another thrill!"

"Oh, they have," George wistfully ogling the redhead as he unlocks his car, "... the thrill of freedom."

There is nothing certain but uncertainty.
(Pliny)

XIII

I HAVE NEVER GIVEN THE ART OF AUGURY MUCH attention, assuming psychic readings, tarot cards and palmistry to be just another venue for entertainment, another poke down the proverbial rat hole. And having no faith in mediums, I have never attended a séance; nor, have I thought it possible to attend one from the wrong-side-in, which is what A.M. has us doing at the A-frame. I must admit, playing the part of the visiting spirit is surreal, the hippies' black lights doing something weird to the smoke at my level until I see things I shouldn't: a buxom redhead with a ten dollar bill trapped under each breast; my secretary Charlene swaying to a Himalayan chant, pointing first one breast and then the other at some kind of ceremonial pot; and my partner George keeping happily abreast of it all.

With my thaumaturge (my "maker of magic") exercising her phenomenal thought imposition, I'm right back where I started: doubting the format's legitimacy.

As George and Charlene drive away, I chasten A.M. for her folly, not to mention her fabrications:

"I didn't know you could tell a lie in our realm. You said thoughts are public domain. So, how could you make them seem something other than what they are?"

"Correct," Aunt Martha chortles, zipping to Charlene's ahead of the bickering couple's arrival. "But I wasn't addressing anyone in our realm. I was talking down, so to speak, giving George some needed advice. Consider this," she adds spiritedly, "have you ever heard of someone lying up? Of course not. They always lie down - which is all I was doing."

"An erroneous analogy," I tease, grabbing the rare chance to rib her, "it's upside-down. Although, there is a venue that allows for, nay, lauds the practice of lying up. In fact, for each successful lay-up, the liar is awarded two points." Aunt Martha confused, her respect for my previous profession producing doubt. "I'm referring to the game of basketball," I explain, any question of her opinions seeming always to sound the trumpet, to rally a quick and vigorous attack.

"A game?" she ponders, her color returning, "y-yes, and that's just what I was doing, throwing the ball into their court, letting them make the next move."

"And how is that?" I ask, A.M. turning things round on me, as usual.

"Well, as you know, that business about a subpoena was fictitious; but I wanted George to be aware of an escape. He can force that other woman of yours to own up to her mistake. He needn't stand in as the father."

"And you thought you could best accomplish this treachery by suggesting her baby lacked a soul?"

"Treachery?" a sudden pique darkening her ethereal cheeks.

"Yes, treachery," I repeat, focusing the blame. "And how did you masquerade as Caesar? The medium could differentiate between male and female vibrations – whatever that means."

"Oh, that was simple," she pooh-poohs, "especially when that pothead was posing as Leander. I employed his inflamed imagination for a while, that's all. Your other woman had his testosterone in such an uproar he couldn't discern the difference, had he wanted to."

"Aha! Then you admit to Charlene's power," I counter, "her ability to make a man do what he would not."

"Ah!" she rejoins, taking my bait with such pleasure I know instantly it's me who is caught. "The good Saint Paul had something to say about that, writing, 'For that which I do I allow not: for what I would, that do I not; but what I hate, that do I.' And again, 'For the good that I would I do not: but the evil which I would not, that I do.'"

Aunt Martha's uncanny memory of the saints, I am soon to discover, is but another trick in her mind-reading repertoire, every jot and tittle of the holy writ – or any other great work - available for instant scan if one knows how to use the galactic library.

"Yes," I admit, recovering, Thelma's Sunday-school lessons not all for naught, "but Saint Paul also wrote, 'Now if I do that I would not, it is ... it-it-'" I stumble, trying to recall the verse. "Oh, now I remember, 'It is no more I that do it, but sin that dwelleth in me.'"

"Which is where I was leading you all along, nephew!" she cries in triumph. "And believe me, wringing an admission of sin from you has not been easy!"

Drawing back for my last punch, I don my most arresting court-room demeanor:

"So you would judge, auntie. But as the great Montaigne maintained, 'We readily acknowledge in others an advantage in courage, in bodily strength, in experience, in agility, in beauty; but an advantage in judgment we yield to no one.' So, I leave it to you to decide," I jab cleverly, "I leave it to you to judge me sinner or saint; notwithstanding the Bible's stern admonishment, 'Judge not, that ye be not judged-'"

"For with what judgment ye judge," she finishes for me, forestalling another memory lapse, "ye shall be judged."

"Which, so saying, should put the fear of God in you," I reply; realizing, even as I cite the verse, that by judging her I'm accusing myself; Aunt Martha's theft of my thought spreading a smile - George and Charlene walking in before she can gloat over her latest advantage.

"Nonsense!" Charlene tossing her comely head, cheeks color-stung with anger. "Believe what you will, George, but my baby has a soul! And a pure one, at that!" she adds defiantly, her hands on her hips suggesting his immediate departure.

"I was only repeating what we heard out there," George retorts, "not making a judgment. And my idea on how to rectify that deficiency ... should there be one, is-"

"Sound familiar?" A.M. thinks, accepting my affirmative nod.

"Well, at least give it some thought," George back-stepping to her front door. "You can bet your bottom dollar they don't call it a marriage bed for the sleep it affords!"

"No dollar will ever see my bottom!" Charlene rebuts, dropping her hands from her hips as if to ward off advance from the rear, "... although, a carat or two might dazzle my shiner."

"Sounds like your treachery is working," I observe, "either that, or George is reverting to his old habits: planning a hard right turn at the church house steps."

"Don't you worry about George," A.M. avers, "he's going to wise up, take a little trip back to Boston ... put some distance between himself and his problems."

"How do you know?" I quiz, following her to Artie's bookstore.

"I read his thoughts, that's why; and he's tired of being refused; tired of being blamed for a problem that promises no relief."

"Relief?" I challenge, "you make sex sound like a kidney function, Aunt Martha. A real pisser. Come to think of it, that's why George left Boston in the first place - he being at all times a pisser or a pain in the ass, according to what he told me - so what comfort can he expect by returning?"

"Melody!" A.M. knocking two books off a shelf to gain Artie's attention – or distract mine. "Let's see what's smokin' here," she cracks with a wink, "or, in the parlance of *The New York Times*, what news is fit to print."

"Can't be much to read from a mind that never reads," I quip, feigning humor to obscure concern.

"And there's not much to be gained by avoiding concern, either," Aunt Martha's proximity giving Artie the shivers. "So what are you worried about?"

"Melody," I admit. "Specifically, that George may be going to Boston to visit her."

"Oh, he's harmless," she assures me; Artie trudging off to build a fire, "there's nothing to worry about there. Look at it this way, dear," A.M. hovering over Artie's wood-burning stove, "if a man were starving, it would be foolish to waste his means on a new suit of clothes. What he needs is a hot meal. And what George needs right now is just that. Nourishment. Nourishment for the soul."

"George needs soul food, does he?" her allegorical approach failing to placate.

"In a sense," her smile widening, "In fact, we could call it his blue-plate special."

"You're just getting in deeper," I warn, not taking kindly to her reference to Melody as a cheap lunch.

"You don't understand," she argues – something she loves to do. "George is blue, right? But Melody's bluer; true blue, if you get my point. So let him make a blue streak to see her. It doesn't matter. She'll blue-pencil his plot faster than he can script it if he starts any blue movie moves."

"Thanks, Auntie," I snort, noting her sudden interest in the paper with which Artie is stoking the kindling, "leave it to you to fetch the blue-bird of happiness."

"And why not?" she crackles. "Looks like your march is going up in blue flames."

"My march?" I echo, out of step with her about-face.

"Thelma's questionnaires, dummy," A.M. nodding at a stack of mimeographed sheets, "he's burning them."

"But they're blank," I exclaim, scanning the stack, "probably just surplus copies he ran off to help her cause."

"Maybe, but at least we can have a peek at Thelma's questions," Aunt Martha's infectious enthusiasm having immediate effect, the idea of researching my pending doom irresistible. "Let's see," she puffs whimsically, scanning a sheet before Artie can wad it up, "it'll be interesting to see where Thelma's interest lies."

"Ok, but clue me in before we start: are we lying up or lying down this time?"

"Down," A.M. ignoring my taunt. "Wow! Look at this," she instructs, projecting her thoughts for me to read, "'Miss Cellaneous March Questionnaire' ... Melvin, you'd better hope she doesn't succeed!"

"I thought her impending success was your impassioned aim," I rejoin, "thought you were gleefully anticipating your nephew's character assassination."

"You're the character making an ass of yourself, not me. But look at these questions, Melvin," A.M. projecting them above the stove as Artie collapses into his armchair, trusted flask in hand, "'Offender's Name, it reads; and, Number of Offenses per Spree."

"Yes, and look at this: under Crime she asks for Frequency of Offense and Duration of Offense; and under Offender Profile one is supposed to rate the Skill in Assault Techniques and Size of Weapon. Judging by the tenor of her classifications, auntie, she has people making war, not love. What kind of message is she trying to send?"

"None," A.M. perusing the form with the distressing resolve of dripping water. "If she were trying to send a message, she'd use Western Union. No, this is covert action. This is General Peabody duping her troops; Thelma, the would-be-temptress, getting the goods on the local lovers. You can bet that for every questionnaire answering favorably for the offender, there'll be one more crime in the criminal, one more offense in the offing."

"You mean she-" I start to say, Artie's long sigh interrupting me, the kindling going up in a wasted rush of flames, a canvas tote of split wood lying untouched at his feet.

"She's compiling a hit-list," Aunt Martha declares, "a list of men to hit on; any 'offender', whose wife or fiancee is disenchanted enough to join her march, fair game for her hunting."

"And all at my expense," I moan, "a man who couldn't survive his reputation. 'O what a vile and abject thing is man if he does not raise himself above humanity,' I lament, quoting an unremembered author of yore."

"Seneca," she informs me, surprising me yet again by her familiarity with the ancients, "knew him in my ... let's see ... my third Roman life, I believe; though I didn't agree with his philosophy."

"I bet you didn't," my lips curling like burning paper, and with the same finality, "I can't imagine you a Stoic!"

"Nor can I this lovable man," A.M. glancing at Artie, then lowering her eyes as if to conceal affection. "Though impervious to words, Artie's anything but unfeeling."

"And just where are you going with this?" I demand, mistrusting her endearments.

"Oh ... nowhere," she muses, eying his silver flask the way one ogles a favorite souvenir, remembering the pleasant times, "... unless we want to follow him into oblivion."

With a sudden gasp, Artie appears to have heard us - or heard something, whatever it was surprising him - his emptied flask dropping to the hardwood floor with a metallic crash as he lurches forward, falling across the wood at his feet with the thud of an ax-felled tree, his stiff felt cap rolling in an arc, then coming to rest under his chair.

Later, when I recall the scene, I remember a flash of light before Artie hit the floor - or a streak, I should say, not a flash; an intense, fleeting glow moving out and up from Artie's falling frame to pass out of sight through the rafters. I've never seen a man die, from the spirit's perspective; but the trauma of Artie's death attacked me like claws ripping viciously through my chest; my own death, unremembered until now, coming back with crushing pain: that moment, alone in the woods; the agony of knowing I was dying, that I was powerless to prevent it, to defend against its pillage, its cruel thievery of my life, my ambitions, my dreams, my chance, even, to make amends for my follies; seeing all - the past, the present, the future; the future as it might have been – all I had done, or not done; my silent scream of terror summoning Martha; hearing her voice, remembering it from my youth ... going back ... back ... Aunt Martha's hand now soothing my brow, my fright, her familiar voice comforting me, telling me, "It's over, Melvin ... it's all over, sweetheart. Artie's got a table reserved in the Galaxy Lounge. He'll be just fine. They'll probably even let him have his flask for a while ... let him adjust to his new surroundings."

"His flask!" I hear myself cry, reaching to where I had seen it drop - only to find it gone. "I had my first taste of whiskey from that heirloom flask!"

"A quick death is the supreme good fortune of mortal life," Aunt Martha stroking my empty hand. "I can remember a few that were otherwise."

"I-I was just-"

"I know," she consoles, "... I know. But having once remembered, it loses its sting, my dear. You'll learn to take comfort in looking back ... back at a bridge you've already crossed. A bridge that, from the other side, once seemed so enigmatic, so foreboding. So impassable."

"Then-then why aren't we allowed to recall this while on Earth?" I ask, trembling from the rush of memories. "Why not take the sting from death altogether?"

"Maybe because we would let down our guard?" she suggests, each of us alighting on an opposite arm of Artie's chair. "We could opt out of trial, of difficulty, by escaping across the bridge. Given the certainty of peace on this side, and the equal certainty of making it safely across, who would choose to withstand all the evils on the lower side?"

"Perhaps you're right," I marvel, regarding the still form of my friend - our friend - sprawled on the floor. "But Artie never seemed bothered," I muse, death playing its usual trick of reminiscence, "I mean, he never seemed aware of evil. It was as though he didn't know it existed."

"Where there is good - all good - there can be no evil," A.M.'s tone betraying her depth of thought. "And Artie was a good man."

"He was that, and more," I agree, suddenly aware of what needs to be done. "We should let someone know about this, pay our respects by-"

"Taken care of," she interjects. "George is on his way," the little bell at the front entrance tinkling as she replies.

"And how did you do that?" I ask, ever amazed at her abilities.

"I-I didn't," a rare humility in her voice, "you can thank one of Artie's angels for summoning him."

"A guardian angel?"

"Exactly. Put the thought in George's mind, made him think he should come look for a book of poetry for Melody."

"You know," I bristle, pulling her with me to leave George behind, "seems to me you've said something about George being with Melody a dozen times today. That's not persistence, Aunt Martha, that's stalking. And I've had enough of it!"

"'Love cloys, unless pain cuts the bliss,' Martial used to say - another one of my Roman compatriots - but by the bridge we were just discussing, you'll soon leave such folly behind."

Indubitably, she's right; and after reliving dying, I'm too discomposed to pretend otherwise.

There are only two kinds of music:
good and bad.
(Duke Ellington)

XIV

WITH THANKSGIVING BUT A WEEK AWAY, THELMA HAS
more on her plate than usual: Arthur Steinberg's funeral to be wept
through, a hyper-creative Simon to be made over, and Melvin's march to
be plotted out. But to get through, over and out of anything, Thelma needs
more than time. And more ammunition. Armed with only two completed
questionnaires, her retaliatory march is promising to be more like a scouting party than a platoon. Another complication is her burgeoning romance
with Simon, the whole of Plainfield beginning to doubt her complicity in
the "commie bugster" affair:

"She's too forgiving," Faithful remarks to Mrs. Rolundo after the
Sunday service, "too eager to make amends. Makes me think there's something astir."

Mrs. Rolundo replying, "Why of course there is, dear, Thelma being
the whirlwind she is."

In truth, Thelma is going in circles, pacing a track in the nap of her
plush hearth rug while attempting to solve enigmas: three poems from
Simon Farley - the latest strokes from his nervous pen the kind of masterly work convincing to all save those comprehending them. Of the three,
Thelma favors *Neither Nor*, judging it a none-to-veiled proposal, reciting it
through her paces:

You are unto yourself what you would be;
But unto me that which you are.
Pray bright may burn your guiding star
To lead you to that end which ends with me.

Pray Great One who from naught envisioned all,
May all be seen in nothing me.
Pray precious one by Love to see
My naught loom large in matters great and small.

Pray too that ever I adornment be,
Gold clasp to hold the vestment true;
Pray then that I in answer to
The why of we, make plain: twas meant to be.

You are unto yourself what you would be;
But unto me that which you are.
Pray look beyond your neither, nor;
Past rule's exception to discover – me!

If indeed he's extending his hand, she's eager to clasp it. Nay, impatient to do so. But caution prevails, the two remaining rhymes so obfuscatory she dare not risk his intent in the first. Of the two, *Fairy Tale* seems to support her interpretation, as well as suggest his dislike for her marches - a right she's willing to right if two rights make a wrong in bed. Just yesterday, she shared her suspicion with Artie, his kind old eyes twinkling as she read him the lines:

One day, by chance, old Happenstance
Fell hapless from his stance.
Try as he might, he could not fight
The slight of reasoned glance.

Like those who wait for luck or fate,
His luck came all too late;
'Cause life demands a show of hands;
Caught fish require their bait.

And we ourselves, like storied elves,

May nap on fancy's shelves;
Till comes the fall, from Humpty's wall,
That walls us in ourselves.

So plant a bean, eat fat or lean;
But keep it Snow White clean;
Or curds and whey may spoil the day
Your way churns out the scene.

The comfort of Artie's agreement invites her back, suggests his opinion on the remaining poem, *The Whippoorwill* (that the whippoorwill is a member of the goatsucker family, Caprimulgus Vociferus, casting no aspersions on her desire to appreciate its majesty), this very desire responsible for her discovery of a frantic George attempting to pound life into Artie's chest.

"What's this?" she screams, "what's happened here?" George's frenetic attempts as startling as the appalling sight of Artie sprawled on the floor.

"Heart attack," George bellows, "or maybe he choked. I don't know. But go get some help, will you?" his strident tone frightening her out of the store.

While summoning the doctor from his tavern dinner, she remembers leaving her poem on Artie's counter, *The Whippoorwill* a subject upon which Artie might have expounded - Artie, on occasion, enjoying the same trails Simon pedaled. But now she'll never know; nor, will she retrieve the poem, her *Opus Mysterium* gone, pilfered by a curious hand, Poor Art's overrun by the meddlesome gawkers a public death attracts.

But when the poem makes the front page of the *Plainfield News*, she thinks better of losing it, harboring a lover's pride in seeing her Simon published. Never mind the poem's notoriety - it being the last thing placed on Artie's counter - and never mind that Artie doesn't read. The mystery of who may have seen Artie last has Simon's poem being recited, the locals theorizing on its relevance to Artie's demise. Even Vincent Tenklei authors an article in which he analyzes the verse for clues. Such notoriety precludes Simon taking credit for his masterpiece, part of its allure its anonymity; not to mention Simon's wish to avoid implicating himself should foul-play be suspected in Artie's death.

But when he discovers a copy of *The Whippoorwill* stapled to a litter bin on the Winooski trails, his hard-thought lines besmirched by a blue jay, he forgoes his self-protecting diffidence, peddling expeditiously for Thelma's farm.

"This is unconscionable!" he raves, the fire in his voice a new excitement for Thelma. "I give you a piece of my heart, and the next thing I know you have it published in the local paper. And as if that weren't enough, I find this!" he shouts, waving the bird-dunged copy in her face. "If an adoring heart is to be ignored, discarded, and trashed like a piece of rubbish, I would think it deserves an interment more sacred than a common litter bin!"

"Only a piece, See-*MOAN*?" she coos, his rage only stirring her desire, "only a piece of your heart? And just when I was ready to pledge you the whole of mine? Who do you think would have cause to post your poetry on the trails?" she asks sweetly, coaxing him through her door. "Could it be someone who adores you? Someone who, like the children of fairytale, leaves you a trail of crumbs to follow?"

"Then ... then-"

"I did it, See-*MOAN*," Thelma's manic smile broadening, "... my way of dropping a hint. And it worked, too," she pipes, leading him to what she calls "his chair", the newly varnished rocker pulled scratching-close to her own. "You're here, safe and snug in your rocker. And I want to hear your inspired recitation. I want to swoon to your words, your voice," Thelma whispering now, leaning over him; the scent of perfume playing the trail of crumbs, "... your voice, like a lute-throated dove, casting *The Whippoorwill's* spell."

Drinking deeply of her shimmering eyes, desire comes flooding as moonlight, waking his troubadour tongue. Taking command of the moment, he waves her to her knees - to a compulsory silence awaiting some Olympian feat - and lifting high her bird-dirtied copy, he lets it fall feather-light to the floor, relying on his memory - his opportunistic memory - to surpass what desire has imagined.

"I-I have renamed it," he stutters, wincing at the implication, "I call it *For the Birds*."

"*For the Birds* ..." she muses softly, "*For the Birds*, for the turds, what's the difference ... just recite it to me, darling."

And so he does; though the lines seem rudely altered, his words, once swaddled in innocent humor, now sharp as piercing swords cutting asunder a last restraint:

> The whippoorwill not consort,
> His pride too big for the swallow;
> Let crow eat all his Wordsworth,
> With rhyme his reason will follow.
>
> The whippoorwill not consent
> To risk robin' his own nest egg
> For hollers in night owl hoots,
> No matter how peli-can beg.
>
> The whippoorwill not allow
> A bird of his feather to flock;
> For time flies hard at his wing
> To a rhythm that wood-ticks-tock.
>
> The whippoorwill not accept
> A package the wagtail has sent;
> Assuming the UPS are downs
> In any stork-naked event.
>
> The whippoorwill cry at night,
> Not a grain of truth in his heart;
> Thinking it's all for the birds,
> Be it bushel, woodpeck'er quart.
>
> The whippoorwill never be
> A raven forlorn in the night,
> Till mockingbird mimics the
> Whip-poor-will's insight – then he might!

His sacrifice made, Simon's rocker envelopes him like a sarcophagus, his skeletal frame rattling back against the dowels. "You know, of course, to whom I refer in the poem?" he asks coyly.

"Nooo," she breathes, pretending diffidence to bolster his courage, "but I'm dying to learn."

"Am I that dense?" he probes, seeking some measure of favor, "do I rhyme so foggily your own reflection is missed? It's you, Thelma," he cries from behind his blush, "you are my mockingbird, my plaintive call to awake and sing ... to redress my lyric plangency ... march to a rousing beat-"

"Then-then you don't mind if I march?" Thelma too pleased to refrain.

"Not if I'm marching with you," he counters.

"But you ... you ... oh well," she falters, deferring to the problems of another day the inconsistency of a man marching against his own nature, "we shall see about that. But right now we have other pleasures to explore," Thelma getting up to find his lap, "other delights for your imaginative mind."

"Yes," he sighs, "yes," such high-flown verse giving wings to his thoughts, her bedposts blurring like the fringe of a voluptuous, flying carpet; Thelma taking him places iambic pentameter has yet to describe – the sensuous trip leaving them too transported, too enraptured for the Earthbound woe of a funeral.

But a funeral there must be, Artie lying in his adopted state as Reverend Rolundo redeems himself by his eloquence, his poise; his non-sectarian approbation for a good man's life in grateful contrast to the kinky kudos of Melvin's eulogy - many of the mourners whispering asides about the reverend's bravery for even daring the tribute. And indeed, he strives to atone for his earlier peccadilloes; his portrayal of Artie as a kind-hearted man, a modern-day good Samaritan, a sower of seeds among the minds of his customers, going far to accomplish this end.

With The Church of the Good Shepherd safely dispossessed of Artie's corpse, the mourners pass on in murmuring file to the hilltop grave overlooking the river, the prayers of the faithful rising like the smoke of incense, their frost-chilled breaths curling eerily about as they trek up cemetery hill. (All, that is, save George and Charlene; those two disappearing before the reverend had even commenced.) "It went as it should," observes the paunch-bellied tavern owner to some of his regulars, "Artie would have been proud of the reverend today," those in earshot nodding somberly.

"And what makes you think that?" an intrusive Thelma demands, quickening her step to encroach on the pace of his listeners. "What makes you think Artie would be any different than when he was alive?"

"Have some respect, will ya?" begs the old man, struggling painfully up the hill, "there's no need to be invitin' the kind of trouble we had here before. And what's eatin' at ya anyhow?" he asks. "Rumor has it you've gone and changed on us, Thelma; you've gone soft on the issues. But now I'm not so sure I believe 'em."

"Yeah," the regulars mumble, "... yeah," signaling agreement with bleary-eyed stares.

Possessed by some puissance before unknown, Thelma bristles at the hint of protest, her voice growing shrill, abrasive:

"If ever there lived an honest man, it was Arthur," she rails, "and since honesty is supposedly synonymous with truth, Artie would not want us touting friendships that never were. Not to imply he had enemies, mind you; but there were a few in our village Artie would have just as soon not fraternized with – and the reverend counted among them," she spouts vehemently.

The stunned men are further surprised by how quickly Simon Farley positions himself at her side – or rather, steps decidedly into her path – his kindly intent obvious to all. "Enough!" he declares, grasping her gesticulating hands. "There are other forums from which we can speak, other venues more appropriate than a man's last moments above the sod."

But where affection has ruled, reason now clearly fails, Thelma shoving him rudely out of her way. "You said you wanted to march with me, didn't you?" she shrills truculently, stomping through the cemetery gate, "then march, damn it! We've got a message to deliver here; a veritable sermon on the mount."

"Oh my God!" Mrs. Rolundo gasps, stepping sprightly to her husband's side, "it's the curse of the dead! Come on!" she implores, tugging his arm, "I won't have you being blamed for this one!"

But if the reverend's presence invoked this torch of discontent, his departure inflames it, Thelma's scorching incantations licking as fire from Artie's tomb:

Never such shameful, foul examples do we find,
But that still worse, untold, remain behind-

she screeches, stomping to a halt before the gaping grave and its dangling denizen, "or so said Juvenal, that great Roman satirist who even now is laughing at our hypocrisy."

"Well! Aren't you the scholar?" a huffing Simon declares, catching up to her as she delivers her quote. "I had no idea!" Refusing him the courtesy of acknowledgment, she continues her raving:

"And if example indeed the reverend be, then believe you me, you don't want to know the untold," she says scathingly. "What Rolundo failed to tell you today, I shall; for our friend here deserves to be heard." Scurrying to the far side of the freshly dug grave, the gray steel of Artie's casket becomes her dolorous lectern. "Unlike the most of us here," she continues, perilously near the cavernous excavation, "this man made a conscious choice to enjoy life in our village, abandoning his former home - his heritage, even - on the strength of his uncommon faith, his belief that Plainfield was the kind of place where one might find life's missing pieces. And ever smiling through those big brown eyes was a heart as big as Texas. As neighborly, too, if you gave him a chance – which the reverend never did. That's right," she fumes, pointing accusingly down the hill at the ever diminishing Rolundos, "you heard me right."

Artie's mourners bending like trees under her windy diatribe – Simon stumbling backward for fear her blazing eyes might reveal some fault of his own.

"I could tell you a thing or two on Rolundo," Thelma's hand outstretched in Simon's direction, "his thing ... those two ... but I won't. I won't because Artie wouldn't. But-but ... excuse me?" Thelma faltering, peering into the autumn sky as though the scrambled clouds are communiques, exclaiming, "Oh, really! And how are things on that side, Artie?" her listeners retreating into a defensive line, Thelma unaware of their movement, "but-but you can still see us here? ... and you're telling me ... you're saying you don't want to hurt anybody? Not even that hypocrite Rolundo? Sorry, I shouldn't have put words in your ... what? ... you want to help us discover what peace is our present portion?"

The cowering crowd moving closer again, Thelma's countenance losing its frightening scowl, her tempestuous tone abating, becoming sweet to their injured ears.

"And especially our dear, delicate artist?" she goes on, "our treasure of rhyme? our own See-*MOAN* Far-*LAY*? ... author of that mystical mystery, *The Whippoorwill*?"

The huddling mourners yielding up such a startled response that even Simon is carried away, their momentary chatter counting as his first public credits. "And being in the position to see beyond our horizon, you take the occasion of your burial to unearth a prophecy? Is that what you're saying?"

Hushed, the mourners inch backwards again, her revelation stoking fear - Simon like a slide under a microscope, his peers nudging him this way and that, sandwiching him between their curiosity and Artie's grave.

"It will?" Thelma's soliloquy continues, "his first book of collected poems will bring him fame? But what is it? ... the title, I mean? ... Ah! how apropos!" she cries, letting go a frightening cackle. "Cycles! ... I like that ... sounds like something he'd try to pedal," she calls back to the scudding clouds. "And what? ... what did you say? that you'll be back to enjoy it? ...that you'll treasure the gift of books this time? ...value the art of reading? And when are you coming?" she asks, turning round and round as though seeking a sign in the sky, "Really! ...that soon!" she shrieks, her pirouetting making her giddy, her stumbling turns, accompanied by eerie peels of laughter, giving the impression of lunacy. "Now?" Thelma letting go another round of preternatural cachinnation, "you're returning now? ... this instant?"

The last of the mourners beating a hasty retreat down the rock-strewn hill - leaving Simon alone with the opportunity to prove his manhood, his protecting love. For when Thelma suddenly drops from sight, he hurries round the blue-gray bulk of Artie's casket to pull her out of the grave.

When the mind doubts, a trifle pulls it to and fro.
(Terence)

XV

ARTIE'S FUNERAL MAKES ME REALIZE HOW MUCH I relished my own service, despite Aunt Martha's meddling, probably because Melody was there; for without Melody - or even George and Charlene - I lacked the tension of personal conflicts to play out the drama. But today is dramatic, nevertheless, Aunt Martha continuing to pull the wool over the eyes of the flock. How she can tell such whoppers through the voice of Thelma I'll never know, the part about Artie disliking the reverend a lie I'm certain will trap her. But it doesn't, the fool on the hill assailing her shivering auditors with such fury and fear she drives them away before truth can redeem the day.

"How can you do this to Artie?" I chide A.M.; the two of us watching Simon pull a dazed and trembling Thelma from under Artie's suspended coffin. "I distinctly remember you claiming criticism as a family right. But even had I granted you that right, it didn't apply here. And what's more, you've managed to leave a man levitating over his own grave!" I add captiously. "Your example of 'leaving it up in the air' is a bit extreme, don't you think?"

"So what shall we do about it?" A.M. asks distractedly, her focus on Simon attempting to escort his weak-kneed lady down the hill.

"Bury him, if we can," I reply, Simon's bandy-legged stride, zigzagging down the precipitous hill, reminding me of Chaplin's Little Tramp.

"Oh, we can all right ... but-"

"But what?" I prod, returning to the problem at hand.

"I was just thinking of Artie," she explains, "his first chance to rest in peace. We'd be interfering; we'd have the whole county astir over his grave. They'd be digging, figuratively and literally, trying to determine how his final let-down came to be."

"You mean-"

"I mean because they didn't finish the job; didn't bury him properly. But not to worry, Artie's about to make land."

"Yes," I mutter, espying two men with shovels approaching from the village below, "I see them trudging up the hill."

"Not what I meant," she corrects, turning to watch the grave tenders. "Artie's coming back to life on Earth."

"So soon!" I rejoin, remembering, suddenly, that Thelma had babbled a like remark. "Then what you were frightening the villagers with is true?"

"Yep," she says curtly, "and coming right back to Plainfield, too ... happening as we speak."

"Barring the miracle of this corpse getting up and walking," I counter, sarcasm edging my words, "I presume you mean the birth of a child."

"Yep," she repeats, enticing further inquiry.

But I don't ask, pretending, instead, to recall those I know to be pregnant. "Let's see," I muse casually, spoiling her pleasure, "there's Melody ... but she's spoken for. And then there's the young Kansas couple, the Comptons, whom Caesar told us about; but they're spoken for, too, I believe. But surely there are others," I go on, ignoring her restive twitch. "But, of course! the wife of the postmaster-"

"How about Charlene," she interrupts, impatience still her ruling planet, "your other woman, Melvin. How could you forget her?"

"I can't - not while you're here to remind me," I growl, feigning irritation, "but surely you're not going to tell me Artie has chosen her."

"Artie hasn't chosen anything," she snaps. "He didn't choose to come over when he did; and once here, he didn't opt to go back, either."

"But I thought we had choices," I argue, "opportunities, decisions. A choice is still a choice whether we act or do nothing ... whether we have our hand on the wheel, or let it spin where it may."

"Right, but one can't exercise a choice, positively or negatively, until one is aware a choice exists. When we are ready ... when we are ready. Until then, our fate is predestined."

"Predestined by whom?" I query, "and isn't that what most people believe? that fate plays the guide in their lives?"

"As to who grants what conditions our destiny, I leave for you to address," A.M. hopping up on Artie's casket. "But as to who petitions for them in the first place, we do that for ourselves."

"But you just said Artie hadn't a choice," I remind her, "so how does that agree with petitioning?"

"Guardian angels. Guardian angels act on our behalf."

"You mean like-"

"Legal guardians?" she finishes for me. "Yes, like legal guardians."

"Well!" I snort, pulling her off Artie's coffin before the chill of her presence can ward off the approaching workers, "you can't do better than an angel on your shoulder."

"And just where do you think that expression came from?" she asks, accepting my lead down the hill, "some dance-hall ditty?"

"Never gave it a thought," I reply, avoiding an argument, "but if Artie truly had no thought or say in his ruling events, then he can count himself fortunate; for, as Sophocles once said, 'In heeding nothing lies the sweetest life.'"

"You and your Greeks," she spouts, making a sudden turn for Montpelier, "as for me, I prefer the wisdom of my Roman peers. In fact, it was Lucretius who wrote, 'All things are bound by their own chains of fate.'"

"So now we have a choice of conditions?" I pose, turning to follow her towards the capital, "the freedom of ignorance, or the chains of fate? If it were me, I would choose ignorance: for, of the two, ignorance can be ameliorated."

"Too bad your other woman didn't have that choice," she quips, leading me into a trap, "but she's broken the chains of fate just the same."

"How so?" I ask, allowing myself to be caught.

"By mending her bitter heart with the love she has for her baby boy," A.M. pulling us up short at the hospital. "Artie has just been reborn as a red-faced, screaming little George."

"Good for Artie!" I exclaim, "... and bad for George."

"Oh?" Aunt Martha taking us in to hover in the powder-scented nursery, "and what would you have her name the child, Melvin, Melvin?"

"Of course not. But George isn't ... well-"

"Isn't going to marry her?" A.M. flitting back and forth among the squalling newborns as though looking for something that might pacify our crying Georgie boy.

"I don't know what I mean," I admit, taking a closer look at the little Artie-turned-Georgie; wondering (even as I search his wrinkled face for Morrison features, any resemblance to me) what my old friend Arthur would think of the switch; of his return as Melvin junior alias George junior, all the while being really himself, the whole confounding tripartite arrangement almost too amusing to accept. "And besides, how can we be sure this is Artie?" I ask skeptically.

"Look right here," she directs, pointing to a small, flask-shaped birthmark on the baby's right hip, "it's Artie all right, signed, sealed and delivered."

"Coincidence," I mutter, taking a closer look, "or a matter of interpretation," I add thoughtfully "The little mark could well be the signature of this child's calling in life ... perhaps psychiatry. This mark could be the projective test of an inkblot, a Rorschach; one which you just imagined a flask."

"Pshaw!" A.M. tugging me into the hall like a punished child. "I wasn't going to let you in on how I knew, but your flippant stubbornness compels me. I read Artie's life pattern while he and Melody were sharing a booth in that New Hampshire diner."

"Life pattern?" I repeat, disbelieving her. "Are you telling me you interpret palms when minds won't yield?"

"You're off the mark a bit," she chortles, smug in her superior skills, "a life pattern emanates from the heart. And with Artie so scrupulously honest, it was a snap to decipher his code ... almost too easy."

"Well, you know what they say about something that's too easy: there's a trick in it somewhere."

"You were the trick, and Charlene turned it," A.M. shoots back, "but Artie is blameless throughout. He's destined to have a better life this time."

"And here I thought his last life was about as idyllic as a man can hope for ... which proves how little I know."

"Idyllic?" her tone suggesting she's sincere. I'm not.

"Yes, with a business that nourished him peacefully ... and with the un-harried, unmarried life of a bachelor, what more could a man want?"

"Well!" she huffs officiously, "from that little snapshot of happiness we can deduce the cause of your melancholy!"

"Explain," I challenge.

"Man must know woman, in the biblical way, for the human race to continue. But according to you, it's just such a prerequisite that precludes our happiness; a kind of mandatory – pardon the pun – prep for the race that despoils our run out of Eden."

"What's this 'our' business," I gibe. "Far be it from me to speak on behalf of your gender," the appearance of a much distraught George O'Malley interrupting our imminent spat before it can fester; his gray, tragic eyes misting as he steps to the viewing window for a glimpse of his squalling junior.

"Not much happiness being evidenced there," I comment wryly. "Looks more like a man being led to the gallows."

"The hang-ups George suffers aren't lethal," she obliges grudgingly.

"Not immediately," I allow. "But maybe he's teary from dread; dread of all the work Artie has left him to do."

"But I'm telling you, he's not going to follow through," A.M. insists, "... he's not going to marry your other woman. In fact, when he's satisfied the baby is normal, that's when he'll tell her; hoping the good report on the baby will cancel out his cancellation."

"What do you mean, 'when he's satisfied the baby is normal'?" I hasten to ask. "If it's true I was responsible for providing the body, A.M., then-"

"Just kidding," she interrupts, "just tricking you into an admission ... King Solomon's ruling, you know: hand you the sword and you-"

"Right," I wince, "and I'm handing it right back, Aunt Martha. As of this instant, you can stop calling Charlene my other woman. Her baby has a body and a soul, but at least one of the two isn't mine."

"Not yours?" she rejoins emphatically, prepared to enlarge on her rejoinder.

"Not my soul," I specify, "not my soul. And rearing the child is not what I'm referencing. It's Artie's last will and testament." A.M. blinks inquisitively, begging me to continue. "George has his hands full, believe me - and not from the complexity of Artie's estate, either. Au contraire, it's the large thing Artie wanted to do with the little he had."

"Sound's familiar," A.M. shooting me a knowing look.

"The property, as you probably know, was leased; his books the only assets Artie owned," I explain. "And therein lies the work: his books are to be auctioned off, the proceeds used to build covered bus stops for the county's school children."

"What can be so difficult about that?" A.M. unsurprised by Artie's thoughtfulness.

"Well, first there's Artie's provision that Simon Farley play auctioneer."

"Comical to imagine," A.M. agrees, "but not onerous," both of us noting George's anxious stare resolving into one of relief.

"But there's more," I go on, "more than just the entertainment of a rhyming auctioneer. The convoluted terms of sale will be what drive George mad."

"What can be so difficult? You make a bid, and if successful, you settle up - pay cash, if required."

"That's what I told him; but he wouldn't listen."

"Didn't want cash? Artie? ... didn't want cold, hard-"

"Doesn't sound all that appealing from our side of the bridge, does it?" I interject. "But in answer to your question, yes and no. He wanted cash on the barrelhead; but he wanted my firm to top the high bid on his law books, The Church of the Good Shepherd the high bid on his religion section, the two tavern owners the high bids on his history collection, the general store-"

"Wait! Stop right there!" Aunt Martha demands. "I see the benefit of legal books for a law firm, of religious writings for a church ... and even Artie's cleverness in soliciting charity from the grave; but where's the connection of history to taverns?"

"Just part of his misconception, his rabble-rousing fantasies about Vermont's history; larger-than-life figures like Ethan Allen playing the agent provocateur in his theatrical mind, Artie dreaming himself back to those splendid times when a man could be a hero and a drunk with equal success."

"And who taught him these things?" she asks; a question acknowledging Artie's aversion to reading.

"The tavern regulars?" I venture, "who else could it be? I suppose the local imbibers would sooner imagine themselves the brave defenders of the Hampshire Grants than the impoverished tenants of New York land barons, and the alcoholic Ethan Allen would personify that fantasy."

"What's the difference," A.M. keeping an eye on George, "in either event, they would still have to earn their keep by the sweat of their brows."

"The freedom to speak one's mind, and then drink that mind into oblivion; a freedom Artie would defend from time to time. But his list of misinformed association goes on and on; another improbable being Thelma. He wanted Thelma to organize a march to raise funds for his women's rights collection. Can you imagine?"

"Actually, I can," she responds. "Provide Thelma with a cause, and she'll deliver the effects. But what possessed you to agree to such an involved procedure?" Aunt Martha knows the answer before I respond.

"How does one say no to a yes man? How does one stay dry in the rain? With Artie, there was no stopping the flow of kindness without splashing a little on yourself."

"Oh, I know," she reminisces.

"Of course you do," I follow, "for in your heart of hearts you know darn well you didn't win all those card games. It was just his way of rewarding you for the company you were willing to provide."

"What do you mean I didn't win?" A.M. defensive; though she would be surprised by an answer. I don't give one.

Our attention shifting to George, who is suddenly effusive, unnaturally affable with the coterie of grandparents, fathers and siblings peering through the nursery window - all with untenable observations regarding the perfection of their newborn kin. George's geniality is stunning.

"What's come over him?" I ask, assuming Aunt Martha can explain. "One minute he's dour 'n gray, and the next he's Dorian Gray, the life of the party."

"That's how he spells relief," A.M. cracks, "one child down and another to go."

"Another?" I repeat.

But my aunt has given me the slip. She's back over the baby, cooing with little George as though his birthmark has a cork. "George senior,"

I break in, joining her in the nursery, "... were you inferring George was going to father a second child?"

"Now how can a man father a second child when he hasn't fathered the first one?" she asks, giving me a wicked grin, "and now that I think about it ... didn't you have a birthmark on your-"

"But you just said-"

"I know what I said ... the problem is how you heard it."

"I'm a Harvard grad, Auntie," I contend, avoiding the birthmark reference by adroit circumlocution, "so I should have the rapidity of mind to untangle a phrase when I hear one."

"Harvard?" she cries, bouncing us through the roof before I know what's happening. "We have to go, Melvin. I almost forgot, Melody needs our help!"

To recall the joy doubles the pain.
(Dante)

XVI

WHAT SUN THERE HAD BEEN, DURING ARTIE'S BURIAL, sinks like a schooner over the western horizon. In its wake, a few silvery clouds nestle a crescent moon; while, quick as a Green Mountain frost, George chills to Charlene and her baby, abandoning them to the care of the less involved. Dogged by a blur of the preceding months, he drives aimlessly along the river, the force of habit sending him back to Plainfield, to the familiarity of Poor Art's Book Mart, its lighted sign like a flashback, memories of past and present conflating in a living scene.

"I had no choice, Artie," George addressing the decrepit wooden sign, as he exits his car for a stroll. "I had to slip out of your service. Charlene's labor pains. No respect, these babies. No respect for the dead ... or the living, for that matter."

A penitent in quest of sanctuary, George saunters toward cemetery hill: head bowed, hands clasped, mind on matters above. Memories break free as he nears the gate, taking wing under a myriad stars twinkling the argentine mist. Nearing Artie's grave, old tombstones glisten under the shadowing moon like a path to the saints' abode, the footprints of angels in sylvan solitude, a peaceful garden where buried souls may rise with the breaking dawn with shouts of joy.

George's imagination discloses incrementally: bordering hollyhocks, caroling robins, nodding conifers, a mountain breeze from scented slopes troubling the ancestral pool, an angel returning some fortunate soul to the cradle from whence it came. Happiness suddenly abounding, the death of a client and the birth of a child somehow conjuring a miracle, the glimpse of a passage, a gap through the range of despair.

Melody, George muses. Melody will understand; only Melody has the depth of soul to plum the darker mines, the brighter climes, the flights of fancy so suddenly all consuming. Melody: her name written across the fleeting, silken cloudscape, an approbatory moon but a sisterly smile as he stumbles upon a mounded grave, a bicycle. A chanting Simon.

Half pagan, half priest under the spell of verse, Simon calls out, "Who goes there?" unbending from the granite slab lying neighbor to Artie's tomb, "be it friend or-"

"There can be only friend in the argot of the dead" George announces, the timid, tenor voice of Simon Farley unmistakable, despite the shadowy haunts. "What cause might one have for alarm? The ultimate price has been paid. There's nothing left. Nothing to be assailed, to be harmed, to be taken."

Paused at the foot of Artie's fresh-mounded plot, his eerie shadow falling long under the waning moon, George's thoughts run even longer as Simon, recognizing his caller, refolds his skeletal frame atop a cold, granite slab.

"Charlene has delivered a child," George glancing about as though every headstone is a shining brass ring, "and I'm debating whether to be, or not to be, the father."

"I ... I admit my inexperience in-in such matters," Simon replies hesitantly, "but I believe you have the cart before the horse. This child of which you speak - if so be it's in the cart - should either be removed from the cart, or the cart should be repositioned behind the horse; for as you describe your quandary, your line of reasoning will get you only as far as the horse you rode in on - which is definitely before the cart."

"It's removed," George states matter-of-factly, "and the little cart is resting well ... perhaps ready for another pull before long. Who knows?" he offers, trailing off.

"And the horse?" Simon believing, as others do, that George is the only horse ever harnessed to the cart in question.

"Caveat emptor," he mutters, giving Simon his first direct look, "buyer beware, for what has been purchased by the price of wrong is not of my stock."

"Stock? as in horseflesh?" a puzzled Simon queries.

"As in the way of all flesh," George waxing philosophical. "As in the way of all mortals ... for this night am I enlightened."

"And what a night it is!" the poet agrees, Simon finding comfort in rhyme more than reason. "But why, pray tell, are you here? Perhaps a summons by our dearly departed?"

"More than a summons, my good man," George peremptory, glancing about for the nearest marmoreal seat, "I'm here by the will of Arthur Steinberg. I'm here to buy and sell, to pay and be paid ... to buy your kind office and to pay my respects."

"Free verse?" Simon mumbles blankly, watching the tall Irishman alight on the nearest slab and draw his knees to his chest like a praying mantis, "I - I didn't know you-"

"Even less than you," George intending no malice for the harmless Simon. "My inspiration springs from the words of others; and the script in question is Artie's will."

"But he had no siblings," Simon objects, "and his parents were deceased before he left Brooklyn."

"Must one have a family to be generous?" George posits - questioning himself, as well.

"Then ...."

"Am I referring to Artie's will?" George interposes. "Yes, I am; for he was more than generous. Indeed, he was generous to a fault: the fault being that he wanted to give what was not his."

Simon draws his own knees up, the posture of prayer somehow befitting Artie's questionable benevolence.

"But I have an idea, an inspiration that may accomplish Artie's wishes," George goes on - in the silvery light, his chiseled face like a Renaissance David, "and I'm going to Boston to allow inspiration its chance."

"Melody Morrison?" a sensitive Simon suggests.

"You are the romantic, aren't you," George observes, taking no offense at Simon's guess, "... probably fell in love by candlelight."

"That, I did ... long, long ago," Simon allows, "but that's not what brought Melody Morrison to mind. It was Vincent Tenklei - or rather, what Vincent told me today before he left the funeral."

"And?" George prompts.

"Melody Morrison invited him down to tour Harvard. He's going this weekend."

"Yes. I know." George pondering the implications. "But be that as it may, you're right; Melody Morrison is at the heart of my inspiration. And what I will ask of her could well involve your aspirations, Mr. Farley; the perfect forum for a demiurgic mind. However, whether my grand design comes to be or no, you may rest assured Artie's magnanimity included you."

"And not only me," a modest Simon replies, "but countless others, as well; for the seeds Artie planted so long ago have since grown into a tree, a tree of knowledge from which many have plucked fruit."

"I heartily agree. Your vision fits nicely with mine. We must nourish that tree, lengthen its limbs, increase its yield."

"*Leaves of Grass* would make for a good beginning," Simon puts forth solicitously, "or leaves of absence for the spiritually minded, a veritable storehouse of practical meditations for harried souls. In fact, I was going to suggest the same to Artie; suggest he compile a metaphysical collection, our good state's history of prophets, seers, psychics and healers, a natural to fund his shelves."

"And a good suggestion it would have been," George muses, giving the starry sky a glance for good measure, "with famous Vermont visionaries like Brigham Young and Joseph Smith-"

"Yes, but the scope of our new collection should not be limited to prophecy," Simon interjects, as though the search were imminent. "No, we should include all the occult arts, both past and present: mesmerism, phrenology, physiognomy, spiritualism, regression, automatic writing, animal magnetism, acupuncture-"

"A man after my own heart," George breaks in, slapping his knees, "animal magnetism ... I like that."

"But Vermont has fathered more than just the occult," Simon contends earnestly, "Hiram Powers, for example; and Dr. Marsh. Dr. James Marsh-"

"Animal magnets were they?" George jests.

"No, sir," Simon answers respectfully, "no ... but they were Vermonters, natives who attracted what was best in the minds of others: Powers sculpting the famous Greek Slave, and Professor Marsh taking pains to publish the prose of Coleridge before the English author was widely read. And we mustn't forget Justin Morrill, either, Vermont's Senator of the hour, securing our nation's land grant colleges; or John Dewey, the great reformer and educator; or Warren Austin, America's first representative to the U.N.; or Admiral Dewey, to mention men of military fame-"

"May as well include Presidents Arthur and Coolidge, if your collection's only criterion is to be a Vermonter garnering fame in his field," George advises.

"I beg your pardon, counselor," Simon admitting error. "Fame is hardly the measure of greatness."

"But what is?" George warming to the little man's idealism. "By what should we measure a man's achievements?"

"Perhaps that's a question best answered by another question," Simon clasping his hands behind his graying head and lying back for a view of Ursa Major. "For example," he continues wistfully, "have you ever enjoyed the little gasps of delight when a lady of your heart admits to a favorite song? ... or a certain sonnet? ... or maybe a particular flower? discovering each to be a choice of your own? Or felt that sweet infinity in the touch of her hand? that delicious unity in her smile?"

The questions could have been asked differently, but they could not have been asked better, George coming at once to the truth. "I have not," he mutters sorrowfully, the moon seeming to lose some of its silver. "... I have not."

"*The King and I,*" Simon says, after a moment's silence, "*The King and I* - Rodgers and Hammerstein - remember the song, *Hello Young Lovers?*"

"I recall the song, if not its origin; but why do you ask?"

"It's about that measure," Simon explains, "that question of achievement. And since you know the song, follow with me the lyricist's plaintive lines as he addresses all the lovers who may have been under the stars that night, telling them to be faithful and true ... to cling to each other ... to cling very close.

"At first, you wonder what he means. By what authority, by what wisdom is he admonishing the lovers. But then he tells them, 'I've been in love like you.'

"And continuing, he cuts to the heart of the matter, recalling what it feels like to have wings on his heels, to fly down the street ... to fly on a chance. And what is this chance? The chance he'll meet his lover ... which, of course, isn't really by chance.

"And there you have it!" Simon's passion evident in his posture, as he sits erect to speak, "that measure we we're looking for. It's the 'not really by chance' that reveals it, the inner light, the infallibility of what Swedenborg called our 'proprium', that mystical something that can make just one couple's love as big as the world it inspires."

"But now you're on another subject entirely," George counters, less from objection than in hopes Simon is right.

"If you mean the soul, George, the spirit - the 'over-soul', as Emerson called it - then, yes; but it requires the union of two souls to create such a love; anything less is ... well ... at best, the animal magnetism you were smiling about."

"And at worst?"

"Not something I've considered," Simon avers. "But to finish the song, what does the songwriter claim as he leaves? That all of his memories are happy. And why? Because he had a love of his own ... a love of his own.

"So, even in reflection, love's power thrives, its measure applies. A life has been lived to its fullest. What more can be asked?"

Even as Simon poses the question, George hears the answer: a desire crying from deep in his tenebrous heart. And he reckons now what founding rock lies beneath a man's dreams, his faith, his achievements - the revelation jolting him to his knees to swear by Artie's grave, by his own honor - his redeemed honor - that such a love will be the measure of his life.

For Melody, the answer was there before the question. It has always been Melvin – the minister's adorable son, pulling her pigtails in Sunday School; the bright-eyed fifth-grader, holding her hand through the matinee; the dashing young rebel, keeping her warm at football games; the Ivy League scholar, stirring more than her mind on long evening walks, the promise in his arms, his kiss, beyond her imaginings.

Perhaps the question has never arisen. Perhaps she has just always known - like the certainty of the changing seasons, or the unchanging songs of the bobolink, the chickadee, the goldfinch, or the faith in the leap of the squirrel, the unswerving path of the milk-cow making her way to the barn – perhaps it has been that simple, that rustic, Mother Nature embosoming them both; for even at Harvard, with its forced rub against a sandpaper world, she has retained her callow way of obliging society's grit without being scarred. And now that she's gladly with child, even her tears are not always sad, Melody agreeing with Ovid that, "A certain kind of pleasure 'tis to weep."

Weeping is the way Vincent finds her, ringing from the street below to announce his arrival. "Have I come at a bad time?" he asks discreetly, hoping she wants, even needs his company. Though propriety disallows his heart a voice, he has always admired this lady, this imagined femme fatale who even now seduces in his dreams.

"At a most opportune time," she assures him, though a daub at her glistening blue eyes leaves him dubious, "you've come just when I could most use company ... and especially if that company hails from home."

"Well, Vermont h-has become like a home for me," he falters, stumbling past the iron-caged elevator, following her up three flights of stairs to her brass-numbered, carved-oak door, "my 'home away from home', as the idiom goes."

"For me, it's a poignant one," Melody unlocking the tall, solid door for his entry. "Since Melvin ... since he went away, I've come to think of Boston as my home away from home, if only because we shared it."

"The way you cushion dilemma," Vincent obeying Melody's gesture to follow her into what had once been a sitting room, its richly paneled walls reflecting Venetian chandeliers, "saying Melvin - uh, Mr. Morrison - has just gone away-"

"Melvin," she corrects, motioning Vincent to cross the room for its view of the river Charles through a tall expanse of leaded glass, the broad and pillowed window seat affording rest. "Call him Melvin. And yes, I refer to his death as a journey, as though he's gone somewhere a little ahead of my own departure. Death is more acceptable that way - by one's heart, I mean," she adds faintly, and with a demure glance. "But do look at the river, Vincent, and Longfellow's bridge ... just there to the right, beyond the trees, bare as they are now ... and the grass, lush in the summer, where we used to sit on a blanket and read our Kerouac - two young Vermonters trying to comprehend the world."

"And making a success of it, too, I dare say," Vincent more aware of the gold in her sunny blond hair than the shimmering crests of the Charles, the innocent blue of her cotton smock than the time-darkened stones of the bridge. "I have always admired you ... the two of you," he adds awkwardly - but she seems not to notice.

"There were fireflies in the grass that summer," Melody peering dreamily past the bridge, "... can you believe it? I remember us watching the city's skyline lose its reflection in the rippling water, Melvin telling me not to look round, to pretend we were on the Winooski when the little trollop lights came out to play - as if they heard him, too, sparkling the grass with their harlotry. It was like magic ... one of those perfect points in time, to employ another idiom; only now the point has begun to flow, to become a line ... a line which I once believed would turn again and become a circle."

"I don't know what to say," Vincent mutters, "except ... except you haven't been here in the summer since, have you? Maybe the fireflies still sparkle. Maybe it's you that-"

"Lost my sparkle?" she finishes for him. "Do you think I've ... oh, what am I saying?" Melody stifling the thought before it can be piteously denied. "I'm very pleased you've come," she begins afresh. "I'll play your cicerone; a quaint little inn out in Concord coming immediately to mind – provided you like beef Wellington."

"Mad about it!" he exclaims, relieved by her turn of the subject, "just mad about it!"

If my bargue sinks, 'tis to another sea.
(Ellery Channing)

XVII

Finding Melody's apartment deserted and dark,
I'm at the mercy of Aunt Martha's sleuthing, her inquisitive thoughts fan-
ning out like cat whiskers to tickle some waiting fancy – the fancy in question surprising us both: a seventeenth-century inn, on the Concord green,
purveying English cuisine.

"So the minuteman's memory lives up to his moniker," I crack, perusing the menu over a stylish Vincent's shoulder, "he risks his life to expel the
British, only to import their fare."

"And you should know," A.M. eying with envy the bottle of Perrier
Jouet iced in silver beside the candle-lit table, "you should know, since the
appellation describes with unerring accuracy your performance as a lover."

"Enough of your crudities, A.M.," I bark disapprovingly, "and especially in the presence of my wife."

"You mean your widow, don't you?" Aunt Martha's undertone shouting volumes, "your pregnant widow on a date with a dashing young man?
one who happens to be conveniently wealthy?"

"Is this why you whisked me down from Vermont?" I huff, chafed
by her rude implication, "this-this meeting of two friends for a congenial
dinner? Vincent was my client, A.M., a guest of our home on numerous
occasions; and I would expect no less of him than to call on my wife in
her bereavement."

"And in her pregnancy?" A.M. unmoved by my umbrage.

"And in her pregnancy," I concur, checking my temper.

"And in your favorite dress, as I recall. That blue-violet, décolleté dress that accents her sensuality, her feminine form, her-"

"And in my favorite dress ... which proves she's thinking of me," I cut in. "So tell me, what help does she need? Why are we here?"

"Rumors," Aunt Martha's response fraught with conviction, spoken as final, a kind of tiptoe readiness to meet opposition head-on, "... rumors."

"Do you think you could be more specific?" I reply; Melody's sexy, pouting lips hinting a smile as Vincent dispenses the golden elixir - her crystal flute now delicately raised, touching the lips I yearn to kiss.

"Rumors and innuendo. Calculated guesses. One plus one making three ... Vincent, a frequent guest of your home; and now-"

"To the point!" I shout, appreciating how we can cross our swords without being noticed by those responsible. "If Melody is about to be blackmailed-"

"That's one very handsome black male with her now," A.M. interjects, "and brilliant, too, wouldn't you say?"

"That he is," I admit, thwarting her thrust by agreement, "more brilliant, even, than the diamonds in his mines."

"Diamonds!" she gasps, "I didn't-"

"And you had me believing you could read minds," I rejoin, surprised she's unaware of Vincent's source of wealth, "not to mention life patterns, diaries and financial statements; and all with just a few blinks of the old third eye."

"But I can," she avers, "except when access is denied ... except for those few cases where guardian angels bar admission to their keep."

"What angels?" I persist, "I don't see any of our winged friends hovering over the bubbly ... or flitting in the candlelight ... or-or-"

"What's the matter?" my aunt displaying genuine concern over my lapse of thought, "haven't I told you guardian angels are of the highest order? They make themselves visible only when necessary."

"Not that I recall," my twinge of shame mitigated by her apparent miss of my fleeting, jealous thought.

"Aaah," she sighs, "I get it. The problem is not the angels unseen, but the one visible: your angel, Melody - the champagne ... the candles - and noticing your name's not on the card she's reading."

"All right! So he's thoughtful - just proves how well I chose my friends, that's all."

"Look," she says in a quiet voice I haven't heard since the night we visited Melody's bedroom, "you have nothing to worry about here, sweetheart."

"Easy for you to say," I complain, "and after admitting Vincent is off limits, too. Some confidence you inspire, Aunt Martha!"

"Not what I meant," her hand on my shoulder with atypical empathy, "and what I was saying about rumors ... you can forget that, too; for you won't be aware of the problem when it arrives."

"Aren't you confusing your philosophers?" I ask, her rare display of compassion having effect, "for now you're admitting Sophocles was correct when he said, 'In heeding nothing lies the sweetest life.'"

"In as much as the life of a babe is sweet - with its parents doing all the heeding - I agree," A.M. removing her hand.

"So, these rumors, these innuendos ... they won't commence until after I return?"

"You guessed it. And I'll be there to correct them, if not to prevent them altogether," she promises, the care in her voice convincing, her ease of mastery, among the tools of meddling, something I know only too well.

"When the crib is again my bed, I suppose I'll be grateful for the benefit of your care. It's not every mother's son who has an aunt with a hazel twig snooping round to divine what's best for him."

"And it's good to be appreciated. - even needed," A.M. licking her diaphanous lips as Vincent refills the crystal, "good to be there in the nursery; there, while the feeling's tender."

"As is Melody," I sigh, noting a tear in her eye.

"That she is," A.M. agrees, "provided the feeling is noble. But right now she's confused: an ache with foreboding, a yearning for the man she can no longer have and a suspicion of the man who would have her."

"But you said-"

"That you have nothing to worry about? George will intervene."

"How comforting," I think sarcastically, hovering behind Melody in an attempt to read her card, "for of the two, George is the one I would more suspect."

"But George won't be drunk," a wistful A.M. rejoins, the presentment of another bottle of Perrier Jouet supporting her assertion. "You should be thankful Melody's driving," she adds, "a safeguard with benefits: one, that she can deposit your Diamond Jim in the lobby of his hotel instead of her bed."

"Aunt Martha!" I fume, "have some respect, will you?" the neat but copious handwritten message in her card doing nothing to support my defense of Vincent.

"And how did he phrase his 'thoughtfulness'?" she asks, observing my furtive glance at the perfumed and ribboned card, "by mentioning that unclouded day? a gathering at the river? the sweet by-and-by?"

"By all of the above," I fret, "by asking my sweetheart to meet him some cloudless, summer evening for a stroll along the Winooski ... to attend a symphony of fireflies ... to frolic along a sylvan path ... to accept ... to accept-"

"Go on," she cries impatiently, "to accept what? his condolences?"

"Hardly," I snip, "'his conditions' would be closer to the mark. Listen to this practiced prose, this attempt to assume the very memories of our courtship: '... your fairy-slippered feet in time with the whispering water, the gay old Winooski murmuring its Indian tongue, the warm spring rain swelling its phrase with the last hidden snow melting down from deer-haunted slopes.' And, as though his lyrical line could snare her, 'the mystical ecstasy in the touch of your hand.' How overt! How obvious! Makes me grit the teeth I don't have. One more crystal flute and she could fall victim to this conniving bastard's intentions. And what's more, he's asking her to accept, as a token of friendship, a three-carat diamond, 'One carat each for the Three Graces you favor', he writes. How juvenile!"

"Yes - in fact it was Juvenal who said-"

"Please!" I growl, "We haven't time for your Roman reminiscences. We have action to take, here and now."

"Did you say three carats?" A.M. gasps, suddenly paler than the ghost she is. "You know what they say, don't you, Melvin? diamonds are a girl's best friend? Well, according to your boast but a toast or two ago,

Vincent is just that: your girl's best friend - the only difference being he has the where-with-all to memorialize the friendship!"

"He's memorializing, all right," I pother, wringing my supernal hands, "his diamond is heart-shaped, like a locket ... a pendant to adorn her cleavage. And would you look at that!" I steam, Melody leaning forward to accept his help in clasping the filigreed chain, bowing her seraphic head as though acknowledging his carnal designs. "What are you going to do?" I plead.

"Same thing as Vincent," she quips, "... admire those perfect breast she's fairly spilling out before him: or rather, envy her the chance."

"I need your help!" I cry, "not your hunger!"

"At last!" a gleeful A.M. exclaims. "At last, you admit your need, acknowledge the worth of my assistance! Well, a little work on an entrée and we should have these two on their way back to Boston in no time."

"Are you sure?" I ask, not wishing my pregnant wife to be ill, "do you know the chemistry of spices? the mystery of herbs? the secret of sauces?"

"Of course," A.M. tugging me to the kitchen, "but what I know best is how to turn a spat, a beef; and Wellington is about to have his Waterloo. Trust me," my aunt knocking over a tray of warm plum puddings for the cover of distraction, "I'll only tamper with playboy's food, not Melody's."

And in truth, it's a good thing she doesn't, Vincent embarrassingly sick all the way back to his lodging; any designs he may have harbored displaced by a rare strain of seasickness.

In lieu of sleep, his baleful night pitches to and fro twixt watering the loo and upchucks.

Time, and the work of changing days, has made many a bad thing good;
fortune has played with many men, and set them firm again.
(Virgil)

XVIII

WHILE DESIRE MAKES A FOOL OF VINCENT, GEORGE IS
a man of action, pacing under the Beacon Street lamps as he awaits some
sign of Melody; pondering, between glances at her darkened windows, the
worm in his apple of life. How can he tell her? Where should he begin? To
suggest Melvin is the father of Charlene's child is not among his options.
Even Charlene would fear such a claim - if only because the pointing finger
would crook in her direction. No, he must leave to time and familiarity the
baring of hearts.

"George?" the mellifluous voice is behind him, Melody appearing
from out of the night like a ministering angel. "I would know that walk
anywhere," she declares, the pleasure of her discovery obvious. "What are
you doing out here? guarding my door?"

"Such an assignment would be an honor," George thinking that reality is in image, only concept in words - Melody's presence a revelation. "I've
been awaiting your return ... wanted to surprise you."

"You have, and happily so," she avers; George trailing her up the granite steps as though invitations are out of vogue. "Would you care to come
up?" she obliges, turning her key in the carved oak door, opening it for him
to hold, "a cup of coffee, perhaps? An Irish? ... if I have the whiskey?"

"My pleasure - if you have the whiskey," he echoes, smiling with a memory, "for if you do, it will be from Melvin's stock, would it not? I mean - you don't-"

"No, I don't," Melody accepting his assistance with an interior door to the foyer, "only wine. And a little champagne, on occasion," she goes on, opting for the elevator instead of the stairs; the small, caged lift requiring George to fold in beside her like the intimate he hopes to be. "Vincent Tenklei is in town. Took me to dinner - only something made him violently ill. I had to rush him back to his hotel .... .

"But here we are," she ends abruptly, stopping the lift at her floor. "Let's hope there's nothing here to make you ill."

"Vincent was-was here?" he falters, following her in, admiring the rich maple floors; the marble sculptures; the framed oils adorning the high, plastered walls; her eclectic, period furniture - the retro ambiance of a Back Bay home recalling his childhood years, "... I mean ... I don't know what I mean. But here, let me help you with your wrap," his big hands grasping her dark wool coat, the flash of her pendant catching his eye.

"A gift from Vincent," Melody turning, fingering the diamond. "A token of friendship, as Vincent put it; something I'd never have accepted from anyone else."

"And why not?" George astounded by the diamond's size - and Vincent's dubious intent. His own intent, had the diamond been his to give.

"Well, because of Vincent's wealth, that's why," she calls over her shoulder, leaving the room to hang her coat, then coming back for his, "... a diamond like this means nothing to Vince, in terms of money; only the thought has value. And that's why I accepted it."

"Explain that to Faithful," he thinks, taking in her arrangement of chairs as he hands her his overcoat, "or worse yet, to all the Plainfield wives who'll envy you the gift and second-guess the circumstance in which it was given."

"I prefer the window seat," Melody hanging his cashmere coat on a Victorian hall tree, "I know it's probably old hat to you, but I enjoy the view at night: the lights of Cambridge shimmering across the Charles-"

"Never," he mutters, arranging pillows on the seat, "it's never old hat to a Boston boy."

"So tell me," she goes on cheerily, opening a rosewood cabinet to peruse Melvin's stock, "do you miss your old haunts? I mean, our peasant village must seem quaint to a big city boy like yourself ... to the dapper man-about-town Melvin told me you are. Ah! And here it is!" Melody displaying a fifth of Jamison Reserve as though the whiskey cast light on her question. "I'll make the coffee. Be right back," she prattles, the lightness in her voice, her spirit, lifting him higher than he's been in months – in years, even; for to be perched in a Back Bay window recalls his youth; and not only his own, but Back Bay's history, as well: Oliver Wendell Holmes once but a few doors down, and across the street, Julia Ward Howe; the Common a block away. The same Common where the residents of two centuries past grazed their cows. A park long refined for the crème de la crème, the likes of Webster, Everett, Parkman and Longfellow maundering under the horse chestnut trees; or marveling at ducks parading across the pond; or garnering, on cool autumn afternoons, a nuance of transcendentalism from tombs at nearby Mount Auburn, some meaning only the dead could reveal.

But then again, Vermont has contributed its own worthy chapters to the annals of New England life, George muses. Witness the conversation with Simon last night, his knowledge of Vermont illuminati, the aspiring poet of spangled Winooski trails taking his own kind of Mount Auburn stroll through a moonlit cemetery, his chaotic attire making him appear, in the frosty November night, as wild as old Daniel Webster, his mental peregrinations no less provoking, no less intriguing than any black-frocked parson promenading on Beacon Hill.

And besides, with three wars won and a century lost, between the Boston of yore and now, there is much to be said for the bucolic life; Vermont, in its simpler life, still fitting the mold of the golden days a bustling Boston has lost. Montpelier's Judge Thompson didn't write his *Green Mountain Boys* for nothing: high-hearted heroes like Ethan Allen and Seth Warner still funding the indomitable will to succeed; the difference, perhaps, being that success in Vermont is measured more by inclusion in the great Book of Life than in the ledger of a Boston counting-house.

"Your Irish," Melody placing a carved, Philippine tray on the tufted seat between them, "... and a little departure for me."

"Thank you!" George starts as though disturbed from a trance. "And what have you in that gorgeous piece of stemware?"

"Port," she announces pertly, "Melvin was forever persuading me, going on about its convivial effect."

"As if you needed it," George flashing his most winsome smile. "You are at once the most elegant and the most exhilarating lady I've ever had the pleasure of knowing."

"Elegant, I shall file away as a compliment," Melody turning coyly to the mullioned window, "... but what to do with exhilarating?"

"Leave that to me," George cracks abruptly; though the slip appears appreciated. "Meanwhile, here's to Harvard, your sheepskin, and ... our partnership," he toasts, tossing in the last almost timidly.

"Yes, to our partnership." She surprises him, clinking crystal to cup. "Is that why you're here?"

"Could be," George glib once again, "for what I have to discuss with you could well be our first official act together."

"My dear George," she chortles, "one would think most any act with you would eventually be ruled un-official, if only by your failure to appear."

"Whatever do you mean?" He seems at a loss.

"Nothing, really," Melody says, his velvety gray eyes arousing a certain caution, "I ... I was just having a little fun at the expense of your reputation."

"Ah!" A froth mustache lightens the moment, after a sip of coffee. "Pleased to amuse; for my reputation indirectly pertains to what I wish to discuss: Artie's will," the mention of Artie erasing Melody's coy smile.

"Yes," she replies, after a pause, "Melvin's death ... it was so unexpected."

"Death, for all its certainty, is the most unexpected event in life, isn't it?"

"Irrefutably," she answers flatly.

"Of course it is," George muttering under his breath, regretting his morbid platitude. "But regarding Artie's will, it's a masterpiece of the improbable; Artie's wish for his inventory to bring more than its legitimate worth is a desire I doubt I can fructify."

"Melvin prepared his will, didn't he?" her tone suggesting discretion, should criticism be forthcoming.

"He did," George taking a moment to enjoy his coffee, to savor the bracing aroma of a warm Irish whiskey, "... though I must say he framed it more from benevolence than from any practical eye toward execution. Artie wanted to draw on the community chest - to force, in a moment of weakness, the purse of his peers, so to speak – to hold an auction of his books that would see each bid bettered by a village business or organization, thus increasing his charity."

"Charity?" Melody's delayed sip of port giving the impression of contemplation, "you didn't mention a charity."

"Right. I refrained so as not to sway your opinion, to allow Artie's ends to justify his means," George glancing back at the Charles to avoid her eyes.

"Well? Go on ... sway me."

"Artie wanted the proceeds to build school bus stops for the kids; something about protecting the next generation of readers, I think; an affable mix of generosity and amour-propre. The reason I say that is because of the brass plaques he wanted installed in each of the shelters, plaques about the value of books, the secrets they hold for those willing to explore - with a promise of reward, as I recall, for the kids who accept his challenge."

"A worthwhile cause," Melody observes, "and one he probably knew every parent would support."

"Maybe so; but Reverend Rolundo is childless - unless one grants a spiritual father the connotation of parent - and neither tavern owner has ever been married; nor has Thelma Peabody. At least, not yet."

"I don't follow-"

"Artie's plan; his terms of sale. He wanted his collections sold to the highest bidder, as one would expect; but with an unusual caveat: all competitive bids must be bested by the aforementioned persons, thereby keeping both his books and his bankroll local."

"A clever idea, indeed!" Melody exclaims, standing up with growing interest. "Artie may not have been educated; but he could never be accused of stupidity. What he's left to be done in a few days is more than his entire life accomplished."

"Now I don't follow you," George flummoxed, twisting in his seat the better to observe her pacing.

"Knowledge should be planted. like seeds," she declaims. " like plants in the hothouse minds of children. For once the bus stops are built, the plaques will be seen every school day - every school day translating into a habit, a subconscious suggestion to read."

"Then you support-"

"Of course, I do," she interrupts, "but with one exception: we must be the winning bidders."

"We?" George cries, getting up from the window seat to face her, "we? as in the firm?"

"Why not?" Melody aglow with inspiration, "why shouldn't we become the gardeners? Artie's hands from beyond the grave?"

"No! You don't understand!" George reaching to take her hand, "I'm in total agreement! What you're suggesting is the very thing I was going to implore you to do!"

"Then, we're partners?" she asks sweetly, allowing her hand to be held longer than discretion allows.

"Partners," he whispers, blushing with the innocence of a boy, the innocence in the blue of her eyes. "Partners in a newfound venture," he adds, searching those eyes for support, "for what I was going to ask-"

"Ask?" she ventures.

"Yes. I ... well," he flounders, letting go of her hand to reclaim his thoughts, "I was going to ask your opinion of keeping the books right where they are; continuing Artie's business – perhaps under a more auspicious name, but under the management of none other than Simon Farley and Thelma Peabody; assuming marriage to be in their future."

"A splendid idea," Melody backing away from his eyes, his presence, for the implied protection of the window seat. "But what's this about marriage? And how would we accomplish the preservation of Artie's business and still meet the terms of his will?"

"Gossip has it Thelma is about to propose. She's won herself a man; notwithstanding the paradox of Simon not being man enough to refuse!" he chuckles. "As to Artie's will, we can meet its provisions, even exceed them, by hiring an expert to give the collection a bona fide estimate. With that in hand, we can advertise the auction locally, then make our winning bids in honor of the 'donors' he specified. For there is one other provision I haven't shared with you as yet: Simon Farley is to play auctioneer."

"No!" Melody cries, placing her crystal on the carved wood tray to prevent spilling her port from laughter. "Our Artie has progressed from philanthropist to comedian? But do go on. Tell me how we can do this-this commendable thing you suggest."

"Right," George sitting down beside her, warming to the cover of mirth, the subject of death transmogrifying into one of amusement. "By playing the locals along – I mean, by not letting them know of Artie's wishes."

"Why? Because they wouldn't attend?"

"That, and the enmity engendered if someone attended in hopes of leaving with one of his collections."

"I see your point. But the same would be the case if we followed Artie's wishes to the letter, right?"

"Right, so it's up to you, or me – or, for that matter, Charlene – to bid at the appropriate time on each of his several categories. There'll still be the odds and ends the public can buy; children's' fairytales, cookbooks-"

"I understand. And we mustn't exclude your fiancée from our charitable endeavor; that is, if she's to remain with the firm."

"You steal my thunder again," George cracks; though the lightening is far from evident, "coming upon a subject before I can introduce it. I was going to ask if you would make that decision without me - as to whether Charlene should stay with the firm, I mean."

"Why, George!" Melody reaching for her port, "do I detect another 'no-show' developing?"

"'Barred from the premises' would be more like it. Charlene thinks I'm vanquished; but I'm merely diminished - and fully recoverable. Yes, I'm having second thoughts. No, let me restate that: I'm having third, fourth ... even fifth thoughts - a fifth of aged single malt much more to my liking."

"And would Judge Whitaker have any part to play in this?" she asks mischievously.

"You know about her" he gasps - blushing as a culpable adult rather than a bashful boy.

"Not to worry," she counters, amused by his rumored affair. "Your friendly relations with a local judge can only improve our win record."

"And I thought I was the naughty one," George grinning his way out of embarrassment, "but no, any decision on the matter of my marriage is strictly mine, not the court's. Oh ... and Charlene's, of course."

"And what about the baby? Mother phoned me with the news, you know; the news I presumed you were here to tell me."

Downing the last of his coffee, he turns the subject. "Perhaps I should call on Vincent ... see if he needs a doctor, medication, some friendly advice."

"A doctor, yes," Melody shooting him a sidelong glance, "advice, no. Any advice you have to spare, you'd best reserve for your own counsel, your decision on what you're going to do before I come home."

"Meaning?" George getting abruptly to his feet.

"Whether you'll be a married man when I return, or-"

"Or what?" he bates, stepping closer to catch her reply.

"Or ... or, not," she whispers to the window, as if the Charles alone should hear.

The only competition worthy of a wise
man is with himself.
(Washington Allston)

XIX

THE CRUELTY OF ANGER IS MINUSCULE COMPARED TO
the cruelty of thought; but my indignation with Vincent has cooled to sympathetic regard. I refuse to leave him alone in his woeful condition, Aunt Martha's dubious tinctures of dish soaps and herbs manifesting with rhythmic regularity – i.e., irregularity. Vincent's confinement to the loo symbolic of my own pernicious evening: the inscribed card, the diamond, the suspicious intent of my erstwhile friend, all poisons I need to discharge.

"How long will this continue?" I quiz A.M., Vincent retching her hasty potion once again, "and please tell me your doctored dish isn't life-threatening."

"The only thing in jeopardy tonight is George's marriage," she retorts, her cocky assurance alerting me to things unknown. "He's admitted as much to Melody; and what's more, he's-"

"So that's why you did this!" I remonstrate, venting a new frustration, "you brought me here so Melody can be alone with George! Unprotected!"

"Wrong, wrong, wrong," A.M. chirps captiously. "Your dearth of gratitude is fast depleting my well of kindness. What I've arranged is for your own good. For the good of your future-"

"For the good of yours, too, let's not forget," I quip. "You've admitted your patronage is self-serving, remember?"

"In as much as we're all God's children, it's in our mutual best interest to improve Her brood," my aunt's fire-blue eyes a flash of warning, "that bit of wisdom summed up in the Golden Rule; something I'm trying hard to practice, despite your incessant bickering, jealous fits, and-"

"Sounds golden to me," I interrupt, reducing her biased diatribe to playful provocation.

"Touché!" she chimes, her fists relaxing into hands on my willing shoulders, "it's about time you lighten up. We've a lot to do and but little time to accomplish it."

"I don't think I can be any lighter," I banter, wincing at Vincent's pained expression, "but since when did time apply to us; or, for that matter, this list of 'to-dos' you're touting?"

"Time is soon to be our dimension again," she reminds me, "and my list pertains to the people and events in our next incarnations - first yours, then mine."

"No one has ever called you a neophyte in the art of fault-finding," I tease, "and rightly so, for now you make me feel ... well ... at fault. I attack your motives, labeling them expedient and opportunistic; and the next thing I know, you claim I'm first on your list of duties. What can I do but apologize?"

"Quite unnecessary," A.M. smiling for having induced my apology in the first place, "and besides, we haven't time for all this maudlin, mutual admiration. Vincent's telephone is ringing ... George is calling from down in the lobby."

"Good work!" I reply, presuming Melody to be alone and safe, "and a timely call, too. Vincent's on the verge of a blackout. Or, maybe a whiteout?"

"It's the same, regardless of pigmentation," she chortles. "That pink stuff pales a face no matter what-" Vincent straining to reach the phone.

"It's me, old fellow," a booming voice resounds, "George. George O'Malley. Melody told me you were in need of a friend tonight. Sick."

"Sick's not the word for it," Vincent groans, "I haven't been this ill since the time in Rhodesia when our well went bad."

"I've brought you a treatment," George confides, "something to doctor the waters a bit. The pink stuff. The little bottle you shake and shake, then gulp to halt the shakes - but you know the routine. May I come up?"

"If you hurry," Vincent moans. "I may not be alive when you get here."

"Sounds ominous," I think for Aunt Martha's benefit. "I do hope your recipe is safe."

"Sure you do," she projects in return, "safe, as in 'safecracking'; for you were the one pleading with me to protect your precious jewel, remember?"

"I remember," I admit, hearing George's knock and suffering a pang of my own - Vincent crawling to the door like a beetle struggling on its back to turn over – a pang of remorse for ever having wished on him such an 'accident'. "I should've remembered: Melody has that effect on men ... she brings them to their knees, their hearts on silver platters."

"Oh, I know," A.M. sighs, throwing up her hands in mock despair. "But it's not every man who emblazons his platter with a brilliant, three-carat diamond," her energized voice trailing off in contrived awe, "... not that Melody is blinded, of course - her vision still acute after three tests in one evening."

"Three?" I bluster, George my assumed number two, "and who, may I ask, is the third?"

"You, nephew," A.M. causing my imaginary heart to squeeze like a fist, "two terrestrial suitors, and one celestial," her abrupt silence announcing the entrance of George.

"That's about as near to an angel as you've placed me," I interpose.

"Surely you refer to Melody," she cracks, "that I placed you near Melody," her cackle infectious, my own spirit catching her delight, "for never would I call you an angel, Melvin! Heaven forbid! Which, as a matter-of-fact, I think it does! But allow me to comfort you just the same. Melody is grieving; and this day, this evening, has been restorative, an antidote to anguish; Vincent's obvious regard - and George's, too - the tonic she needs; one any woman needs. A woman never forgets how to flirt, even if position precludes it. The opportunity to practice from time to time is all the satisfaction required. And it's important to qualify what little pleasure Melody allows herself with these gentlemen."

"Pleasure?" I break in judiciously. "Gentlemen? Really, Aunt Martha-"

"Yes, these two gentlemen connected to you," she continues blithely, "said connection giving her license ... allowing flirtation its charm, its innocence. It's almost as if she's flirting with - with you."

"My dear aunt," I reply, after a moment's reflection, "I do believe you could convince a man of most anything. So, why not convince these gentlemen that Melody is untouchable; is nothing more or less than a beautiful lady in want of protection?"

"Because, she isn't," A.M. counters, turning away from the irksome scene of George administering capfuls of his pink panacea. "Not that she isn't beautiful, mind you; but she doesn't need their protection, Melvin. Recall, for example, her shrewd disruption of Thelma's questionnaires, Melody's clever idea of planting bugs raising the fear of discovery in the most callused heart. No, she doesn't need protection, my dear. What she needs is you."

"But I-"

"Not your old self," A.M. reacting to my wince of guilt, "not the tainted man you became; but a babe-in-the-woods, an innocent child with a clean slate between his cherubic hands."

"So, let me be certain I understand," I respond, commiserating with Vincent as he groans on his bed. "I return as my wife's firstborn, and these two 'gentlemen', as you erroneously call them, will be content to count on her as a friend. Or, to put it another way, be content to count on her for nothing else."

"Should men ever be content," she parries, a cat-like grin squinting her sly-blue eyes, "fancy will have folded her tents, desire pulled up her stakes, and the entire circus of gods among men gone off to some better realm."

"Comforting," I observe with a wry smile, "although a bit discriminatory, don't you think? Your circus troupe smacks more of a cabal of coquettes than a company of clowns. But what of these two?" I ask, returning her attention to the quack O'Malley and his pink-lipped patient, "What role will these two clowns be playing, once I'm back under your circus tent?"

"Formative ones," she mutters vaguely, "or informative, as the case may be."

"I thought reform is the purpose of my return ... another chance to get it right. But no, you're hinting these role models here will be pointing me in all the wrong directions."

"Wrong?" she quibbles, "What's wrong with Vincent; other than his forgivable infatuation with Melody?"

"Okay," I rejoin, "but it's dreadfully obvious why you omit George from your defense. His guilt is tacit-"

"Tasso?" A.M. squinting as though reading at a distance-

"Because the shaken soul, uncertain yet
Of its return, is still not firmly set."

"What?" I'm half amazed, half disconcerted. "You forsake your Roman peers for an Italian poet some fifteen centuries later? Or am I misinterpreting your interpreting?" her epigrams, her seeming sapience at every turn, so unlike her last mortal stint that it's only her cunning at avoiding my questions that belies her most recent identity.

"The First Crusade," she says with an impish grin, "I was there, a little scamp chasing a knight in armor; those men in gray turning red a young girl's cheeks. And when Tasso came out with his epic *Jerusalem Delivered*, I just had to meet him, his account reading like a travel guide of my former, vagabond life - though at the time of Tasso, I was a scamp once again: the mistress of an Italian bishop."

"From whence hails your self-assumed proficiency in judging the male anatomy," I retort, "your lover's bishopric enlarging your reference, if not your pretense."

"A pun's a pun, I suppose," A.M. sidestepping my long-awaited retaliation, "at least, it works in English – which is more than could be said for your-"

"Drop it!" I snap, "and I'll spare you another mistake. You're off on a lame foot, the language of love easily understood in any tongue – speaking of which, Vincent's tongue is ghastly, the size of a fist." My comment sparked by real alarm.

"Maybe he has allergies," A.M. avoiding blame, "how was I to know? But now that George is here to care for him, we'd best be returning to Plainfield. Your friend will recover. I can see those things, you know: the so-called future-"

"Plain-Plainfield?" I stutter, our sudden change of course bewildering. "If Vincent is safe, then why not check on Melody before you assure me of her future, just in case some little something in your master plan goes awry; something inconsequential; something immaterial. Something like those bubbles Vincent keeps coughing up."

"If only for your peace of mind," she allows, laughing at the sight of Vince licking a blister of pale bubbles from his swollen lips, "... and to leave poor Vincent in peace."

"Peace?" I challenge. "I doubt it. And so much for the erroneous idea of 'resting in peace'. Especially if every newcomer here has an aunt like you for a guide."

"So what's it going to be?" Aunt Martha dismissing my gibe. "Which one shall we unman: Melody's bed, or Thelma's march?"

"Crude, but to the point: Melody first, then Thelma," I quip tersely.

"Leave it to a man to twist the simplicity of two choices into a smorgasbord of confusion," she scoffs, "but if it's both you want, then it's both you're going to have," her nod towards the Charles setting us down on the Boston Common.

Besmirched by chimneys of the evening past, the gray and muted sky falls heavily about us, my astonishment to be on the Common checking my objection. As sullen as the sky appears, the Common is cheerful, the misty pond a perfect stage for our play of thoughts – until I think of where I'd rather be, my preference effecting instant change, the predawn sky flushing with fairy fire, the city's marble facades receding, diminishing, catching the patina of some ancient cathedral town as the Common's pristine beauty, all dew-drenched and still, harks back to an era when ladies promenaded under hats, when boys walked in awe of their fathers – little girls in awe of the boys - the transcendental aura of the gas lighted scene resurrecting my stifled desires:

"W-what's all this about?"

"You thought of Melody, didn't you?" Aunt Martha asks matter-of-factly, "... remembered the tree ... your tryst in the rain?"

"That I did," I admit, "but is that what caused-"

"It is," A.M. taking a seat under the old horse chestnut tree, sole witness of my proposal to Melody. "Your memory has become what we refer to as 'golden', as sweet as any fairytale. And in a way, that's what it is. For marriage can be euphoric; although, from my perspective, I think a woman often marries what she idealizes in a man. She plays the princess in the fairytale; and later, is hard pressed to continue the pretense when reality has tarnished her dream."

"Which is exactly what I don't want to happen," I remind her, "Thelma's march is a risk we must prevent."

"We?" she echoes, smirking in her own sense of precedence, "is this your way of showing gratitude for my assistance? This incessant reference to we?"

"But I am grateful, Aunt Martha," I insist, "and I'll be even more so if we – you - can preserve her propitious memory."

"Still want to be her prince, do you?" the first ray of dawn dazzling the dew-dripped limbs like so many diamonds in our mystical, autumn bower. "Well, perhaps you can have your wish; though not in the way you imagine. For when Melody's travail gives life to a son, she once again has the perfect man - only the dream never fades. And if the princess is older, she is also wiser, because this time the prince is real. Where passion may once have died in her arms, it is now very much alive; a commitment beyond any need to possess; both mother and son ever ready to die for the other should circumstance force the tragedy. She will always be his light in the window; and he, her Sir Galahad."

Moved by her sudden sincerity, I ask, "How can you know these things with such certainty? You never married ... never gave birth to a child; either, or both, it seems to me, a prerequisite for such bold authority."

"You refer to my life as your aunt, I presume," her tone plaintive, her drill sergeant eyes gone holy mother soft, "but you forget that I've had many lives. And time is a great storyteller."

"I haven't forgotten," I said, "though I'll admit I've been wondering why I have yet to recall any of my own; for surely I've had a similar past, haven't I?"

"Similar, no. Varied, yes. But you can't recall them because you don't need to. You're a good student, sweetheart ... all your lessons have been well learned. All except one."

"Fidelity?" I suggest, presuming guilt.

"Actually, no," she answers slowly, surprising me. "Had you loved completely, the negative of infidelity would not have developed. Love is your continuing lesson, not its misapplication. Love, Melvin, when it's truly consuming, cannot be misapplied. Do you know why?" A.M. becoming animated. "Because there's nothing left to be wrongfully given; nothing left to be thrown away."

"But I did love Melody that way," I argue, "I loved her completely; and I never made a conscious choice to cheat on her."

"No, but the weakness was there just the same – and by the way, you need to know that it was you being cheated, not Melody. You were the one suffering the guilt, not her."

"But how could I be so weak?" I ask, suffering blame even as I pose the question.

"Commitment," she explains, the role of castigator empowering, "you held back just enough of yourself for a doubt to thrive. And once taking root, it split your resolve like an ax. Simple as it sounds, the same heart that reacts to love tells us what love is. So when that heart is divided, it can also be deceitful, the one part engaging in an errant romance while the other denies its existence."

"Held back some part of myself?" I muse. "I can't imagine what that would have been."

"Ambition can play such a sleight of hand. It can deafen the caring ear. Once a pedestal is shared, the thing worshipped is no longer unique."

"But what ambition I enjoyed was wrought solely by her inspiration," I counter, "not by rivalry."

"Oh, I know ... and how I know," she laments, reaching to pluck a dripping diamond, "for I, too, have been the victim of accomplishment ... or rather, the victim of the pride which so often diminishes accomplishment. Before you know it, pride is all you have left to show for your efforts; your regard is for the achiever instead of the achievement."

"I-I think I follow," I answer haltingly, "but there is no uncertainty in my current ambition. It's nothing more or less than to be with Melody. And not only with her, but of her; for her; from her-"

"Then, you are ready," she interrupts, caressing my cheeks like a doting grandmother, "your transformation is at hand." And with that, we are hovering like pleasant dreams by Melody's bed.

Asleep, she rests peacefully on her side, one arm about a Teddy long remembered - a prize I'd won at Vermont's famous Tunbridge Fair - her golden hair in wisps about her cheeks, their pinch of color like a blush, a glow of innocence, a certain quality Mr. Rockwell knew how to paint – Norman's productive years in Vermont something of which we could all be proud. But, as Aunt Martha has just defined it, pride is not what I'm feeling as I gaze worshipfully at my sleeping wife. Stealing over me, like the golden shafts of light breaking over the Atlantic horizon, is an awakening, a nascent ability to disremember my former role as Melody's prince - a performance, I admit, deserving a fall from her pedestal. I am ready. Ready for the "clean slate" Aunt Martha mentioned; and the cherubic hands, as well.

"There is something mystical about a woman with child," A.M. whispering as though Melody might hear, might awake to distract my ear, "... something divine."

"Like the Madonna?"

"Not what I meant," she corrects. "No. It's as though woman conceives in the flesh, then forgets that lowly union to wing aloft, to breathe divinity, to create with the gods her gift of life beyond mere mortal means. And where that gift is born of love, that love aspires to deify the child; what mortal passion may have wrought, now sanctified, ordained, blessed by a chaste and sustaining ardor."

"You make birth into a religious experience," I say with warm agreement.

"And so it is, in as much as the cause is redeemed by the effect. For you see, Melvin," she goes on earnestly, "I've suffered from the cause ... from its wrongful worship; my battle with the passions, my attraction to the bed and its pleasures, the irritant in my judgment of you and your like mistakes."

"You needn't apologize," I think with new humility, "not to me ... not with my own failures so recently exposed. But surely you don't mean to imply that 'the bed', as you put it, is to be avoided."

"Of course not!" her eyes limpid, tear-cleansed, "of course not! In fact, the bed of love is to be desired, to be sought after; and once found, to be held in reverence, to be regarded as sacred. Temple sacred; though I'm sure you'll agree it would hardly be respectful to pile refuse before a temple door, which is what you were doing when-"

"Got it," I break in, not wishing to hear my sins recounted. "But now that we're on the subject - and I'm virtually in bed with Melody - I find it odd to feel no attraction ... I mean, there's an attraction ... an overwhelming desire; but-"

"I know," A.M. eager to explain the enigma. "What you are feeling is the very power of creation, the same love holding the planets in orbit, a love surpassing mere physical intimacy. It's the pulse at the heart of it all, sweetheart; the love of all loves: your mother's call ... her waiting womb. That little infant is you, Melvin, curled safe in your sacred cradle, in the warmth of your mother's love."

"Oh! And how I love her, too!" I whisper.

We are columns left alone
Of a temple once complete -
(C P Cranch)

XX

IF AUNT MARTHA'S VICTIM FEELS ANY BETTER FROM
the sunlight freshening his room, George can't discern the improvement,
Vincent's clothes like chainmail as he moans in the effort of dressing. But
with each man discreetly disappointed by the other's presence, the weekend's awkward beginning finds redemption in Melody's company: Vincent
buoyed by her gift of smiles and George playing guide for a tour of the
sights. This, to his advantage, too; for with Vincent confined to the back-
seat, George has Melody alone at his side.

"Where to, my man?" he calls over his shoulder to Vincent.

"Why don't you make the choice, George?" Melody interjects, the
flash of her pendant catching his eye. "If Vince isn't up to a walking tour of
Cambridge, we can still enjoy a drive about town. Or perhaps a drive out of
town?" her wink putting to trial his peevish thoughts - for in her garden of
delights, he and Vince are but two hired hands and he dare not be judged
the lessor one.

"To Concord we go!" George rubbing his hands together with an
air of satisfaction and enterprise. "It's the least we can do for Vincent.
Otherwise, he'd have only the memory of a shipwrecked night; a night we'll
help him forget by exploring Concord under the bright and steady sun."

"Aaah, steady is just the word I need," Vince sighs from the back seat,
a wan smile accentuating his tubercular aura, "... but what about the little

figure on your dash, George? Saint Christopher, is it? why are his hands clamped over his eyes?"

"Are you suggesting George drives as fast as he lives?" Melody's laughing blue eyes disarming the question.

"Perhaps Saint Christopher doesn't approve of the face in the rearview," George postures, gunning into the Beacon Street traffic to an immediate blare of horns. "Then again, maybe it is my driving!" the swell of laughter dispelling any trace of enmity.

Conducive to gaiety, sunlight sparkles the ice adorning the high woods of Concord, the dazzling trees in merry disregard of the tepid ocean breeze down in Boston. Even Hawthorn's house seems inviting, and Alcott's; the two snug against a hill, a path along its crest worn deep by Nathaniel belaboring some dark imagining. And Emerson's house just down the road, George recounting Thoreau as guest, as handy-man and gardener, as teller of tales to the household's young and to a world that would someday listen in.

Wending among Lexington's farms, George's discourse follows freedom's trail to the winding hillocks overlooking Fresh Pond, the picturesque lake once affording Bostonians their picnics, its winter surface the ice for their tropical trade.

And on to Mount Auburn, the famous cemetery a visiting Dickens once asked to see before any other New England monument, the hallowed site holding dear to its breast the tombs of New England's finest - the likes of Channing and Brooks, of Howe and Booth - lamps forever lighting the world by their exemplary lives.

Then, along the widening Charles, to Cambridge, to Harvard Square where the spreading elm once shaded a young General Washington; and around the corner, the pale and stately Craigie House where Longfellow penned *Evangeline* as he peered over his lyre-shaped garden into the candled window of his famous neighbor's study - Professor Worcester's prodigious lexicon provoking the Dictionary War, a pitched battle twixt his own and Mr. Webster's more spartan edition. A generation of Harvard fellows preferred the professor's masterly work, George explains, touting Worcester's dictionary as an erudite choice.

Motoring past where Washington Allston ended his years before his great *Belshazzar's Feast* - a vast canvass the artist spent most of his artistic life painting - George brings his car to a halt on Bunker Hill, the view of Boston apropos of the morning's trek.

Gazing up at the commanding, battlefield obelisk - its cornerstone laid by Lafayette - Vincent is pensive. "Forgetting all its factories," he says at last, "its wealth of goods ... hope is America's export of choice to millions of the world's oppressed. My people would die for such freedom - and have - which makes me feel I'm on hallowed ground."

"I agree," Melody turning to address him. "We Americans could do with an occasional removing of our shoes, as well; a looking back at the price of our freedom. As paradoxical as it seems, it's the very flowering of our freedom that obscures its roots; its heady enjoyment that leaves us forgetful."

"Yes ... like the rose," George offers, starting his car for the drive down to Back Bay.

"The rose?" Vincent mutters, an exchange of quizzical glances confirming Melody shares his bewilderment.

"Yes, the rose," their contemplative guide affirms. "Bewitched by its beauty, its perfume, we reach to possess, forgetting the thorns."

"Sounds more like something for the poet than the soldier," Vincent observes, "perhaps a romantic lament?"

"We should allow him his expression," Melody defending a George she's never known. "There's something to be said for the freedom of hearts ... and the happy choice to yield that freedom when another would make a compact - the thorns unseen, unfelt, till the moment of dissolution."

"I'm reminded of General Patton," Vincent taking in Boston's endless wharves from the heights of a bridge - reminiscing his youth through the long silence of absence, "the general's assertion, 'In war nothing is impossible, provided you use audacity.' Perhaps what we idealize in our heroes is nothing more than a cavalier disdain for the obvious; a reckless disregard we mistake as bravery."

"Memory can be capricious, Vince, but how did a delicate rose lead to the rigors of war?" Melody asks.

"Oh ... I don't know," he muses, "maybe it was Bunker Hill ... or maybe the tea party your audacious Mr. Adams supported. Then again, it isn't a battlefield I have in mind."

"Oh?" Melody prodding his explanation.

"Never mind him, Melody. He's off on one of those romantic laments," George interrupts, playing guard to her innocence, suspecting what manly profession Vincent might make should he find his elusive audacity. "What Vincent needs is a little cheer, a little help to come out of his shell. And I know just where to find it - America's oldest oyster bar, not far from the old North Church."

"Oysters?" Vince grimacing in his mobile infirmary, "nothing raw, please ... and nothing that smells of the sea. I don't think I'd survive it."

"Then it's the North End," George counters, eliciting a feeble response from the rear. "There's nothing fishy about a good Chianti with brick-oven bruschetta, and my old friend Luigi's mostaccioli."

"Anything's better than-"

"My sentiments, too, Vince," Melody contributes. "I can vouch for George's choice. You won't be disappointed."

"You've had the pleasure?" George veering off by Callahan Tunnel to ease through the North End's narrow streets; its bustling trade appearing mostly out-of-doors: an old-world array of vegetables and fruit, of baked goods and smoked meats, a veritable salmagundi spilling out between junk and antiques, the ubiquitous ristorante suggesting old Genoa - even the maze of shoppers, milling purposefully in the streets, exuding the energy of an ancient, seafaring town.

"I have had the pleasure, thank you," Melody gushes, "many times - but always with Melvin," her trailing qualifier spoken as if anything pleasurable requires his accompaniment.

"Then-then you would prefer not to-"

"Oh, no!" she protests, cutting him off, "given a choice, I would choose Luigi's; if only to rekindle the memories."

"All pleasant, I'm sure," George mumbles, coming to a stop between two gesticulating youths. "Luigi's boys," he tells Vincent, "valet service; though it's a mystery to me where they go with the cars. As you can see, there's no place in sight to park them."

"Maybe a parking barge docked at a wharf?" Vincent suggests, recalling his view from the bridge.

"Now, there's a thought!" George reacts approvingly, "leave it to a visitor to solve the natives' problems; the old 'forest for the trees' thing, I suppose."

But once inside, the pell-mell pace of men and machines is forgotten, Mario Lanza crooning *You do Something to Me* as a rotund Luigi accosts them. The old man's jocular persona suddenly on guard, a wary enthusiasm twitching his well-manicured mustache as he ponders how George has managed to woo Melody from the gentlemen accompanying her before - Melody unforgettable to a man who makes a habit of women.

"How have you been, Mr. O'Malley?" an astonished but affable Luigi inquires, "... or need I ask?" he adds with a wink, leading the trio to a private booth, his choice suggesting what he would want could he but have the luck of the Irish.

Behind a lattice of ivy, and partially hidden from an intimate, half-moon bar, the booth's cushioned seats are provocatively dark under a glass-shaded candle, the ivied partition allowing a one-way view of linen-draped tables grouped cozily before a glowing hearth.

"Luigi's idea of ambiance," George whispers, noting Melody's apprehensive eyes. "Expressed simply, he thinks a man should want nothing more than a warm fire, a bottle of wine, and a hot dish – especially if the dish is blonde."

Blonde or no, George has a problem. Unlike the tables in the adjoining room, a booth has but two sides. If he sits across from Melody, he'll have her eyes, her attention; leaving Vincent the pleasure of her nearness. But if he sits beside her, Vincent will be the man she addresses, her partner in conversation; making his own proximity seem second-place.

"I-I can't. I can't do it," Vincent cringing under the shadowing ivy. "There's a patron out there with a steaming plate of mussels. As savory as I'm sure they are, the mere thought of being near them is threatening me with nausea. I'm going back to my room ... back to rest. Perhaps you'd allow me the pleasure of your company at dinner? I should make a better candidate by then ... I-I think."

"But of course," George volunteers, "and if you insist on leaving us, why not take my car? We'll catch up later by taxi," his eagerness to hasten Vincent's departure prompting Luigi's offer:

"Good idea. I'll have my boys bring the car round."

"But he doesn't know the city," Melody objects, sidling closer to Vincent, supporting him with an affectionate, one-armed hug, "and as poorly as he feels, this is no time to send him exploring."

"You're right," Luigi's admiring eyes taking her in, "and for my good friend here," he adds, clasping a chubby hand on George's arm "I'll have one of the boys drive your ... your-"

"Client," George offers, the word hanging a veil of formality between Vincent and Melody, "Mr. Tenklei is a client, a client of the firm Mrs. Morrison - or, Melody, I should say – will soon be joining. In celebration of that event, we're showing Mr. Tenklei about town." The mention of 'Mrs.' adding a smile to Luigi's approving gawk. "Melody and I will accept your kindness, as will Mr. Tenklei," George taking every opportunity to portray Vincent as a business acquaintance apart and distinct from the friendship he shares with Melody.

"Is there something amiss here?" Melody asks cordially - Luigi waddling off to summon his boys. "This is the second time, Vince, you've abandoned our repast by some allusion to 'nausea'. Is it me, or the choice of eateries that drives you away?"

"As for last night, I put the blame on Bacchus," Vincent parries, leaning unsteadily against the lattice, "and today, who knows? But of all the immortals, you, my dear lady, are the goddess I would most desire at table."

Acting quickly to dispel the exquisite tension the remark has strung, George places his big hand on Vincent's forehead as though checking for fever. "My dear boy," he says doltishly, "I believe your illness has gone to your head," his forced laugh drawing the others in.

"Ah!" Vincent recovers, surmising George's intent, "and how easily am I overcome! But do sit down," he insists, the aroma of garlic announcing Luigi's return. "Enjoy your ... what did you call it, Melody? your 'repast'?" the casual use of her given name a parting dig at George.

But with Vincent gone, George forgets the gibe, relaxing in the balm of her presence - Melody regarding him with confidence, her Delft-blue eyes vouching her trust, any manly desire standing in check of her faith, her unguarded acceptance of a friend.

The candlelit privacy of the booth, and the gradual awareness of an accordion playing *Hello Young Lovers*, recalls George's moon-struck meeting with Simon; the music in harmony with his willing heart, the very words on his lips as enchanting as the Chianti they share. Revealing what he tries to conceal - his boyish charm, his sudden shyness, his blush at her slightest subtlety - he signals what he doesn't admit. And as Luigi surprises them with his signature antipasto, George betrays his heart, telling her more with his eyes than his words can hope to hide.

And she, comprehending, with feminine clarity, what unspoken course he has charted, thinks better to trim the sails than to pray for diminishing winds; her every look portraying contentment, her every word breathing hope; what tension courses between them stretching the net of safety, allowing her time to heal, to revisit the past, to mend the scar of Melvin's death by whatever means she choses – the diversion of Plainfield an easy digression to take.

"Whatever became of Thelma's Thanksgiving march?" she asks, George's flair for the incredible returning as though he possesses the magic to cause it.

"Cancelled," he declares pompously, his smile a kind of casual nudge to accept whatever comes with it, "... assuming it was ever scheduled."

"How ... how can you be so sure?" Melody queries with the hesitance of doubt. "Thelma Peabody happens to be the subject of one of my most vivid childhood memories; her screaming insistence, one Easter Sunday, that we 'Little tots of the church should scratch the dust for our Savior's blood rather than scamper through the grass for pagan eggs' still haunting me to this day. One can never be sure of Thelma - sure of whether her motives are in agreement with her actions."

"Are you suggesting Thelma does things against her will?" George spearing a thin slice of prosciutto protruding from a nest of olives. "If so, perhaps we should reconsider the bookstore's-"

"It's her will I question, not her faithfulness to it," Melody interjects, her own antipasto untouched. "Ever since Artie told me of her plan to march for Melvin, I've suspected a motive other than what the action suggests – one of her blistering banners, perhaps; one that besmirches rather than lauds."

"I'll check it out," he promises, topping her glass and refilling his own. "I'll be back a day or two ahead of you ... time enough for discovery ... time enough to protect the untarnished memory of-of our much loved and-and much missed departed," he finishes awkwardly - Luigi's fresh mostaccioli appearing in a cloud of steam, the rich marinara making Melody thankful she hasn't squandered what little appetite she has; the old man proclaiming:

144

"A meal without bread is like a bed without sheets. No matter what you spread-"

"Mrs. Morrison," George hastily interposes, employing the formality of her surname to counter Luigi's familiarity, "Mrs. Morrison is a native of Vermont, not Boston, and as such, will not fully appreciate your metaphor. But as to your bread ... now, that is something she can appreciate, and no doubt will, as soon as you serve it," he adds, contriving to praise, even as he reproves his host.

"Thank you," Melody whispers - Luigi galumphing for the kitchen. "I can't imagine - and indeed, don't want to – what he was about to say. But-" With a moue of distress, she fumbles for her silver to divert his attention.

"Well?" he prods, his attention on nothing but her, "do go on ... don't leave me in the dark."

"I was going to say," she admits coyly, " ... I was going to say, you can be the gentleman when you choose. I mean, it isn't as though you have erred beyond mending, you know."

"Erred?" he repeats, his cheeks streaking a trace of guilt.

"Perhaps that depends on one's upbringing, one's environment," Melody advancing a vague apology. "After all, what I may hold in moral question may be another's fervent creed; and accordingly, who am I to judge? And just because a man doesn't seize on every opportunity to brag on his newborn son-"

"Allow me," he breaks in, hurrying to quit his reply before Luigi's untimely return. "Allow me to address that-that ... well ... I would hardly call it a problem, now would I?"

"I don't know. You tell me," she quips.

"OK. Let me put it this way: if I were to stand trial for my life so far, Melody, it would be you whom I would most prefer as judge. For where you would be blameless, such lack of guile would be the very virtue promising mercy. And mercy ... or at least the compassion one regards as mercy ... is what my confession requires; what that dear little baby-"

"And is that what you would be expecting from me?" she interposes, her blue eyes bashfully downcast, "... the tender hand of mercy?"

"Just your tender hand would be more than I deserve," he answers, bringing a deep blush to her high-boned cheeks, "much less your mercy. But regarding the child-"

"Piping hot!" cries Luigi, huffing to the booth with his vaunted bread, "brick-oven baked and cornmeal dusted. My customers tell me, Mrs. Moralson, that it's the North End's best," he brags.

"Morrison," George corrects, making room for the cloth-lined basket and the generous dish of olive oil, balsamic vinegar and fresh oregano Luigi unfailingly provides, "it's Mrs. Morrison, as in Van Morrison, the other Irishman of worldly fame."

"Oh yeah?" a lusty Luigi replies, "but then again, she ain't no '*Brown-eyed Girl*', now is she?" Melody's beauty emboldening him. "In fact, Mrs. Morrison's one of those blue-eyed goddesses, that's what she is; the kind one might catch sight of in one of those high-flown Greek temples."

"The reasons I count you as a friend are manifold, but making a move on my beautiful partner is not among them," George scolds, reaching between candle and bread to pat Melody's hand.

"Well, you can't blame me for trying, can you?" the crusty old Italian chuckling as he makes his way past the lattice.

"He isn't-"

"Angry with me?" George finishes for her, "of course not. And how could he be when he knows he overstepped propriety?"

"Then we'll leave it at that," she says evenly, a smile disavowing her tone, "we'll forget the impropriety of the proprietor and enjoy the delights of his establishment."

"Beginning with you," a stricken George retorts.

Looking up, she appears amused. "Yes ... a beginning; and one that won't lead you to harm," the lush refrains of Al Martino's *Here in My Heart* negating any need of reply.

No man is rich enough to
buy back his own past.
(Oscar Wilde)

XXI

"WOULD YOU LOOK AT THIS?" AUNT MARTHA PRAT-
tles, both of us browsing through Artie's locked and dusty store like a
pair of intrepid intruders, two thieves with nothing better to filch than
a knapsack of useless trivia. "It states right here," she goes on, "right here
in this old *Arcane Facts of New England* that the first recorded hanging in
Massachusetts was that of a teenager, one Thomas Granger, for the carnal
assault of a mare, a cow, five sheep, two goats and a turkey. I dare say," she
chuckles, returning the book to its shelf, only to blow off the dust from
another, "you may not have survived the ordeal of a Puritan life had you
been a boy of that period."

"Bestiality is a far, far cry from even the worst of my faults, auntie,
and you know it," I cavil, shooting her a malign glance. "And besides, it's
you who lived among the beasts of Rome, not I."

"It's just the weather," she apologies, thumbing through a leather-bound edition of *Bowditch's Practical Navigator*, "just the weather playing tricks on our sanity."

A plausible excuse, too, as it's desperately cold outside, the Winooski's
sluggish slabs of ice as gray as the dusky sky, the swirling snow sifting
silence over the valley, silvering the stubble of a summer lost. What color
once bloomed from earth's nurturing breast is long unremembered in
the stark and numbing chill. With Thanksgiving but a day away, Mother

Nature is joining the celebration, enchanting the warm windowed-views of rosy-cheeked children eager to brave the slopes; and of old-timers, too, content to remain behind, relishing the warmth of lullaby hearths to the wistful remembrance of youth; to the savory scent of venison roast, of turkey and hot apple pie.

"Weren't we going to check in on Thelma? cast your spell on her march?" I ask hesitantly - the snow, drifting in irresolute patterns against the windows, like a hypnotist's chant, prompting but vague, a fleeting suggestion that I need to discover the edges.

"What am I, a witch?" she quips playfully, replacing the mariner's manual with a disregard screaming her ignorance of first editions, "your personal genie?"

"If you're the lamp sent to guide me," I gibe, reluctant to fly in such poor visibility, "then why not be the genie, too?"

"I am," she chortles, flitting over to Artie's display window to better enjoy the white-icing treat outside. "And to prove it, I'll let you in on a secret: Thelma's still asleep - dead to the world, as it were - her restless arms holding tight her one last hope for a man."

"Is that why you knocked that first edition of *Human Sexual Response* from its stand?" I ask amusedly, stooping to retrieve the disheveled book before its pages are permanently crimped. "I'm referring to the Masters and Johnson treatise partitioning intercourse into four separate stages. Was it disbelief that made you knock it off? Disbelief the stages of excitement, plateau, orgasm and resolution are something a man can produce? Or was it your overt disbelief in the sensuality of senior citizens? "

"You can knock it off yourself," she barks, the accuracy of my barb etched in her face. "You've got us all wrong, sweetheart. After all, why do you think they call us sexagenarians?" she poses - disdaining my answer, should I give one. "I can assure you it's not for the yogurt and bran we consume before going out on the prowl."

"Right," I retort, "the word comes from the Latin sexageni, meaning 'sixty each.'"

"Ha!" she scorns, "there you have it, Melvin; for that's fifty-eight more than you had when you abruptly quit the race!"

"Race, march - I don't care what you call it;" I respond, returning to my present perturbation, "I just want to be sure Thelma Peabody doesn't pull one of her infamous placard punches on this straight-man nephew of yours."

"If it's placards you're worried about," A.M. rallying to my concern, "then I'll show you what she's prepared so far-"

"So far?" I interrupt, such a chilling thought making my light head swirl like the wind-blown snow. "Do you mean there's more to come?"

"Nothing of the sort," A.M. emphatic, waving her attenuated arms like a director before an orchestra of flakes. "You do see what I've done, don't you?" A.M. pointing her phantom baton at the storm while turning to me for praise, "I've made her march impractical. And I did it for you!"

"You-you have to help me here," I stammer. "Our Lord walking on the water is a miracle I can believe, if for no other reason than He who created the water should know how to employ its properties. But, you?" I guffaw, "you, my erstwhile aunt? Are you claiming to possess such power, too? or such knowledge?" I amend, "since knowledge is power? But wait!" my thoughts drifting like the snow, "I think I grasp your meaning! You're saying if our Master walked on water, the least you can do is walk under it; the fact that it's frozen, and falling harmlessly about you, something only He can explain!"

"Do you want to waste your morning smarting off?" A.M. smirks dismissively, "or see what Thelma has to make you smart?"

"One can never know enough," I submit, "... take me to task, if you must."

"Then we're off to Thelma's basement," she announces; just the thought of being underground – though it takes us to Thelma's instantly - making me uneasy, like standing in a quiet room with a crooked picture.

"It's really cold down here," I grumble, shaking my ethereal limbs in hopes of a little friction. "I didn't realize we're still subject to such mundane effects as changing temperature and inclement weather."

"Actually, we aren't," she assures me. "It's just your imagination, your recall of how cold once felt ... of how a damp cellar once chilled you ... of how the grave-"

"The grave?" I interject, shivering uncontrollably.

"You don't remember, do you?" she mumbles to herself, switching on Thelma's basement light before I can remember I don't need it.

"I don't; nor, do I-I wish to," I rattle.

"Not many do," A.M. posing dramatically as she slowly turns a pole-mounted, lace-fringed placard to a full-frontal view, "not many stay behind," she adds, giving the weird, feminine sign a flutter, "not many stay buried in self-pity, responding, instead, to the light calling them into the clouds."

"Which is hardly the call of Thelma's placard," I observe, wincing as I read it aloud:

MOTHER! MOTHER!
A name that blesses
lest the 'M' be set aside;

OTHER! OTHER!
A name that curses
the women it may deride.

"What's this about Mothers?" I quiz, too cold to pick up the trail.

"From Thelma Peabody's twisted perspective, it's not so much about mothers as it is about the charismatic letter 'M'," Aunt Martha's twist of the protest placard sending a mason quart of apple butter crashing to the floor.

"T-The letter 'M'?" I shiver, "a-and charismatic?"

"Sure. Don't you get it?" she shrills, bouncing upward to avoid the shards of glass. "The letter 'M' stands naked in shame ... like Hawthorne's scarlet letter. It's the letter of your initials, Melvin. All that gibberish about Mother, and Other is just smoke from another fire. And do you know why?" her cold blue eyes staring me down in hungry anticipation, "because this isn't Thelma's placard ... it's Charlene's!"

"But where's the charisma?" I parry, denying her the satisfaction of my guilt. "Where's the magnetism? the charm?"

"That's your memory," she snaps, disappointed. "I mean, not yours, but the recollections of those you left behind, what they recall of the recently deceased Melvin Morrison; the bright-eyed, big-hearted kid they portray all too kindly in the screening room of the dead. But then, we're all so inclined," she allows, "even me. Why, I can remember when your father died, how I was forgiving him even before he thought to look me up, forgetting all the times he took dead aim at me with those hell-fire sermons of his; how he all but called my name in his scorching, accusatory delivery; how he-"

"The more you go on about it," I interrupt, "the less it would seem you've forgiven him."

"Right," she mutters, turning abruptly to retrieve another sign. "Helen the organist composed this one," A.M. safely negotiating, for the moment, the over-stocked shelves of Thelma's home-canned fruits. "And if it makes you feel any better," she adds pretentiously, "Helen and Charlene were the only Other Women who completed Thelma's questionnaire. All the rest were frightened off by Melody's commie bugster ploy."

"Only two?" I chime, my shivers subsiding, "then Thelma isn't marching today, even had the sun shown hot on the Statehouse lawn! So much for your snowstorm trick," I cry, "and so much for you taking all the credit, too. By your own admission, Aunt Martha, it's Melody I have to thank for Thelma's failure, not you."

"Read the placard" she growls, jabbing it in front of my third eye, "... read it before elation runs away with your prudence."

"As if!" I retort with scorn - reading it just the same:

March for our own dear Melvin,
And his midnight ride for to see,
The plight of the Other Women
Who come not by land nor by sea.

"I see you have a new cause," she declares, almost indifferently, her cold shoulder holding me at fault, "a cause beyond my help. Perhaps Melody can get you out of this one, too."

"What's there to get out of?" I ask, peering about my former Sunday-school teacher's cellar with ardent curiosity. "If there's to be no march, these protest slogans are harmless."

"Harmless?" she echoes acidly. "Would you say they're as harmless as Thelma's private gallery in the corner behind you?" her chilling remark prodding me to turn about.

"So what?" I voice weakly, Thelma's color montage of muscle men, grotesque in their posed positions, spread out across the dank stone wall like decadent trophies. "It's her private vice. No one else will be the wiser."

"But how does this discovery make you feel?" she asks scathingly. "After all, she was your spiritual mentor, you know."

"That's all in the past now. It's something she'll have to deal with herself," I cavil. "And with the advent of Simon, maybe she'll tear down her secret temple, her altar to Adonis ... put it behind her here and now ... correct her karma, as it were."

"Or un-correct Simon's," she snips witheringly.

"Short on forgiveness today, Aunt Martha?" I ask, suggesting her own correction.

"Short on patience," she responds, letting the remark double as an apology. "And I must admit I kept my own gallery when I was mortal; though it was all in my mind, not my cellar."

"Which explains why it's still with you," I tease. "But I can appreciate that; for it's a natural thing to do: imagining your perfect mate; a kind of mental measuring stick attempting to abet the heart; abetting, that is, till one meets the truly perfect mate - a mate who may or may not be what one has imagined; but who will, in any case, be immeasurably superior."

"You have set me up to tell you," she replies, after a pause.

"Tell me?"

"Yes ... tell you about Charlene – oh! and George, of course! Charlene has announced the breaking off of her engagement."

"To George?" I ask stupidly, her news disturbing my short-lived sangfroid.

"To everyone. She's announced it to everyone who'll listen, complaining of George's inattention, his drinking bouts, his promiscuity, his-"

"Go no further," I interject. "You've said enough – enough to raise alarm on another front."

"Concern for your child?" her eyebrows raised approvingly.

"Never! Ever!" I declare. "Charlene, if she's nothing else, is a splendid, doting mother. I know, because I was looking over your shoulder when you called up her record, her life pattern."

"Touché!" she shoots back, unwilling to give me advantage, "but I thought you were after something else ... something other than her qualities as a mother."

"What else would I have been interested in?" I pose.

"Oh ... love, perhaps? Perhaps you were curious - after marring your record on the subject - as to whether Charlene would have been a better mate."

"If you think that, you're dead wrong!" My retort peremptory.

"Dead, yes; wrong, no. There's always that question lurking in the shadows of an affair. I should know. I've had my share of them down through the centuries."

"But wait," I interject, preventing her dissertation on concupiscence, "does George know about this yet? He's been down in Boston for two days, and won't be home till later today. So-"

"He doesn't; though the news will be welcomed when he hears it."

"Conflict of interest? Are you suggesting George will be only too happy to recuse himself from a case of diapers?"

"You got it," she laughs, "... before it gets down and dirty – which reminds me, you haven't seen Thelma's placard yet; the one she prepared expressly for you."

"Do I want to?" I ask, too late to catch another mason jar as she reaches for Thelma's composition. "Thelma's going to wonder what happened down here, with a trail of broken glass and sticky fruit leading right to her gallery."

"Maybe it'll suggest her penance," A.M. twirling the largest of the three placards for me to view. "It'll take more than a little chastening of the soul to wash out the stain of this one," she exclaims, reading it aloud for emphasis:

Be not deceived; God is not mocked: for whatsoever a man soweth, that shall he also reap.

For he that soweth to his flesh shall of the flesh reap corruption; but he that soweth to the Spirit shall of the Spirit reap life everlasting.

"But it's not her composition," I quibble; though none too pleased by Thelma's selection for my memorial, "it's from the book of Galatians, an epistle Paul wrote to the church in-"

"I know," A.M. breaks in, using her expertise with the heavenly index to find the passage before I can cite it, "6th chapter, verses 7 and 8," she continues pedantically. "By calling it her 'composition', I mean she cheapens its purpose, misapplying Paul's message to-"

"Cheapens?" I return the favor of her frequent interruptions. "Are you inferring the Holy Bible is debased when Thelma quotes it on my behalf?"

"I'm not inferring it, I'm affirming it!" she rages, suddenly irked in my defense. "She's hypocritical! No, worse than that, she's demoniacal to fault your peccadilloes when, as the good book says, she should remove the beam from her own eye before fishing for the splinter in yours."

"I appreciate your bias, Aunt Martha," I tender, hoping to calm the tempest, "especially when I'm on the long side of your equation. But I must remind you that no harm has been done since the march is not to be. There is no cause now for anger."

"Oh?" she whines, capitulating ever so slightly, "and what are we to do about Thelma meddling in our new incarnations? Can you answer that one?"

"Meddling, did you say? And here I thought you ranked first among meddlers. Be that as it may," I say, softening my aspersion, "Thelma may be a lot of things, but she's no Methuselah."

"I read life patterns, remember?" A.M. as morbid as her subject.

"'That which is, already has been; that which is to be, already is,'" I philosophy, quoting some remembered Bible lesson.

"Ecclesiastes 3:15 - and I'm here to tell you," she appends menacingly, "to warn you: we haven't seen the last of Thelma Peabody!"

What is allowed, we scorn; what's
not allowed, we burn for.
(Ovid)

XXII

Up before the discontented dawn, before the
nervous past can find him out, George escapes Boston Jesus clean. A strange
and new elation, this boy in a man's body, a childhood memory reviving
his deadened heart - an August night, under moth-fluttered lamps, the
envy of his pals for the excitement of Mexican jumping beans. What strife
remains in the dark of his mind, fades slowly away, his bygone failings like
swords in the frenzied hands of gladiators annihilating themselves in the
past, the present unscathed by their violent passing. A rebirth, it is; a new
beginning; a grafting to the vine of a superior vineyard, the Winooski River
valley seeming all of this world he will ever need.

And Melody.

Thoughts of Melody are sanguine, yet they summon Charlene, her
rancor like a siren before a storm. And the innocent babe, the little boy
born under his name? What hope has he in a hopeless home? What peace
under Damocles' sword? For even as he thinks of Charlene, it's as though
she's beside him in the car, her slighting eyes, her scorning smile, her biting
words so heavy on his mind he stops for a cup of coffee, stops to escape the
oppressive air, to feel anew a divine autonomy, the silken freedom of the
evening before.

The quaint New Hampshire diner is like a coddling aunt, an order
of blueberry griddle cakes and Vermont maple syrup reminding him of

his farm - the great oak table he rescued from the barn, a table on which to spread the fruits of a life well-lived with one's mate, one's children, one's community; the joy of sharing the very fuel for his flight of fancy.

As he butters his pancakes, he recalls how he's never been afraid of superlatives, using them like keys to his lovers' hearts, believing all the while he was immune, untouched by the sentimentality. Too selfish to love, he once promised himself he'd never give his heart; and now he's breaking that promise, being untrue to himself. Or is he? The question brings a chuckle as he imagines being in a drugstore, standing in line with the women, believing what he reads in the Valentine cards.

How is Melody so different? What magic does she wield to transform a man? And willingly, too, he thinks, savoring a bite of blueberries; for where once he'd known Ovid by his poems, now he's met him in her eyes! And the mystery doesn't end there, Ovid writing his *Art of Love* just before the birth of Christ; his *Metamorphoses* a few years afterward. Is there significance there? Is Melody his own Madonna? He hopes not - some vague imagining bringing a blush at the possibility. Of this only is he certain: having known her, he dare not demand of his God any greater happiness!

Oracular, this move to Vermont, this transmutation of failure into fortune - fleeing his old misdeeds, convinced there could not be despair where hope has never been, only to discover hope has been there all along, awaiting his arrival – the result answering fully to the zeal awakening it.

At first, it was Melody. But the shame of his past decried his passion - Charlene, with her ready problem, the scapegoat for atonement. Ironic as the rich being drawn to charity, his misplaced desire; his need, in hand with sympathy, going off to get lost in the dark.

Nor is his mistake any easier on Charlene. There are moments when she seems amiable enough, patronizing him like the English listening admiringly to a good Irish tenor. But there are others when she moves through the void of his presence with magnificent indifference, a look of fatigued resignation meeting his embassy of words. Answering him neutrally, if she answers at all, her contemptuous dignity, her bumptious manner, sends him off to sulk in the gloom of a hopeless distance.

Despite this first and failed attempt at love, he will not raise the flag of defeat, his flight to Vermont offering more than the chance to rusticate. Making bold to prosper, the conflicts wrought by cloistered minds hold his interest. For all that's been said of America's opportunities, few of her fortunes were made by the sweat of the brow, he decides – and a good thing, too, since a pioneer he is not. In Boston he'd found no objective meriting the trouble of effort, but now he suffers the madness of enthusiasm; his clients going away convinced of victory, nursing within them the enmity already at their hearts.

By nature nonchalant, he's become punctilious, winning by the fright of detail; a record he's building assiduously, wishing for the firm a prestige as becoming as his soon-to-be partner. Melody is his cynosure, his talents honed by her promise, her rarified sense of the man he can be leaving him breathless with expectation – expectation having its counterpart in an imposed obligation: Charlene. For even as he feigns an interest, his eyes are a valediction, his smile a pejorative, Charlene reducing love to the pittance of the mundane, the material, the bud of romance nipped by the mere mention of her name. As long as he's the answer to her problem, she's a fallen woman - one who may never get up. The ordeal of his best intentions has left her wounded. And himself, too; worst of all wounds being those of the heart. If it were not for Melody, he might just as well be considered posthumous. Expelled from the orchestra, he has no desire to reapply. He doesn't miss the dissonance.

But in Melody's presence, music is a time machines, a love song taking him back to innocence. And if he can believe what he so ardently fancies, there are moments when she glimpses in him the face of Raphael. He imagines her lost in a reverie - one including him - her countenance brightening with a gleam of her former happiness. Perhaps pity is a path to her garden; or maybe compassion. She's suffered enough from her own misfortune to have a wellspring of empathy for his. Maybe she'll understand if he tells her; will think more of him if he admits the baby isn't his; will think him saintly to have borne the public blame.

Perhaps she'll even apologize for having inquired, for having asked why he didn't bubble with tidings. Not that she needs to. God, no! An apology from her would be like Jesus admitting a sin, the undoing of perfection, a profaning of His very worship.

And therein lies the difference. He worships her.

Oh, he wants to touch her, too; to feel the woman inside the goddess; but he wants the goddess to remain unmarred, to forever be his quest. Remove the aspiration, he reasons, and he'll be but the animal he's been before.

Dreaming of Melody gives him a sense of belonging, of home; remembering Charlene, as though he has no home to go to. And in truth, he's been everywhere but home of late, succored more by tavern hearths than the fire he's tried to spark. But today is different. Halfway between the Boston of old and his new, Vermont estate, his thoughts of Melody somehow hallow his waiting farmhouse - or is it just the falling snow on the gentle mountains as he crosses the Connecticut River?

He can't decide. But once he turns at his gate, makes the first tracks in the new-fallen snow, he's certain of the change, of the gentle force behind it. After shaking the snow from his boots, he builds a three log fire the way Melvin taught him to do, ruminating on the evening Melvin spent with him here – and Melody – the memory casting doubts like shadows from the quickening fire. What if Melody had the same memory? What if she were here by the warming hearth, only to think of Melvin?

"Melvin, my friend," he says to the smoke-scented room, "you're gone ... and still you linger. We're in different worlds, with a grave in between, and still you make your presence felt," the sound of his own voice covering the knocks at the door until the caller begins to bang, a glaucous-eyed Simon Farley puffing on the ice-glazed panes in an effort to peer within.

"Didn't know they made snow tires for bicycles," George quips as he opens the door, his irritation melting like the flakes on Simon's parka. "What brings you out in weather like this?"

"Has to get deeper than this, or be ice underneath, before my Schwinn knows the difference," Simon showing himself in to pull a cane-bottomed rocker closer to the fire. "And besides, any effort was lost in my worry," he adds with an air of mystery, "... my worry over you."

Reclaiming the comfort of his wingback, George remains silent, experience advising against reply.

"Thought you might need some company," Simon tries again, "what with your fiancée taking potshots at you," this last aside, armed with violent significance, alerting George to the matters at hand.

"Charlene?" Shrugging as if bored by the thought, George leans to thrust a poker in the fire.

"Yes ... and after the heart-to-heart I had with you in the cemetery the other night, I thought ... I don't know what I thought exactly," Simon trails off, George's silence having its effect. "It's just that we were alluding to love ... ."

"Love?" George repeats curtly, a scream coiling tightly in his chest, "yes, well ... it may not be for everyone."

"I'm sure you like apples," Simon retorts with lock and key finality.

"Who doesn't?" George wary, leaning back in his chair.

"Why, no one that I know of," Simon cocking his head as though George has asked the impossible, "but I chose apples because I want you to think of something pleasant; something you thoroughly enjoy. An apple just came to mind. I can imagine how it must be down in Boston," he continues, the fire's warmth inviting him to shed his parka and hang it from the cresting rail of his rocker, "... how a fellow might be perusing the aisles of a grocery store and chance upon an arranged display of hand-waxed apples cascading from woven baskets ... and how that fellow might choose an apple from among the three or four he handles-"

"Something wrong with that?" George quips, having done exactly what Simon is describing.

"Not a thing. Not a thing. And that's my point - or part of it. For everyone – and that includes you, Mr. O'Malley – everyone should be able to savor the sweet crunch of a ripe apple. It's just that some of us ... well -"

"Well, what?" George prods, an unvoiced judgement in his eyes.

"Some of us are just more fortunate, I guess. Here in Vermont, we pick the fruit right off the trees. In fact, we can even choose the tree from which to make our selection. And that's how it is with love, too. Don't you see?"

"As a matter-of-fact, I don't," George capitulates, "although your allegory makes me want to."

"It could be the same apple – whether it's displayed in the big city grocer's, or still hanging from the tree; but the enjoyment of that apple, it seems to me, must surely be more complete when experienced in its natural environment."

That Simon could be referencing Melody is more than George is willing to dare; but to be sure, he redirects. "And just what did you mean earlier when you said Charlene was taking potshots at me?"

"Like I said, I came out here because I thought you might need some company, continue our graveside chat - entre nous, of course." Simon gazing at the crackling logs, fumbling in his shirt pocket for a frayed and folded notebook page, then tendering it in the direction of George. "There's nothing like a good book for company when a body needs a friend ... or maybe a poem. I-I composed one for you ... thought it might speak to your hurt, your anger ... or maybe to both. *Just This Abides* I call it. Hope it helps-"

George reaching to take his gift - comprehending, at last, the purpose of Simon's call. Unfolding the crumpled page, he reads the neatly printed lines aloud:

Old chapel bell, toll true tonight,
Ring round my hurting heart,
An ancient spell to set affright
The ghost who stole my part.

Sway slow and true your iron sides
To brush the midnight skies,
Till darkness drips from whence it hides
To wash my mournful eyes.

Old chapel bell, be clear of mind,
On you I yet depend;
Though beats in you a heart in kind
With cold forsaking friend:

The lips that sealed a wedding vow
Beneath your belfry there,
And you rang then, as you do now -
Yet now I'm much aware;

That all who answer to your call
May come in joyful quest;
But you and I know that's not all
In truth your tolls behest.

Your hardened heart hangs ever cold
Above those chapel doors,
A clanging cold, a banging bold

To deafen promise goers;

Till once beyond your iron lip
A pledge is soon forgone,
And Libra's scale begins to tip
Unfairly then for one.

So chapel bell, toll true tonight,
Ring true to wiser ears;
Ring out with harsh and bitter slight
The pain of bygone years.

Sway slow and true your iron sides
To celebrations past;
Till ringing still, just this abides:
One truth, one love to last.

Only the fire offers comment, a whiff of smoke, as George rises slowly from his chair. Rummaging among books on the mantel, he finds what he's in search of. "I, too, composed something on the subject ... only the subject isn't Charlene," he clarifies, voicing his scribbled lines:

I hold you in the arms of dreams,
caressing you with wild imaginings.

Light as unknown trouble,
my feet run certain to your being.

Where orange water drinks the dregs of day,
I grasp the silver cup of empty night;

and bearing it expectantly,
am never friend to disappointment.

You ask of me remaining days ....

I surrender, knowing well that
night is more eternal thing;
that dreams have life beyond the sun.

Farewell to shadowed world

made stark in glare of light;
for silver cup of empty night
is calling –

Calling me, filling me;

Enchanting me with you.

I hold you in the arms of dreams,
caressing you with wild imaginings.

With a flick of his wrist, George tosses both works into the flickering
flames; each man appreciating the finality of fire.
The gift of silence.

Never confuse a single mistake with a final mistake.
(F. Scott Fitzgerald)

XXIII

WITH THELMA'S MARCH ALL BUT DEAD AND BURIED, I
let my worry fade like a misplaced memory - as misplaced as the Comptons
appear to be, arriving from Kansas in the middle of a Green Mountain
snowstorm. And on a holiday, too, with no one to greet them save George.
George excels in his role as executor, his commanding presence, his evident interest in their affairs, easing the young couple's move.

"The old farmhouse I purchased was shoddier than yours," he shares,
fashioning hope from experience. "The old place hadn't been occupied in
years, and the lack of maintenance cried aloud at every turn."

"George is right," I remark to A.M.. "He's stretching the truth a bit,
but he's inspiring the Comptons, creating a vision of possibility, a glimpse
of the future."

"Needs a nursery," A.M. grumbles, "got to add on a wing, if I'm going
to nest there."

"That's called 'connective architecture', I believe; although I miss the
connection between wings and your next incarnation."

"You'll think otherwise when we meet again," she snorts. "I'll be a
heart-throb, the beau ideal of every dashing young man in the county."

"I hope you're mistaken," I reply archly, feigning a fume, "I won't be
a dashing fellow, if you're a heart throb." Aunt Martha ignores my froth,
donkey-tugging me to Old Faithful's farm before another razz can fizzle.

"Thought you would want to be here when Melody arrives," she brays, "see how she takes the news about George."

"You mean about Charlene, don't you?" I suggest, admiring Faithful's sweet-tart apple and fresh pumpkin pies, remembering our good times together. "It's Charlene who has the new addition, not George."

"It's Artie, smarty, and there's nothing new about him save his name. Besides, Melody already knows about the baby. I'm referring to George; to George being let off the hook, so to speak; the old 'plenty of fish in the sea' metaphor-"

"So the choices are infinite?" I interject – not that my effort is warranted, Melody turning into Faithful's drive even as I'm turning the inference.

"Look at Faithful, would you?" Aunt Martha gasps, wresting my gaze from the beauty knocking snow from her boots on the porch. "Look at her eyes, dancing with the frivolity of a waltz, the glow on her cheeks like candles burning golden over some gay gavotte. Sometimes, Melvin ... sometimes I think it's the most miraculous idea God ever had, expressing love through motherhood."

"Granted," the easy swing of the heavy wood door, the big, rumpling hug following the removal of Melody's coat, the rapid patter of affectionate exchange, all leaving me large-eyed for love. Faithful's wrinkles, profuse about her eyes and mouth, move with a life of their own, crisscrossing and overlapping in seeming disdain of her powder, her smile the main distraction.

And Melody.

Leaning back in Faithful's hungry arms, she displays her diamond, its very enormity exuding danger, its precarious suspension from the filigree chain emblematic of life's fragility.

"Vincent gave it to me," she whispers, searching for sanction in her mother's eyes, "... Melvin's client."

"I-I know who Vincent is," Faithful replies with uncertainty, "... but why? I mean, fortunes rise and fall like hemlines, so he must be prospering of late; but why would he share his fortune with you?" astonishment etched in her face.

"Friendship?" Melody ventures, attempting to quell her mother's shock, "in memory of Melvin's friendship?"

"Men don't give each other diamonds, darling ... but then again, it isn't polite to return a gift, now is it?" Faithful's chuckle all the approbation Melody needs. "Too bad it wasn't given by George," she adds, reluctantly ending her embrace.

"George?" Melody echoes, as though aghast at the thought, "George?"

"Maybe Charlene wouldn't have dumped him," Faithful explains - Melody's face as red as a sledder's wind-chap.

"Dump him? But-but why, Mother?"

Interposing on the scene, Aunt Martha directs my attention to a car pulling up behind Melody's. "She can ask him herself," she says, "... infinitely more exciting that way."

"What's he doing here?" I grouse, George's tall frame emerging from his car.

"Just you wait," Aunt Martha's mirthful tone putting me at ease. "You have a pleasant surprise in store, one to merit your approval," George rapping loudly on the rear porch door as I ponder what Aunt Martha's concept of pleasant might be.

"George!" Melody exclaims, opening wide the door as though acknowledging his imposing stature, "we were just-"

"About to have some warm apple pie," Faithful breaks in, aborting Melody's about-to-be-gushed admission, "... and a fresh pot of coffee. Would you join us?"

"Be delighted," their surprise visitor accepting Melody's help with his coat, her slender fingers, playing delicately over the soft cashmere, part of the mise en scène his eyes don't miss. "And pardon me for presuming upon your hospitality," he adds, his wistful eyes following Melody - something Faithful's eyes don't miss. "What I stopped by for was ... well, I was hoping Melody would be here. I want to take her to see the impromptu show on the capitol lawn."

"In a snowstorm?" Faithful incredulous, attending to the assembly of her percolator - one Melvin had bought her, insisting her antiquated drip pot be discarded - "and ... and on Thanksgiving Day?"

"Yes," George affirms, accepting Melody's offered chair, its timeworn arms embracing the old table as if Caesar is expected home. "Yes, the snow and the holiday spirit enhancing the show, lending it romance - if-if I'm using the word correctly."

"That depends," Melody selecting an opposite chair as his eyes beg explanation, "... depends on whether you think the 'show', whatever it may be, is romantic; or, whether the picturesque capitol, the snow, the holiday, the gathering of friends, all make the recipe for romance ... and damn the show!"

"Melody!" Faithful exclaims, laughing as she joins them at table, pie in hand, "what would your father say if he heard you swear?"

"I never knew him," George intervenes, "but from what I've been told, he would be going straight for the cause, ignoring the effect," Melody's twinkling blue eyes acknowledging his aid.

"That he would," Faithful deftly knifing the still-warm pie into six large pieces, the aromas of flaky crust, of apples, cinnamon and allspice, turning the sluggish percolator into a foe. "And if there were goings-on down in Montpelier when Caesar was here, he'd be the first to check it out."

"Why not accompany us, Faithful," George clasping and unclasping his hands, then withdrawing them to his lap, "... if the coffee ever decides to brew."

"Patience, my dear," Melody addressing his eagerness. "You know what they say: 'the longer the wait, the greater the satisfaction.'"

"That depends," George counters, mimicking Melody.

"On what?" Faithful asks.

"Well ... like an engagement," he postures, maneuvering out of a pending embarrassment, "... I'm sure you've heard."

"I just arrived!" Melody responds, determined to hear his news first-hand. "Have there been developments?"

"You might say that," George concurs, "or better said, the picture will not be developed. The camera's broken, Melody. Charlene and I have-"

"Made a decision?" she interrupts, struck by an inchoate sundering, like a promise broken before it can be expressed, "might we say a snap decision?"

"Honestly, no. I mean, yes. I was going to break it off with Charlene upon my return from Boston, but she beat me to it. Apparently, she told everyone in Plainfield, except me."

"But-but you weren't here," Melody mutters, the thought of absence, of a man not being there to play his part, reminding her of someone else. "Where's Thelma?" she asks suddenly....

Melody's question shocks me into a fright. "Is that your surprise?" I scream silently, A.M. smirking with amusement. "Is that what you deem pleasant? My march to crucifixion?"

"Now, who said anything about you, Melvin?" A.M. zapping the percolator with a burst of energy. "Gotta get these folks on the road before the show's over. Don't want you missing your surprise."

"Knowing you, it's probably one I'll wish like hell I did miss," I complain, unconvinced by her apparent nonchalance.

"Funny you'd say that," my aunt's casual act more like magnificent indifference. "Fact is, wishes are what hell is made of. Did you know that?"

"Changing the subject doesn't work with me," I counter with fisted defiance, "only honesty."

"Give me a break!" she shoots back, pointing a skeletal finger at Melody. "Where was this fixation with honesty when you were-"

"Enough!" I interject, pleased to see the coffee being poured, the pie served. "I'll check my temper, if you'll check yours."

"Deal," she simpers - her old fascination with George drawing her so near to his chair that he asks for a coffee warmup before his first sip. "What a doll!" she coos, "what a perfect specimen!"

"Yeah, like those little containers the lab technician gives you to take into the bathroom." But she seems not to mind my aspersion, the party of three donning coats to depart for the show.

"Want to wait and enjoy it with them?" A.M. asks, as they trek through the snow for George's car.

"Let's meet them there," I suggest, somehow knowing it's the answer expected – Thelma's placard, unexpected, announcing our arrival at the capitol.

Adieu to the blues,
"I Do" is the news.

What comes in twos,
Is not a ruse.

"Not her best," I guffaw, relief spreading through me like nitrous oxide, "but Simon's a made man, if ever there were one."

"Made a man is closer to the truth," A.M. arm-pumping a gleeful YES! "Told you, didn't I? Promised you a surprise, didn't I?"

"You did, Aunt Martha; and forgive me for doubting you," my apology in mid-sentence when I espy Vincent, mummy-like in blankets, strapped to a gurney, held at a forty-five by two Godhard professors, the better to afford him a view. "Let me rephrase that," I add, grimacing at the sight of Vincent still suffering from the potion my jealously authored. "There are areas of expertise in which doubts have merit ... one of them being-"

"He'll recover, I tell you. It's in his life pattern-"

"But you told me you couldn't read his life pattern; that his guardian angels wouldn't allow it," I cavil. "Some faith you engender, Aunt Martha, risking a life for a whim!"

"Add a 'P' and you've got it," she snips, "for a wimp is what a jealous man is!"

"Never mind me," I cry, "it's Vincent we need to help."

"Help is on the way," A.M. dabbing her eyes as though my censure has reaped her tears - George's car emerging from a blind of snow. "Watch your Vincent now," she sniffles, her twitching lips breaking into a smile as Melody exits the car.

"Heaven help us!" I hear Melody cry – Vincent unfastening his restraints to go wobbling to her side.

"What did I tell you?" A.M. asks stiffly. "Damn men. You're all alike."

"Including George?"

"I said men, not gods," A.M. flitting to George's entourage just as Simon appears from behind a capitol column, traipsing down the steps under a placard of his own design - a roar of Hurrahs! prompting Thelma to turn and discover the cause:

If I write the lyrics
And you make the music,
Together we'll have a hit.

But first you must promise
To quit all this protest,
And march to a legal writ:

I do!

"You were right!" Melody gushes, tugging at George's sleeve, "The show has romance! And what's more, so does the supporting cast!"

"Can a marriage proposal be anything less?" Vincent queries from his blanket shroud.

"Indeed it can," George stepping abruptly between Melody and Vincent, "... as my experience proves. However, in the case parading before us, marriage makes a certain business proposition more enticing."

"Oooooh, that's right," Melody catching his inference, "we have another show coming soon, don't we?"

"Another?" Vincent gasps, terror in the shine of his eyes.

"A mammoth book sale," George explains, to Vincent's immediate relief. "And one you don't want to miss. Simon's to play auctioneer."

"You don't say!" exclaims Faithful, her sideboard sessions with Simon suggesting bibs more than bids.

"Artie's will," George informs. "Got the last laugh on us, didn't he?"

George's assumption rousing Aunt Martha's objection:

"Hardly! Artie's the butt of the joke, his little shiner being wiped by his executor."

"As though George would change a diaper," I laugh. "I doubt he has much to do with the little tyke since he and Charlene have-"

"That's another surprise in the making," Aunt Martha interrupts, "and one heck of a convoluted one, too; but a surprise just the same ... and it's all for you."

"For me?" I respond, doubting her altruism. "This is beginning to be pleasurable, this student-teacher thing we've got going; and especially when the teacher turns out to be a queen," I blandish.

"Queens can give titles, Melvin, but they can't make a gentleman out of a serf. We can all, however, be noble of our own accord. And that is my gift: another chance for you to be noble."

"No surprise there," I mumble, taken by her remark.

"But it is," she affirms - for once, her blue eyes ignoring George. "'Greater love hath no man than this, that a man lay down his life for his friends,' said our dear Lord; and soon you will see that you've done just that - if only you live up to it."

"Now I am confused," I quibble, Melody's beauty making it difficult for me to think in the abstract. "First, you say I must lay down my life; and then you say I must live up to my death. Seems to me it's got to be one or the other."

"Think of it this way," Aunt Martha's sudden display of patience confusing, an attribute of which I'm unfamiliar, "sometimes, it takes the death of one idea to birth a better one; the failure of one experiment to lead to a successful one. Get it?"

"I think so," I nod. "A bad man must die for a good man to be born? A kind of celestial quid pro quo between the morgue and the nursery?"

"No, that's not it!" she shouts, her supply of patience apparently minuscule, "but perhaps you've stumbled upon something I didn't know."

"Here we go with the Roman empire again," I tease, my surprise reduced to annoyance.

"And why not? 'They wail more noticeably who mourn least', claimed my good friend Tacitus. Let's see you put that in your pipe and smoke it."

"What's there to mourn?" I rejoin, aware she's referencing my separation from Melody.

"Nothing," she replies, a sardonic smile prompting my alarm. "You've discovered your surprise-"

"Enough!" I bellow, the word 'surprise' having lost its allure.

"Just enough!" she howls, mimicking my ire, "just enough to impregnate Charlene!"

Loneliness is but the fear of life.
(Eugene O'Neill)

XXIV

MONTPELIER HAS SEEN NOTHING LIKE IT SINCE
Admiral George Dewey's homecoming after the Spanish-American War.
Even the governor is in attendance, and all the legislators who aren't snow-
bound - Thelma Peabody's pugilistic presence, marching to a bickering
cadence across the capitol lawn, a tourist attraction for as long as anyone
can remember. And today, her wedding promises to live up to her legend.
That vows are to be exchanged in her literal tracks only adds to the bizarre
milieu, hundreds of guests hoisting placards in remembrance of her causes.
(Most of them lost!) Real Men Are Neither is not among them, nor is Make
Up, Not Out, both omitted in respect for the occasion. But a plethora of
others bob and nod to Thelma's epigrammatic career. If God made man
from dirt, behind every good woman's a cloud of dust, reads one; and A
vote counts, but a cause multiplies, notes another. Among the favorites
are issues of more recent dispute, problems as diverse as unwed mothers
and DDT bringing Thelma's pen to bear: A hitch in time saves nine, and
Putting pests-aside, a bee in the bonnet's all the buzz you need, proclaiming her personal views.

   With the happy event hastily scheduled for the Saturday after
Thanksgiving (Thelma taking no chances after her previous stand-up),
Mrs. Rolundo has demonstrated her industry admirably by organizing
'placard parties' among the ladies' auxiliaries, reviving, on the subject of

hairdos, such treasures as: Wanted: Dread or a Hive, and Don't split hairs, chop heads! And wilder yet:

> Had Francis Keys your dread-full locks,
> our stars would all be bangles;
> But Franklin, my dear, didn't give a damn,
> choosing bald among the eagles!

that old Ben lobbied for turkeys, not eagles, apparently beyond Thelma's literary purview.

As if hundreds of pole lofters aren't puffery enough, Simon is in on the act, as well, hiring children to distribute handbills of his own inspiration. To some, it's unclear whether his poem is in commemoration of the weather, or of Thelma's protests. But Thelma suffers no such ambiguity, demanding Reverend Rolundo read it aloud as she stands in vestal white, on the capital steps, beneath the outsize bronze of Ethan Allen:

> Gray sky of somber morn,
> Furl fast your grievous standard;
> Hush bugler's damping horn,
> I'll hear what Pan has pandered.

> Roll out the cheering blue,
> Bedazzle day with promise;
> For I to Hope am true,
> Be damned your doubting Thomas!

> No ears have I for fife,
> Nor bands of tardy tapping;
> Let fly the song of life
> To hands of hardy clapping!

> Draw quick your drape of drab,
> Let rise my canty curtain;
> For I have dreams to grab,
> My play's rehearsed and certain.

Though fool you may the few
Who cower 'neath your cover,
Here's one who knows the blue,
That laughing lets you hover;

The better to compare
What soars above your sorrows:
The clime of your despair
To many merry morrows.

Gray sky of somber morn,
Mark hell a lost retreat;
For I am Faith reborn,
Hark well - my joy's replete!

the Right Reverend Rolundo's resounding recitation giving the verse, like the statue of Ethan, a larger-than-life persona.

If all else seems a spectacle, the ceremony has the air of a miracle, the exchange of vows commensurate with a sudden shower of snow, a myriad frozen flakes swirling round as though Providence is tossing rice.

"Always did have a good sense of timing, that Thelma," observes Faithful, the bride and groom wending merrily through the well-wishers, "always knew where to be, and when; which is more than I can say for Simon."

"Simon had his moments, too," Melody recalling his success with the bugs, "you might say he knew where not to be, and when. But you can bet he'll be at the reception."

"He'll be carried along by the throng whether he intends to go or not" Faithful banters, accepting George's help into the car, a fanged wind etching her face like the crinkles in a crape myrtle blossom.

"The reception's at Thelma's farm, isn't it?" George asks.

"At her maze is more like it," Faithful titters, "her tiered rows of mountainside garden enough to shoo the pests away in confusion."

"But it works, Mother," Melody responds. "Thelma's coerced old man gravity into playing her gardener, making him water her veggies with the turn of a single tap. Too bad we can't appreciate her handiwork under two feet of snow."

"Nor Charlene's in her two arms of ice," adds George. "Which reminds me: have you given any thought to her employment?"

"It could be awkward ... for the two of you, I mean. That's something you need to decide, not me. Mother called on Charlene twice this week, hoping to see little George; but Charlene made a point to refuse her the baby, claiming he was cross, or sleepy, or some such nonsense. Mother thinks she's jealous of me being with child – which makes no sense at all."

If you only knew, George muses. "Perhaps the auction should be her last official duty with the firm. When should we schedule it?"

"Over the Christmas holidays, perhaps? Although, it's not my schedule that matters anymore; it's the auctioneer's. He's the one with his hands full, now," her observation prompting laughter.

"Believe it or not, Simon assured me that next weekend would 'Just do me dandy," says George.

"Oh? and me, as well," Melody surprised by the rush of events, "a good excuse for another weekend home before the Christmas holidays."

"Thought I was reason enough," Faithful feigning injury from the back seat.

"You are, Mother, it's just nice to have an excuse sometimes. If only reasons are facts, then excuses are imaginary; and one never knows when a little imagination might come in handy."

"According to Napoleon, it reigns supreme," George throws in, after an affected harrumph. "The Emperor once said, 'Imagination rules the world."

"Which solves the mystery of why Artie chose Simon to play auctioneer. Maybe Artie saw his chance and took it," Melody following George's lead - the sight of Thelma's snowcapped farm, behind a colored chain of cars, corralling the trio's attention.

One week later, a chain of cars again surrounds the action. With Artie's book values professionally appraised, all that remains of George's duty is to help Melody bid for the firm - not an easy task. The ever erratic Simon is making 'auction' seem descriptively oblique, 'theater of the absurd' falling nearer the mark - especially for the uncategorized items. Under an upraised, tattered edition of *Children's Garden of Verse*, Simon squawks:

"What-am-I-bid? What-am-I-bid? Do-I-hear-five? A five-five-five? There-a-five, now-a-ten? A ten-ten-ten? There-a-ten, now-a-twelve? A twelve-twelve-twelve? Do-I-hear-twelve? Going once ... going twice ... SOLD! for ten dollars to Miss Charlene Mally."

But Simons' calling of the bids are not as disconcerting as his penchant for versing in between. Free rides like:

A peek-a-boo and a buck-a-book,
And a sheepskin for your trouble;
A rock-a-bye and a baby's-book,
And they're off to make your double.

Just make-a-bid on a chil'en's-book
And your stock'll be-in-silken;
Or don't cry wolf when the goose won't cook,
Or a cow they're still-a-milkin'-

taking the crowd by surprise, then by their purse, as he preys on their fear of ignorance - even George aghast at the bids his hype is hiking:

So what-am-I-bid? Pray, what-am-I-bid?
Do I hear a five-or-a-fifty?
A fifty there, and a sixty here-
And a babe that won't be-a-milkin'-

But when Simon strays to the abstruse, chanting:

Buy a book on a brook,
Buy a book on a farm,
Buy a book on Brook Farm, too-

George takes a turn at the mic, sending Simon off in an arcane fog.

"Brook Farm was a Boston area utopian experiment in communal living, in case you aren't familiar with Mr. Farley's reference," George begins, "but here's a work of more modern times, though its subject harks back to Brook Farm's era." George holds up a copy of *The Search for Bridey Murphy*. "Being of Irish decent, I've read it myself," he continues, brightening to the afterthought as though endorsement might author demand. "It's the story of an American lady who, under hypnosis, recalls a past life in Ireland-"

"Three ... I bid three," Melody interrupts, drawing closer on the makeshift podium to inspect the book. "Melvin's copy?" she mouths with surprise, noting his scrawl on the flyleaf, "must've donated it to the library's book sale-"

"And then Artie ended up with all the books that didn't sell," George finishes for her, "... free!" his half-whisper keeping the observation from the crowd. "No wonder he made money ... and with so little effort."

"Considering a change of profession?" Melody teases, handing the book back to George as an old dairy farmer startles them with a shout: "I'll match that, and raise it a dollar!"

"This is an auction, not a card game, Mr.---"

"Buck. Mr. Buck," Melody coming to George's aid, "one of Artie's poker partners. Probably thinks you-"

"Raised the ante?" George's cheeks dimpling with a grin. "Well, he's right if he thinks you're in the game."

"Five!" she offers brightly, forcing his return to business, "I'll go five on *Bridey Murphy* ... and then raise your ante later," she trails under her breath.

And raise it she does, Melody in sudden discomfort, her baby stirring in her womb as though threatening an early entrance.

"Do I hear six?" George rallies, his back to her obvious cramps, "six? six? then sold for five dollars to Mrs. Melody Mor-, to my partner, Melody."

"Partner? then you should take better care of her," bellows Mr. Buck, pointing a barn-calloused finger at Melody, "shouldn't be workin' a little lady that close to birthin'."

Thankful thinks otherwise, her gratitude for George's quick response effusive as they enter the hospital. "My daughter's fortunate to have a friend like you," Faithful says, holding a snow-dampened cloth to Melody's brow. "You'll make it easier for her to come home-" George failing to reply, just the thought of Melody's return leaving him word-struck.

Foolish consistency is the hobgoblin of little minds.
(Emerson)

XXV

"YOU HAD ME IN A FRIGHT DOWN THERE, MELVIN," Aunt Martha rousing me from a troubling trance, "had me convinced you were making an early run for your rebirth."

"Run for it?" I repeat groggily, a faint recollection of thumbing through *Bridey Murphy* and thumping my mother's belly somehow merging under an ER lamp. "Wh-where are we?"

"We were in the hospital - you were toying with your birthday package," she scolds, "trying to make it Special D."

"Oh ... now I remember!" I gasp, glancing round to ascertain my whereabouts. "It was that damn George again, making moves on my mother ... I mean, my wife. I had to do something to throw him off track."

"Honey, there are no tracks here except the one in your mind," A.M. protests. "If you're not careful, it's going to derail you before you leave the station. And another thing, Melody is your mother now, and as such, she can't be your wife; a distinction you'd better accept before heading back south for milk."

"Who, me?" I ask impetuously, "me? abreast of the times? Never have been and never will be. I'm a Vermonter, remember?"

"Books read the same no matter where they are," she snips, "though Vermont makes for a darn good reading environment."

"Which is not why you burned all those midnight candles in Poor Art's Book Mart, now is it?" I retort, fueling her fire.

"Nor why you blew yours out at the office," she shoots back, damping mine. "But never mind our past mistakes; it's the clean slate we have in store that's important now. Especially yours."

"Oh, yeah?" I challenge, still sullen over George. "And what makes you think so?"

"It's not what I think, young man; it's what I know!" she declares. "Too much care has been taken, too much editing of too many life patterns to have you spoil the production. The surprise I've promised you is a masterful stroke, a finale to please all involved."

No less perturbed than she is persuaded, I'm ready for a war of words. But just as I give a supercilious harrumph, my eyes take in a sight knocking the proverbial wind out of my airy chest - A.M. jerking me back to Star View Station and the Galaxy Lounge to pull up barstools on either side of a new arrival.

"What in heaven's name!" I exclaim, as bewildered as the traveler sitting stone still between us, "w-what is she doing here?"

"There's a major shift going on among a few life patterns right now - a reaction. In fact, you could call it a chain reaction, since you're the cause of it all."

"Me?" I cry, staring incredulously at the woman between us, her astonishment rendering her speechless. "But-but I left her behind months ago."

"If you define 'leaving' as physical separation, yes," Aunt Martha signaling the bartender for drinks, "but if you mean your spirits ceased to compound the good or ill achieved when you were together, you're mistaken – yes, two glasses of your best port," she interposes, sending the bartender on a mission. "You'll discover I'm right when she sips her drink," A.M. continues, "it's her connection to you. A glass of port will loosen her tongue; her reaction to an action you took late one Wednesday night when she was-"

"Point taken," I interrupt – the lady between us turning her head as though I'm addressing her.

"This is a bit much just to make a point, isn't it?" the new arrival finding her tongue, her deadpan expression dead-ending me.

"So, how did you find me up here?" I ask foolishly. "Some people will go to the ends of the world just to-"

"That must be where I am, if you're here," she interjects, a sip of port reviving her. "Then again, if I'm with you ... I-I must be-"

"Dead?" Aunt Martha's tone as bitter as failure, "but you aren't, sorry to say."

"Who is she?" the now-coming-alive-imbiber asks, hitching a thumb over her shoulder at A.M., "my conscience?"

"Always were insightful, weren't you?" I respond, avoiding a direct reply. "I'm surprised you don't recognize Martha Morrison," I chide, as I signal the barkeep for a glass of port. I don't want to miss the opportunity, if my aunt is buying – not to mention the incredible age it's likely to be.

"I'm getting the picture," my auditor responds, casting a furtive glance at A.M., "I'm in hell, right? for what torment could exceed the company of two Morrisons?"

"She's got some major negativity to discharge," A.M. prattles, going on as though the suddenly much distraught woman isn't present, "some substantial bitterness to work through."

"You make it sound like a tour of duty," I retort, sandwiched awkwardly between women refusing to speak to each another, "or maybe I have a bad case of dyspepsia."

"Not to worry, she has family on the way," A.M. disregarding our subject's presence, the approach of a little prune-like woman prompting me to offer my seat, the frail figure wringing her withered hands over some long-lost hope, her pinched smile the only hint of imminent reunion with Charlene.

"Charlene's grandmother," A.M. informs me, sliding off her stool to accompany me to the exit, as the barkeep calls, "Your tab, ma'am?"

Halting at the diaphanous door, Aunt Martha's lack of propriety deepens my distress. "Charge it to him!" she yells back, jabbing a finger where Adam's rib is supposed to have been, "it's his turn to treat, not mine." Whispering, she adds, "those Southern boys always make the best bartenders, topping off a lady's drink at will - the lady, too, if she's so inclined - and expecting not a cent for the gins. Or grins."

"Didn't know I had a tab," I remark, circumventing her Southern blockade. "Furthermore, I don't know how I'm going to pay."

"Looks as though your other woman's grandmother is going to settle your tab," A.M. whirling for the egress. "Maybe you didn't notice, but she accepted the port you ordered for yourself. In my book, if someone commandeers a barstool, and the drink in front of it, the bill's been commandeered, as well."

"Now that you mention it," I tease, relieved to be out of the lounge and lost in the jostling throng of intergalactic pilgrims, "Artie once told me about your barroom feats, how you'd accept an offer to dance and end up at another table – and on another's bill – with the uncanny regularity of another round."

"Call it another dance, another round ... call it anything you will," she sidesteps, "but the disoriented Charlene we left in the lounge proves change is inevitable."

"Rrrright," I growl. "I was going to ask you about her - how she came to be traveling. The last I knew, she was going nowhere fast."

"Funny you would put it that way," A.M. titters, tugging me to a bookstore-cum-gift shop to escape the press of the crowd, "it's funny, because nothing's changed. She's still going nowhere fast. And even when she does go, it will still be nowhere. Some of us are inordinately stubborn, requiring multiple incarnations to admit a single fault."

"Not what I asked," I redirect.

"I know, and I'll address that, too," she promises. "If there's anything quick about your lady friend, it's her temper. That, and her driving. The two don't mix with ice. She had quite a crash, I tell you – but would you look at this!" A. M. holding up a pair of gossamer wings. "Training set. Big sellers to the outward bound. Guess folks figure it's never too late to straighten up and fly right."

"Aren't wings in fashion here?" I ask, trying on a pair of exceptionally large flappers. "I mean, if one is upwardly mobile, aren't wings a prerequisite?"

"Yes; but like love, they can't be bought," A.M. donning an extra-small pair. "And just like love, the less one thinks of one's self, the more one's wings will grow."

"That explains how a mother can be an angel," I remark wistfully, unclasping the over-sized fakes from my arms. "Melody is definitely an angel, an orphan of beauty among a bevy of beast," Aunt Martha sliding me a wink of delight, her bright eyes sparkling with a joy of which I've heretofore thought her incapable.

"My dear nephew, I believe you're ready to be readied!" A.M. returning the extra-small wings to their hanger, only to sidle up to a revolving display of what appears to be backpacks: gossamer contraptions, in a variety of shapes and sizes, emblazoned with pithy maxims. Just Say No to Snakes, reads one; and another, No Apples a Day Keeps the Devil Away.

"Auntie, have we stumbled into a celestial bank of slogans?"

"You might call it that," A.M. chortles, holding up a capacious selection with Study to Show Thyself Approved inscribed in orange letters across six of its many sides. "You'll need this for your course in human causes, your prep school for advanced returnees."

"S-School?" I stutter, fear of celestial classes never far from my attention. "Do I have to?" I groan, "can't I just move on without the certificate? I've learned the basics empirically. In fact, there should be a test for travelers like me; one that earns the graduate a certificate without the boredom of classwork."

"Step over here!" Aunt Martha imperious, leading me to a wall of reference tomes and textbooks, her selected backpack secured under one arm. "Just show me a book you don't need to study," she barks, "just one."

"That's easy," I say, noting the section on law, "take, for example, Peter Lombard's *Book of Sentences*, a work which accomplished for theology what Gratian's *Decretum* did for canon law. But how far do you want me to go back?" I ask pompously, "and on which discipline do you wish me to elaborate? We're in the middle of the twelfth century with these two, both of which were influenced by earlier Roman law. And if that's what you'd prefer, one of the first compilations of secular law, the *Codex Constitutionum*, or *The Code*, was compiled in the sixth century by Justinian's commissioners; although the work was centered in Constantinople, capital of the Byzantine Empire, and was not generally known in the west until-"

"Melvin, Melvin, Melvin," A.M. shaking her head as though I'm to be pitied, "when will you learn? When will any of us learn? Law - true law - is the opposite from that of which you so amply demonstrate your familiarity. Remember our discussion of Plato? It's the essence of law that's taught up here, not imperfect representations. Not mistakes. And only when one discovers the ultimate deduction of deductive reasoning, the sole rationale of rational inquiry, can one truly grasp the purpose of law."

"Then why are they up here?" I quiz, suggesting the mistake to be hers. "Why would imperfect representations be shelved in a perfect library?"

"Back to Plato again; though in this case, I must confess your Greeks have it over my Romans," she exhorts with a chuckle. "But to continue, a shadow can be employed to prove the existence of its cause, a mistake the existence of perfection. Where mortals have attempted to legislate good behavior, we learn up here that good behavior is like the shadow, the result of something higher than a commitment to a code. It's internal. It's within the perfect self, a disinclination to stray from the bliss of perfection. So, in the cause of higher education, these books serve as shadows."

"I want a blue backpack," I say submissively, shelving the tomes I'd believed could free me, then returning to the revolving display. "Orange is for orangutans, and I'm-"

"Not a monkey?" she interposes, handing me the backpack.

"Monkeys are primates," I correct, pleased to know something she doesn't. "Orangutans are anthropoid apes. But as I was going to say, I'm not one to ape. I'm my own man. Do my own thinking. And blue is-"

"The color of my eyes, and your mother's," she breaks in, handing me a smaller version of her first selection, its slogan If Blue is True, What is False? in bright white script. "Don't think you'll be needing as many books as the orange one holds, anyway," she says with a wink.

"Thanks, Auntie," I mutter, pondering the backpack's question.

"You'll take a crash course up at True-Blue U," she informs me, charging my gift to a card of gold, "I hear the campus is divine."

"You've never been there?" I query, surprised her curiosity hasn't earned her a tour.

"No, but your Emperor Justinian teaches Philosophy there - something to do with his atonement, I'm told. Aristotle still chairs the Department, of course, but Justinian-"

"I was going to mention that," I interrupt, eager to be back on a familiar subject, "Justinian, I mean; for although Justinian did much for the law, and, in his opinion, much for Christianity, his reign was austere, his ban on paganism extending to the centers of learning - including the University of Athens - spelling an end to the Platonic Academy."

"But just as nothing is ended, everything is begun," she muses, leading me back to the busy concourse. "The Platonic Academy – or the essence thereof – is alive and well, and enjoying the enthusiastic participation and patronage of its one-time enemy. Go figure – or so said my old friend, Euclid-"

"No!" I cry, stopping her dead in her tracks, "don't tell me you knew the great Greek mathematician-"

"I didn't," she giggles, pulling me along to join the flow. "I was testing you, checking to see if you were still with me."

"And where else would I be, Aunt Martha? Hey! Wait just a blessed eternity!" I exclaim, abruptly bringing her to another halt. "Weren't you just telling me that books read the same no matter where they are? So how can Lombard's *Book of Sentences*, or Gratian's *Decretum* read any differently than they did eight hundred years ago?"

"Great question...and by asking it, you've passed your entrance exam, Melvin," says a gorgeous, dark-haired, olive-skinned maiden.

Sitting yoga-style opposite my beautiful companion, we're shaded by the most spectacular tree I've ever seen, its overarching limbs like a father's arms, protective and trustworthy. I don't question where I am, a flash of memory prompting me to bid my femme fatale a pleasant day and set off in search of something far more beautiful, far more rewarding than a mere pleasure to the eye: Aristotle and his theory of rational inquiry.

Men are subject to an illusion regarding matters apparent to the senses ... for things have changed their nature in the very moment we see or touch them.
(Heraclitus)

XXVI

CHRISTMAS IN VERMONT IS LIKE SEEING THE WORLD through a small boy's eyes: the carpet of snow across the roll of George's meadow a magical ride in the offing; his ice crystal pond, under a pinnacle moon and chandelier stars, a shimmering palace ballroom - that Cinderella might glide into view as likely as cookies and milk; the aroma of chocolate and hazelnuts begging his indulgence, his belief in the conjuration; the abracadabra fire in his hearth charming a visiting Melody.

"Mother made the cookies," she says - George slouching in his chair, enjoying a Currier and Ives fantasy, a scene fitting nicely the tinkling of bells, the clipity-clip-clop on his ice-hardened drive. "She thought you might like them, and I'm sure you'll appreciate them even more after a sleigh-ride," the elfin scuff of her stocking-feet on the parlor rug, the per-fumed scent of her golden hair, as she leans near his ear, enhancing his reverie; Melody's delicate touch on his shoulder like a wand to awaken her prince. "Silver bells, George ... silver bells. Do you hear them?"

"Sleigh bells?" he mumbles, the hearth-glow in her porcelain blue eyes bringing him back to the moment. "Surely not ... not unless you-" George erupting from his chair in disbelief.

"It's Mr. Buck; the old farmer who raised my bet on *Bridey Murphy*, remember?"

"Remember?" the edge of eagerness on his every word, "that's all I do anymore, Melody! You stoke my reverie like a glowing hearth!"

"How sweet," Melody backing away as though the fire is causing her blush. "But let's not keep Mr. Buck waiting. He has chores to get back to. Cows to milk."

"And what about you?" George scurrying for boots and a coat - Melody tossing him a cap with muffs, a sheepskin affair that makes him look as young as he feels. "What pleasantries await you this evening? Is Christmas Eve a night of tradition at your mom's? maybe goodies she always bakes? special gifts? stuffed red stockings dangling like loaded questions from the mantle?"

"You've got the picture," she laughs, donning her gloves to wipe a circle of frost from a front door pane, "and so does Mr. Buck," she adds cheerily, acknowledging him through the glass. "Looks as though he's put more hay on your side than mine. Must think you Boston boys get cold feet when sitting next to country girls."

"And how do you know it's my side?" George opening his door to the earthy scent of a horse, Mr. Buck's Morgan standing as proud as his bloodline of two hundred years.

"Because a lady's side is always the nearer one; or don't Boston boys know that?"

"Boston?" Mr. Buck calls out with alarm. "Train station, maybe ... but Boston?"

"You tell her, Mr. Buck," George mutters, giving Melody a hand to help her up, "thinks she's one up on me just because-"

"One on the way, did you say?" the old farmer interrupts, cupping his ear at George, "but of course. It's the only reason I let her hire me. The way I seen it, you wouldn't be tryin' any of your funny stuff while Mrs. Morrison's with child," he huffs. "I've heard the talk, ya know; stories 'bout your-"

"Now, now, Mr. Buck," Melody scolds, her chill-reddened cheeks merry in the frame of a fur-lined cap, her twinkling blue eyes anything but reproving.

"At least I'm worth a laugh," George grumbles, trekking round the sleigh to clamber up beside her.

"And what was that supposed to mean, George O'Malley?" she asks, offering him help with the hay-mussed blanket.

"Mr. Buck's reference to my 'funny stuff'."

"Oh," she says with relief, "... that!"

"I didn't mean anything," he banters, happy just for the excuse of her nearness. "The old farmer said it, not me. But now that it's said, what are my options?"

"How does Poor Art's strike your fancy?" she asks, Mr. Buck reining his Morgan in the general direction of the village.

"Tickles it ... though it appears Mr. Buck's making the choice without us," George intrigued by his breath becoming visible in the frigid air, "... but whatever our destination, it won't be Poor Art's."

"That's right!" Melody chimes, smiling at his fascination with winter's effects. "I keep forgetting, Simon Says is somehow out of character with my memories of the place."

"You mean your memories of its former proprietor, don't you?" George pausing in awe of a snow-laden spruce, its evergreen arms stretching out as though embracing the past, the bygone era of a horse-drawn sleigh enchanting the thought. "But why visit the store on Christmas Eve? A last minute gift?"

"Perhaps; if your referring to Thelma's regard for Simon," she titters girlishly. "But, no. Thelma's hosting a surprise party for Simon, a grand opening, merry Christmas, one-month-of-marriage celebration, all-in-one. I thought us duty-bound to attend. Hiring Mr. Buck is my gift. He can give rides to the children while their parents socialize."

"I thought ... I assumed we-"

"We were going elsewhere?"

"Milk and cookies?" George managing a smile, masking his expectations, his mistaken belief the sleigh was a Christmas card, a reaching back to a time untainted, a heart untaken.

"Milk and cookies, as promised; and a treat for Mr. Buck - provided you keep rum in your cabinet. You don't mind, do you? Your place is on his way home, so why not?" she adds, explaining how her 'gift' includes him. A matter of convenience. The proper thing to do: Morrison & O'Malley arriving together as the partners they're soon to be.

"Sure, why not?" George muttering in a glacial tone as they enter the village, its snow-shoveled walks appearing as rips in his gift-packaged night; the gold-glistened lawns under candle-lit windows, smears on his oil-painted dream; the night-mellowed sound of frost-wreathed carolers, a needle deep-scratching his heart. "Why not?" he repeats, "... why not?"

But once inside, the warmth of Artie's wood burning stove, the cheer of punch happy chatter, the heart healing balm of belonging, of being part of something other than one's self, quickly repairs the damage, the ribbon of hope tying him round like the gift he'd imagined; Simon's suggestion of 'spiking nogs' over the old wood stove taking him back to when he'd hurried into the store to find Melody the gift of a book; only to discover Artie on the floor by this same wood stove. Perhaps he should complete that quest, he thinks, accepting Simon's trembling toast - Plainfield's newest entrepreneur off to a shaky start, his palsied patter, after the party's punch, turning the long spike of his eggnog into the proverbial nail in his coffin, Simon dropping to the floor in a sprawl reminiscent of Artie.

"Damn!" George exclaims, looking for a place to set his drink, "what stories this stove would tell if only we understood crackle!"

"Cackle's more like it," interjects a thin, young stranger, relieving George of his glass. "Does the man always drink like that? I've been watching him since I arrived ... fellow drinks like a fish. Do you think he's all right?"

"Until he comes to," George eyeing the tall stranger suspiciously. "Don't believe I've had the pleasure," he says, offering his hand.

"Just up from Boston," the young man parries, ignoring the offered hand, the press of locals gathering to gawk cutting short the exchange - George's call for a pitcher of water scaring back the more audacious ... the splash on Simon's shock-puckered face scaring him back to the party ... Simon's bloodcurdling scream of "Th-elll-maaa!" scaring her back to his side. And Melody, too, George unaware of her polling the guests for the stranger's identity.

"It's that old demon Rum," Melody shaking her head in an effort to appear disapproving, "give him half a chance and he'll lay you out cold."

"You mean half a gallon, don't you?" George suggests, perceiving by her whimsical tone that disapprobation is merely pretended. "That young man ..." he continues, glancing round for the stranger, "... I don't see him now; but he told me he'd been observing Simon, making note of his predilection for firewater-"

"Yes, but no one knows who he is," she interposes, moving aside so Reverand Rolundo can help with Simon's resurrection, "... it's a mystery-"

"Have faith, young lady," Reverand Rolundo admonishes, stooping over the unconscious Simon as if to decide which spirit to conjure. "Our Lord tells us that where two or three or gathered together in His name-"

"Mr. Farley would still be with us if he'd kept it to two or three," a nasal voice whines, the unknown Bostonian reappearing from beyond the ring of ogling partiers, "but it's not to be. For Simon Farley, it has always been wine, women and song; the only variable in his dissolute life being which one of the three held dominion over the iniquitous moment."

"You are badly mistaken," Reverend Rolundo barks preachily, protecting his most pregnable parishioner, "and it's Far-*LAY*, not *FAR*-ly," he corrects, "your mispronunciation proving your ignorance of our dearly departed, even had you not miscalled his character. But that you might believe, I shall give you proof," the minister extending his hands as if to fend off Simon's rush from confinement. "Lazarus, come forth!" he bellows, his hands outstretched as he whirls to lay them on Thelma. "Loose him and let him go!" he commands – only an irate Mrs. Rolundo and a worried Helen the organist surmising correctly: if anything's loose it's the minister's tongue.

"Simon ain't Lazarus, and you ain't Christ," a smoldering Thelma snarls. "My hubby just didn't appreciate the power of my punch, that's all – which is more than a certain little woman here can say about you!" her tyrannical tone just the antidote Simon needs, the inebriate celebrant staggering to his feet to assume the pose of recitation, his slurred attempt raising general alarm:

Ssh-give it to me ssh-traight
Whish-pered Helen,

Or don't ssh-give it ... a-tall.
Amen.

Ssh-give it to me hard
Ssh-poke up Helen-

Thelma quelling the swelling murmur with a slap on her husband's back, the force of her blow – and of Simon's verse – sending Simon and the reverend to their knees.

"That's proof enough for me," cracks the stranger, a twitching smile contorting his face, his darting dark eyes giving Melody a haunting impression, a memory too hazy for reflection, "only the proofs in the punch, not the parson ... and I reckon it's 90 at least!" this last observation bringing Melody's phantom into view, a muffled cry alerting George to her need of his arm:

"Cookies and milk?" she mutters, "is Mr. Buck still ready at the door?"

"I doubt he's had time to leave," George replies, "but I'll check."

"No ... no ... no," she says in soft but determined syllables, "I'll go with you. just ... just keep your arm-"

"Melody?" George calling her name in dismay, "are you ... ?"

"I think so," she answers piteously, accepting his help to the door. "I'm afraid the cookies and milk will have to wait. Another little treat's trying to interpose." Melody puns, making an effort to hide her pain. "But with the roads like they are, Mr. Buck and his Morgan are a safer bet than a nervous driver behind the uncertain wheel of a car; and as luck would have it," she adds, seeing Mr. Buck still in place-

"Call it luck, if you will," George breaks in, his strong and willing arms carrying her to the sleigh, "but I call it Christmas. What better time to deliver-"

"Deliver me to the hospital!" Melody cries, instructing the ever-vigilant Mr. Buck; the old man snapping his Morgan to a brisk trot as he shouts back his plan:

"We'll follow the river a ways," he barks, "follow the lower Winooski trail, then cut back 'cross the fallow fields. Have ya there 'fore a motorcar can navigate the snow-bound roads," he promises, calling crisply to his horse as though the Morgan can second his pledge.

"Did Mother-?"

"She did," George whispers, his arm comforting, his shoulder assuring, "she's coming with Mrs. Rolundo. I saw them tracking through the snow for the reverend's car as we all passed under the streetlamp."

"Not the reverend!" she wails, wincing from another pang, "Mother shouldn't be riding with a man whose vision is distorted by some two thousand years. I think the old winebibber actually thought he was Christ before the tomb of Lazarus!"

"Not to worry," George's well-intentioned squeeze causing another wince, "he wasn't with them. The last I saw of the rev, he was on his knees before the soot-covered stove, whimpering like a child left out in the dark."

"Oh. Good," she manages, "... good," her pains occurring with more frequency, thieving her attention – George, too, momentarily distracted: the river valley, just hours before so opalescent in the turquoise dusk, now fairy-wing pale under the silver moon; the numinous night, the tinkle of bells, making sacred the nearness of Melody; his lofty imaginings poetic, his hopeful heart entreating the stars, his belief that his reach can exceed his grasp earning him a glimpse of heaven, of ultimate peace, of the very ideal he yearns to attain – Melody's moans calling him back to the moment, to the urgency of mortal dilemma:

"It's coming!" she cries with alarm, "the baby's coming!" her keen cry alerting Mr. Buck to reign his Morgan to a snorting halt along the frozen river's bank, decades of hay-manger deliveries affording the old farmer a needed confidence - the cover of snow, the crisis of birth, precluding any awareness he may have otherwise had that he had stopped under the same silver maple where Melvin Morrison died.

THE YEAR
2000

The present contains nothing more than the past.
And what is found in the effect was already in the cause.
(Henri Bergson)

XXVII

As I said once before, I've never given the art of augury much attention, believing such things as psychic readings, tarot cards and palmistry to be just another form of entertainment. But as such, it seemed a clever idea to hire a professional, a Boston hypnotist, to provide the entertainment at my New Year's Eve party. And for a number of reasons; among them, that the eve of the year 2000 was momentous, the beginning of the third Christian Millennium; another, that it would be my last party in the apartment I share with my stepbrother, George, Jr. (alias Little George), and my last party as a bachelor, as well (my pending marriage but a month away); and lastly, that I'd just finished reading *The Search for Bridey Murphy*, a book I found among my mother's eclectic collections, the frayed hardback infecting me with a mild curiosity of hypnosis. The book presented, as factual, a modern day American woman recalling, under hypnosis, her past life as an indigent girl in Ireland. Recounting it convincingly, too, with a proper Irish accent; although the lady had never visited Ireland, nor had friends of Irish descent.

The book intrigued me, reviving my never-too-reticent inquiries into how I, a black man, could be born of a white mother and father, my mom's well documented and hopeful research into her own and my assumed father's genealogy revealing not a clue to the mystery - though my stepfather George has long suggested a mistake was likely made by a defunct

Boston sperm bank. According to George's theory, my deceased father, together with his inimitable foresight in providing for my well-being, provided for my being, as well. And though my mother eventually supported George's postulate, I've always rejected it as preposterous, believing it far more likely Mother was seduced (in a drunken state, of course - probably the reason she seldom imbibes) by the man who gave her the monstrous diamond I once embarrassed her with as a child.

Ironically, my childish prank occurred at yet another New Year's eve party - Mother's guests including the diamond giver - during which I discovered the delights of her jewelry case. And being under five years of age, it seemed the right thing to do at the time: masquerade as a little girl and traipse in front of her guests behind a pendulous, three carat diamond. What I remember most is how it perturbed my soon-to-be stepfather, George; and prompted the diamond giver to leave the party. But I'm straying from more current events, recounting my New Year's Eve celebration.

The Boston hypnotist (I'll call him Dr. X) arrives early, and in a state of hysteria – the very moniker he gives Vermont. Apparently, Dr. X has a preconception of Plainfield as a quaint little village with an innkeeper in desperate need of guests, said need epitomizing the lack of regard the good doctor tenders my state. So, when he learns there's no room at the inn, he panics. I don't, securing him a bedroom en suite with the Comptons, the parents of my fiancée Dorothy. It's an arrangement I'm soon to regret, Dot. Com (my fiancée's nickname) blaming me for all the spooks the spellbinding doctor unearths; Dot.Com, according to Dr. X, "The spunkiest spook of 'em all". And if it weren't for my sister Pamela's support, and that of my stepbrother Little George, Dot.Com would probably dis-engage me, Little George (who is actually 6'4" and older than me by two months) saving the day by suggesting Dot.Com's collaboration with me on a book, noting the fame she's sure to garner. Fortunately, she believes him; for, if there's anything at which Little George excels, it is books, his encyclopedic mind filing away everything he reads.

My party is at once a successful soiree, and a social snafu: the subject of Plainfield gossip, Godhard lectures, Montpelier coffee-houses, and even a free weekly newspaper or two – one of which eventually gets into the hands of a young Appalachian revivalist making a name for herself over the airways; my party, in her fundamentalist's jargon, hosting the minions of hell with Dr. X playing Belial. (More on that later.)

Dr. X strikes a vein – my jugular, it seems – regressing me to a life fraught with ruinous connections to my guests. My journey begins, innocently enough, with my offer to be the doctor's first subject. If the host can be hypnotized for his guests' amusement, I venture, they'll be obliged to follow my lead. But despite my best intentions, I steal the show, providing my friends such hair-raising, mind-boggling entertainment that the old year passes and the new one arrives without the faintest flick of an eyebrow, my audience sitting as solidly about the doctor and me as the megaliths on Salisbury Plain – some of them turning just as gray from my startling revelations.

Stretched out on an old sofa my folks had salvaged from the attic over their Plainfield law office (Mother swears it had been my father's), I'm already unwittingly in the past, the doctor taking up his mesmeric ritual where my father once practiced his, the old sofa resuming its role as an altar to dark skills and thrills.

"Breath deeply," Dr. X instructs, his pipe tobacco voice a smoky sing-song, "ten deep breaths, then close your eyes. Relax ... relax," his cherry scented breath corralling my focus. "Relax and let go, as I count backward from ten to one ... count down till you're totally calm ... completely at peace when we reach number one ... relax ... feel the tension leaving your body ... a soothing flow of warmth, of peace, bathing your lower extremities ... your toes, your feet, as I start my count at ten ... warmth, peace, moving up your ankles, your calves, spreading gently over your shins, as I count to nine ... spreading ... relaxing ... gentle, soothing warmth moving up your thighs ... your pelvis, as I count to eight ..."

The numeral eight the last word I consciously remember (the rest 'remembered' on the doctor's recorder), the word 'pelvis' sending me into a mental spin, into a memory locked deep in my tenebrous past, the numeral 'eight' playing the key and Doctor X the hand that turns it -

"Elvis-Pelvis," I mutter, Doctor X ready with his mic. "Miss Peabody says he's satanic ... but Aunt Martha ... Aunt Martha says ... Aunt Martha!" I abruptly scream; or rather, try to scream, all the tension Doctor X has charmed from my body returning to collect in my throat, my hoarse attempt at a scream sounding more like a pillow-muffled whisper.

"It all began the day of my funeral," I whimper, "Aunt Martha literally dragging me over my casket, forcing me to look at my body, to accept my death ... and more importantly, my continuing life -"

But I've already related that part, and most of what happened in between – between my life as Melvin Morrison the attorney, and my reappearance as Melvin Jr. on the snowy bank of the Winooski River – so I'll return to the present, to the year 2000.

Simon Says book store has been my favorite haunt for as long as I can remember, my mother taking me there to buy fairytales and picture books, all of which are still safe in my bedroom bookcase. And although I have no memory of Thelma Farley, Mom says she used to rock me in her sun-browned arms while Mother browsed her shelves. But Simon Farley is another matter, a recent memory; one of those 'foundation blocks' one realizes, as an adult, was there when the building of character was in its critical stage. A local celebrity by virtue of *Cycles*, his prize-winning collection of poems, the wizened Simon was every young rhymester's confidant, the veritable proof persistence pays; his economic freedom, he assured his young admirers, hard-won after years of composition. His was a romancer's tale I chose to believe, despite Mother's assertion it was Thelma's persistence, not Simon's, that got him published.

Later, my faith in Simon's persistence theory saw me through Harvard Law School with an almost religious expectation of success; albeit, my definition of success has gone through several metamorphoses. Disregarding the changes, I am successful; and successful, as Simon defined the term. I'm happy. Happy with my almost-now-and-hopefully-soon-to-be-profitable Black-N-Blue Bar-B-Q, my riverside smokehouse and bar; and marginally happy with Dot.Com, provided she survives Dr. X; which is something the deceased Simon hasn't done, his life dredged up in the local press in a kind of third round of *Twice-Told Tales*.

"Ran across him in the cemetery one night," remarks my stepfather, while peering over the top of the Sunday paper, "lying cold as a ghost, he was ... lying atop the stone next to Artie Steinberg's grave."

"What did he have to say for himself?" Mother asks matter-of-factly, the trauma of my party numbing her to the preternatural, the pleasure of having Little George and me over for Sunday dinner dampening her doubts.

"That was before he died," explains my stepfather, "before the locals decided Little George is Artie reborn, that his father is really-"

"Now, now," interjects my mom, feigning the bland emotion of greeting-card sentiment, "there's no point in bringing that up when the only one who could tell us for certain has been gone for twenty-some years."

"Uh ... that would be me," offers my sister Pamela, "I'm supposed to be Charlene reincarnated; but I can't help you, my memory fades out near the age of two." (Pamela is the result of my mother's second draw against the deposit account my father left in the Boston sperm bank, and, according to the "revelations" garnered at my party, the current embodiment of Melvin Senior's seductive secretary.)

"How could a man be certain back then?" replies George, ignoring Pamela and addressing Mom. "DNA wasn't even-"

"I wasn't referring to him," Mother breaks in, any reference to my supposed father requiring such emphasis when George and my mom are talking in front of us kids, "I meant Charlene," she avers, the mention of the long deceased Charlene getting the same emphasis. Not that their strange behavior has any effect on the three of us, for we've talked it out - especially Little George and me - agreeing that we're abundantly blessed to have not only each other, but two such loving parents. And besides, if there are any scores to be kept, we're even, George, Jr. and me each claiming a stepparent; the fact that my father and his mother died young - and suddenly - balancing the score. Now, we feel even closer; or, I should say, the fact that we want to feel closer makes us believe what my party touts: that my supposed father is his actual father - meaning I am his father - that I was the former partner of his stepfather, while Little George – Artie - was our client. Which makes it logical, or genetic, if you will, for Little George – as Artie, his stepfather's client - to become my son-cum-stepbrother; the whole convoluted chain binding us closer than identical twins.

The one exception is Little George's frequent spells of nightmares starring Dot.Com; terror dreams from which he awakes mid-scream, admonishing me tearfully to break the engagement, assuring me she's a drunk, a card thief and a scamp, if ever there were one. Only when he's awake and fully composed does he rationalize his behavior and employ such nebulous phrases as "distortions from behind the veil", or "old sins so long forgiven." It's then he advises me, with downcast eyes, to "go on ...

marry the wench. Who knows? perhaps it's in your karma this time around to reform her."

But my sister Pamela has no such reservations, her own dreams revealing marriage as an ideal – one in which her shining knight, yet unknown, spirits her away. Caught up in the festive preparations for my wedding, she unabashedly assures any who'll listen that she'll catch the bride's bouquet – even if it means knocking down her peers. Pamela's assertion is disturbing because she usually keeps her word. I say "usually" in deference to a glaring exception. I'm referring to P.M. (my sister's moniker among family and friends) promising to cover for me with Dot.Com while I enjoy an innocent night of flirtation with an ex-girlfriend, a Harvard grad visiting from Louisiana. P.M. doesn't cover; nor do I enjoy the evening. P.M. blames Dot.Com for both failures. I know better, Pamela's cute little asides, in moments of trial, always more accurate than entertaining.

P.M. tells Dot.Com I'm reworking my Black-N-Blue menu, adding hot specials that literally headline my evening's activities - items like "Bayou, Get-Two" and "Blue-Fun-Due for Two". And her allusions to two new desserts only exacerbate Dot.Com's worries, "Get-It-While-You-Can Flan" and "Blue-Brown Betty with Hard-To-Get Sauce" screaming my clandestine fun. It's enough to send my fiancée storming into the bar with her own menu suggestion: scratch the hot chick-dish appetizer of the night, "Illegal Tenders", and blaze a trail for home.

And there are aftershocks: Dot.Com, half-lit at my bar, imploring me to sell the restaurant and use the law degree I'd worked so hard to earn. It's a most compelling argument, I admit, Dot.Com asserting, "As a black attorney in the 'whitest' state in the union, you'd stand as stark as an exclamation mark behind your every win," and "you, of all our local stock, should feel most painfully the bickering and slights stirred up by Vermont's civil union law. After all, being black should have taught you something!" (I'm always amused by my Dorothy's blindness to her own brand of bias.) "The protest signs, 'Take Back Vermont', and its opposite, 'Take Vermont Forward', or the onerous one down on the border with Massachusetts, the one that reads, 'Leaving the Bay State and entering the Gay State', should inflame a crusader like you, Melvin. You could develop a following," she exhorts, waving her empty martini glass, "find a timely path to the governor's mansion, if only you'd raise your standard! And with your parent's support -your mother's, in particular," she adds abruptly, "being the most popular state representative-"

"You mean my stepdad's support," I interrupt, her diatribe putting me on edge. "Not that I don't admire and adore George, mind you, it's just ... it's ... ."

"Well?" she prods with a threatening scowl.

"Well ... it's just that George, by his reluctance to accept what we learned at my party, makes me feel as though I have no depth; as though I just dropped out of the sky like a stray raindrop. A raindrop that'll eventually evaporate into the great formless mist. And not only me, but the rest of us, as well."

"Ah!" she retorts, her flashing black eyes giving me the fright of close lightening, "do we have a little storm cloud brewing?"

"Are you suggesting you're pregnant?" my humorous attempt to ameliorate only darkening her glower – Pamela's breezy entrance dispelling the clouds.

"So, what do you think?" my sister bubbles, parading inappropriately in her bridesmaid's gown, "am I not the perfect pick in this dress? the nobody-else-has-got-a-chance knockout choice for the man of my dreams?"

"That depends," rejoins a sullen Dorothy, turning over her empty martini glass as a signal for a fourth free drink. "Depends on whether or not your knight errant has returned from his quest-"

"That's exactly what's bothering me," I interject, ignoring the overturned glass, "that's what's irking me about George's unbelief. According to my past-life regression tape, P.M., here, is the reincarnation of Charlene returning from her quest, an unfulfilled quest, the poor lady dying in a car wreck on her way to see Mother-"

"Calls for a toast!" Dot.Com. screeches, shoving her glass across the bar - P.M. adding, "Yeah ... and you'd better watch out, bro, for a seductress I still may be!"

"Not my point," I scold P.M., getting Dot.Com a coffee instead of a gin and serving it with a stern admonishment, "and not yours, either, if you know what's good for you. No, it all seems to add up, when you think about it: Charlene was about to risk her own reputation for the sordid satisfaction of revenge. She was going to tell my mother that she'd played around with my father; but the angels prevented it by an assumed accident. And before that, my father was about to scar my mother's trust by admitting infidelity; but the angels prevented him, too. Now, Charlene (Pamela) and my father (me) are back together under the care of the very lady we were about to injure. Such ineluctable 'coincidence' proves love can never be overcome. Never outdone. Love always wins in the end. And without the first fist raised, without a harsh word spoken-" ·

"What's that have to do with George's unbelief?" Dot.Com grumbles, accepting the coffee with cross resignation.

"Don't you get it?" I ask, disgruntled over her lack of understanding. "George's offer to marry Charlene was more than a gentleman's gesture to a lady in distress. It was an offer to her unborn child, an offer to give it a name, a father, a start in life equivalent to all the other little tots in Plainfield with married parents. And what happens? he ends up adopting the boy, standing in as his father, despite the tragic death of Charlene. It's as though his offer was made and accepted in the next world, too; a pledge of love transcending the-"

"Don't tell me," Dot.Com blathers, "love can never be overcome. Never outdone. It wins every time. Right?"

"It did this time," I affirm. Look at us. We're all back together, the dark chains of adultery, of pseudo-romance, no longer shackling our hearts. Brothers and sister in one happy family; our regard for one another unselfish, our highest concern for the others' good."

"But Daddy does want that for us," P.M. argues petulantly, accepting my offered soda. "Our happiness is always his, what did you call it? his highest concern?"

"Never said it wasn't," I mumble, surrendering to the misdirection of her usual inattention.

"Fathers can be like that," Dot.Com sardonic, stirring a second dose of sugar in her coffee, "concerned with getting high. My Dad has regaled me numerous nights with tales of the old hippie commune and the weed that choked out their flowers; or of Thelma Farley and her thrill-seeking feats of intervention-"

"Thelma Farley went after the pot smokers?" I query, amenable to any subject that might cheer my dear Dorothy's mood.

"At least that would have been commendable," she rejoins, amid noisy slurps of coffee, "but, no. Dad claims Thelma took an immediate and inordinate interest in me when I was born. Like I was her grandchild – could she have had one – her intrusion into our home an almost daily affair; her threat of some curse by Jehovah Herself, if she wasn't named my godmother, the straw that broke the camel's back."

"Wow! Your dad had an affair with an Arab?" P.M. taking leave, momentarily, of her reflection in the backbar mirror. "I didn't know camels were ever-"

"How do you account for Dorothy's ebony eyes?" I break in, trading a wink with Dot.Com, "or her raven hair? Mr. Compton doesn't have either."

"But that old woman who wanted to be your godmother ... what was her name?"

"Thelma," Dot.Com intervenes.

"Yeah ... Thelma," P.M. turning back to the mirror, "her stepson does - or did, I suppose. For though his hair is salt and pepper, his eyes are still as black as Dorothy's."

"So let's be sure of your implications, sis," I reply, pretending to ponder as I perfunctorily wipe the bar. "You're suggesting the deceased Mr. Farley's son - the son he never knew he had until the boy was in his thirties – came wondering up from Boston, a tall, thin stranger in search of a father his ailing mother disclosed on her deathbed; only to have an affair with Dorothy's mother?"

"Really? A Bostonian?" she quips. "Do you really think that's where my knight will come from? Some summa cum laude-"

"Some sooner, some later," I interpose, "and for their sake, I hope it's the latter."

"That's right, sweetheart," Dot.Com joins in, a smile softening her face, her eyes, her entire demeanor becoming empathetic. "Marriage is a commitment, dear, not a complaint you can rid by prescription."

"Oh, do tell," P.M. retorts acidly, giving me a glance forewarning disaster. "Then what were you doing, Miss Commitment, with that young Doctor Brigham I saw you kissing last night?"

There is no merit in a faith whereof human
reason furnishes the proof.
(Augustine)

XXVIII

GEORGE O'MALLEY HAS ENJOYED OVER TWO DECADES
of enhancements since moving to Vermont - some voluntary, some not -
but marriage to his widowed law partner is his epiphany, a veritable act
of ennoblement. And though it took him more than five arduous years to
win her hand, Melody Morrison-O'Malley remains his raison d'être, the
joy of his desiring, the model of motherhood for each of their three grown
children - none of whom are his. Conceived by the miracle of modern
science, Melody's son Melvin, Jr. and daughter Pamela are the progeny of
a love forever sacred, forever separate; Melody retaining, by the vogue of
a hyphen, her widower's surname for the benefit of their children. And
with the death of Charlene Mally, and the subsequent passing of Charlene's
mother six years later, Little George joined the family by way of adoption,
an act almost unnoticed by the children at the time, their bonds formed
long before Little George became 'legal'.

And so it was with Simon Farley - his son, from a youthful affair,
coming up from Boston to discover the dad he'd never known, Simon's
sensitivity gradually fostering in the hardened young man a latent tenderness, a likeness of his father that would have never been save for the old
man's gentle guidance. Seeping through the Bostonian's crusty façade like
a penetrating oil, Simon's kindness proved practical, indeed, when dealing
with his stepmother Thelma.

For Thelma had never changed. Love merely redirected her energy, making Simon, Simon's son, Simon's work and Simon Says, her new quartet of causes, her incessant promotion of which prompted the natives to look back fondly on her more impersonal marches and placards. But succeed she did, seeing Simon published, then selling her farm to buy him his namesake bookstore; even living long enough to approve, begrudgingly, of Simon Junior's management; a "guarantee", as she called it, on Artie Steinberg's dream. When the school bus stops fell into disrepair, she nagged Simon Jr. to make a name for himself by organizing a drive for their mending. And not only of the structures, but of the brass plaques Artie had bequeathed for display, Thelma insisting they be polished and permanently encased in frames bestowed by the family store - Artie's original inscription conveniently in harmony with her motive:

> Simon says 'cause he can't read
> Is why they call him Simple;
> As they will you, if you don't heed
> The call of learning's temple.
>
> So study well the printer's art,
> Buy books and read them through;
> So, Simon says, will you be part
> Of Future's well-to-do.

"Simon Says the Bus Stops Here" was Thelma's last public drive, the fiery old lady expiring on the Statehouse lawn like a saint on a mission from God. But hers was an act that could not be topped, her death and funeral remembered like D-Day; her demise only enhancing the tales of her feats - Simon Senior not missing a beat, his compositions in Thelma's honor increasing the bookstore's traffic, former visitors returning to gawk and buy at her shrine. "Vermont's own Emma Goldman," Simon was wont to claim, "a woman ahead of her times" – to which George countered privately, "If we could but know the times ahead, I'm sure we'd be glad she's behind them."

Life evolved for George in a similar fashion: a going private, a smoothing-out, a quieting-down, a mellowing appreciation for the peace of rural life; his knack of finding controversy now political instead of personal; his law office, with Melody in the Legislature, more a think-tank for the establishment than a bastion for the unhappily wed.

Accordingly, it's an out-of-the-ordinary social disturbance when young Doctor Brigham comes calling for an audience, his discordant demeanor suggesting a war afoot in the brush.

"It's about your son," he announces officiously, slamming George's office door for emphasis. "I've come to appeal to your reason, to your long years of hard-earned wisdom."

"Out with it, my good doctor," George taking subliminal advantage of the chair lodged comfortably behind his desk. "And which son might that be?" he asks, motioning for the young fellow to select one of the armless chairs floundering on a sea of green carpet.

"Need you ask?" the irate doctor fumes. "I mean ... after the debacle of the century, that ruinous party that has folks second-guessing everything from the past life cause of their present ailments to the karma of their long failed loves -"

"Ah ... so it's Melvin," a dispassionate George observes in his most professional tone. "From what I've heard – and you admit – the stage of those goings-on was a frivolous party, not a forum for serious research; and as such, I suggest you're overreacting."

"Hear my complaint before you conjecture!" bellows the doctor. "If I treated my patients with such disregard, presuming their maladies before hearing their symptoms, I'd be-"

"Dishonoring my oath," George finishes for him. "But the difference here is that we haven't a malady worthy of treatment. And should there be those who think otherwise ... placebos should set them aright."

"Go ahead," Doctor Brigham grumbles, "sugar-coat it all you want; but in my expert opinion as a doctor of psychiatry, your son's party, whether intended or not, has had ill effects on our community ... on my patients - well, on one of my patients - specifically, Miss Dorothy Compton."

"Melvin's fiancée, no less," George nodding thoughtfully. "And short of violating a trust, what dilemma, may I ask, has my son's party caused? For if a 'cause' is to be acknowledged," he appends prudently, "it would certainly be the party, not its host."

"It's a case of mistaken identity," the doctor redirects, his ire subsiding to controlled discontent, "of misplaced affections. Dorothy - uh,

Miss Compton - is unaware of her true feelings, the myth of her past-life personality superimposed on her persona till her judgments are no longer her own. To be quite candid, Mr. O'Malley, she thinks she's in love with your son."

"And I suppose you're here to attest otherwise?" George parries, his big gray eyes growing larger with surprise and amusement. "Or is there some dark side to my son of which I'm unaware?"

"Oh, heaven forbid!" exclaims the fidgeting doctor, "this has nothing to do with skin color!"

"Then to what does it pertain?" George prods, pressing the young man's point, "is she in love with you?"

"She is!" the doctor resounds, getting to his feet as though a salute is in order.

"A-And you?" George genuinely surprised by the "problem".

"In love with her," he affirms, still standing at full attention. "I am, indeed. And I'm here to beg your permission ... ."

"Yes?" George manages, befuddled by the doctor's admission. "Go on ... ."

"Well, not so much your permission as your cooperation," he continues, relaxing enough to reclaim his seat. "I think it would be better for all concerned if you spoke to Melvin about this; let him hear it via the safety of family, rather than the competitive challenge of a suitor. But we must act with haste!" he adds, the hint of a smile alerting George that the doctor assumes his complicity.

"Haste? In psychotherapy?" George acquainted enough with the science to know haste is considered quackery. "To discover Dorothy is under your care is surprise enough," he counters, "but now that I know, all that's warranted is my support for her choice of disciplines. Of course, had I been in your shoes, I'd probably be looking for the hypnotists again, searching for another past life to dispel all the problems in this one! In the interim, we have the moment, don't we: the here and now to laugh and cry; to err and amend; to fail and succeed? And that includes our institution of marriage, Doctor Brigham, of which I am a most grateful alumnus. So, no, I cannot be party to your haste; nor, can I interfere in another's choice of heart. In your profession, doctor, you should know such a pursuit will fail," George's tone stern, but paternal. "You should know that the heart can never be coerced."

"But that's just it!" an animated Doctor Brigham argues. "It's not her heart that's making the call here. It's her pseudo-personality; the dupe, if you will, of her own suggestibility."

"Correct me if I'm mistaken," George replies, after a moment's reflection, "but didn't Melvin and Dorothy announce their engagement months before the party? And if so, then just who are we to surmise responsible? the hypnotists? Is that good doctor the practitioner of magic, as well? Might he have transubstantiated into an idea? one he foisted on the couple in question? only to come round many months later as the hypnotists who 'discovers' his 'victims'?"

"You're going heretical on me, Mr. O'Malley," the dumbfounded doctor rejoins, "postulating the preposterous, suggesting what even the hypnotist wouldn't dare."

"It would be interesting to know who you were supposed to have been before ... how your past life, or lives, may have interrelated with the others. Perhaps you were Dorothy's suitor 'way back when'; perhaps you're unwilling, now, to accept that you're not."

"For your information," Doctor Brigham retorts haughtily, the friction of George's suggestions heating him anew, "in my profession, some of us learn the art of self-hypnosis; and being personally prepared, I took the liberty of regressing myself the other night – set up the session in advance on two tape recorders: one, with the instructions and questions; the other, for my responses, my pleasant trip back, my waking refreshed."

"And?" George quizzes, enjoying what he has no belief in – or at least, no pragmatic regard for, his long ago encounter with Marvin the Medium tainting any future opinions.

"As it turns out, my subconscious received a suggestion from my conscious mind even before I put myself under. I 'recalled', as the true believers phrase it, a past life as Dorothy's benefactor ... well, sort of. I imagined I had been the old bachelor who willed his farm to her parents, creating a home for Dorothy."

"Fred Compton?" George delighting in the coincidence. "I met that old gentleman before he died. Melvin's father introduced me to him - one of my first clients here. In fact, I prepared Mr. Compton's will."

"Melvin's father, did you say?" the doctor poses, half standing as if the conference is concluding. "I'm too young to remember him, but my folks say he was quite the charmer; a dashing young man. And wealthy, too, as I recall ... something about diamond mines back in Africa-"

"Another case of mistaken identity," George banters benignly. "But I will - if you want me to testify ex parte – mention our little meeting to Melvin. Or better yet, to Melvin and Dorothy jointly. That way, there can be no secrets; no mistakes wrought by misunderstandings. I think that's what we have here, Doctor Brigham: your misunderstanding of a very charming, but complex young lady."

"It's my field, Mr. O'Malley!" the doctor defensive, stepping stiffly to the door, "not yours!"

"Agreed," a grimace replacing George's smile, "and one that needs plowing under, I'm afraid. But with psychology being your 'field', as you so ardently assert, surely you're familiar with Sigmund Freud's admission: The great question that has never been answered, and which I have not yet been able to answer, despite my thirty years of research into the feminine soul, is 'What does a woman want?' "

Dr. Brigham's mouth is agape as he quietly closes the door behind him.

But there's no time for reflection. As campaign manager for Melody, George is busy enough on the complex issues threatening her reelection. A sweeping tax reform (the legislature's euphemism for 'increase') has constituents up in arms, as well as the recently enacted civil union law allowing gay marriages.

And as though native voters can't decide for themselves, there's been an influx of out-of-staters in recent months, militant special interest groups picketing in front of the capitol, their bible-backed chantings and evangelical rantings making Thelma's remembered antics seem, if not tame, at least comedic.

One out-of-stater in particular seems to have a monopoly on the media, her charisma charming newspaper editors and newsroom producers alike; her compelling rhetoric attracting even the learned. Melvin among them. That she's an ordained, Pentecostal revivalist counts least among the reasons he lobbies the Church of the Good Shepherd for her invitation to speak.

A kind of special edition, it is; a Wednesday night prayer meeting with "Wednesday" and "prayer meeting" deleted; "night", by the gifted tongue of the beautiful young orator, taking on the wild grandeur, the hunt-or-be-hunted forest peril of the Appalachian Mountains from whence she hails. "Minister, helpmate, mother," she declaims, "and in that order. Such is my purpose in life; anything more of transient worth-" all the men in the attentive congregation imagining otherwise.

Putting aside her physical charms, suggest some of the old-timers, her spirited delivery brings back memories of an earlier minister. If you close your eyes, you can imagine young Melvin's grandfather back in the pulpit, they say; Rev. Moses Morrison stoking hell's fire with the plentiful sins of parishioners.

Melody sees it differently. When the young firebrand retires to her parlor for cookies and milk - as is the family custom after Wednesday night meetings - that sweet soul allays her smitten son's fear: my concern that Miss Minnie Ruth Taylor is incorrigible.

"Her redemption is fait accompli," Melody promises, soothing my troubled brow. "With a mind so searching, so engaging, the discovery of a higher path is inevitable. Besides," she adds discerningly, "if you're that bothered by this pretty West Virginia belle of yours, I'd suggest some missionary work is in order. Heap 'Coals of fire' on her head, like the good book says, and before you know it, 'The lion will lay down with the lamb.'"

"Which might be just what the missionary has in mind!" George Senior contributes, his gray eyes twinkling. "You're fortunate to have a Bible scholar for a mother, young man," he teases. "When I was young - and could have used such a line - I had no one to tell me the Bible could be employed as a romantic adviser. However, since we're on the subject-"

"Which we aren't," my mother interposing with one of her infectious laughs, "but since you are, what wisdom have you to share?"

"The wisdom of modern science," George parries, "or in your case, Melvin, modern séance."

"George!" Melody scolds, looking about for any sign of injury on my siblings' faces. "It was just a gala, dear, not a galactic encounter."

"Ah! But you misjudge me. All of you," George compounding our suspense. "I wasn't referencing the party at all; only the aftershocks felt by a certain sensitive young doctor in town ... though I promised him I would only discuss what he 'felt' with Melvin and Dorothy - in private."

"Yeah, Private Dawson was making eyes at me in church tonight," Pamela alleges, "must think I prefer a man in uniform to a-"

"Learn to listen, will you?" Little George scolds, reaching to slap his sister playfully on the back of her hand. "Now, what's this about Doctor Brigham?" he asks, turning to George.

"Who said it was-?"

"I saw him leaving your office this morning," Little George explains, "and then later, with Dot.Com at the Montpelier coffee-house. Serious as a double espresso, he was ... leaning over his demitasse, staring hungrily into Dot.Com's eyes like they were the last two sugar cubes on Earth."

"Oooo, steamy!" Pamela eyeing me for a reaction.

"I'm ahead of you all on this one," I say, my blush suggesting otherwise, "... but it's not something amenable to oatmeal cookies ... not a treat to be passed around-"

"I wouldn't pass on a treat like Doctor Brigham, either," Pamela spouts, inaugurating the salvation of laughter; my secret, if I have one, tucked safely away in the shell of propriety - even George Senior saved from breaking a trust.

"So, what do you propose we do about this Miss Taylor, Melvin?" George asks, making a mental note to arrange a meeting with Dorothy and me as soon as possible. "I happen to know Judge Whittaker will grant a rapid ruling on the legalities of 'preaching on public property'. Perhaps, if you take the sermon away from the sermonizer, the message away from the messenger-"

"Or the law away from the legalist," I quip defensively. "Maybe we'd have a workable solution, a common sense approach to the public good."

"Does that mean I can be bad in private?" Pamela sponsoring another laugh, "or does that apply only to ministers?"

"It did at one time," George responds, regaling us with the story of the long deceased Rev. Rolundo and Helen the organist.

"B-But I thought I told you about those two," I gush, "... thought it was on my tapes."

"Oh, it was, son," Mother assures me, "but Dad and I knew about it years ago; or at least suspected it, the late hours the reverend sometimes kept with his organist not unnoticed by the village faithful."

"There's my proof!" I cry, jumping triumphantly to my feet. "My story's validated in the patchwork panes of the village church, its windows stained by the sins of a minister whom even you admit was guilty - the old reverend's indiscretion something I'd never heard of before!"

...And if I perish, I perish.
(Esther 4:16)

XXIX

IT'S NOT WITHOUT DIFFICULTY MY STEPFATHER PER-
suades me to bring Dorothy in for consultation, what I learned from
Pamela at my Black-N-Blue bar, and from Little George after church, convincing me my fiancée might be grazing in other pastures. "Marriage is a
ceremony invented by man to honor a rite ordained by God," the winsome
Miss Taylor had preached so persuasively the night before; her definition
of "rite" - limited to the purpose of conception - sending me on a flight
of fancy, imagining what it might have been like had the evangelist and I
been raised as neighbors, as Catholics, the thought of our marriage, of our
twenty children (all asleep in other rooms), overwhelming me with bliss.

Church is supposed to be inspiring, I rationalized, a moving experience, a kind of coming together of flesh and spirit – such "togetherness"
making me blush conspicuously on the aisle end of a front row pew.

Recalling my blush prompts me to analyze my engagement to
Dorothy, or more specifically, my relationship with Dorothy; for she, too,
has made me blush - though never from thoughts like the ones I had in
church. Rather, my blushes are usually brought on by her faux pas, or her
overindulgence; the latter, I've heretofore accepted as my fault for allowing her too much of a good thing: superior gin on an all-you-can-drink-
for-free tab. But suddenly, I'm shunning the blame, taking to heart some
of Miss Taylor's more convincing arguments - her hazel eyes mysteriously

demure, as though embarrassed by what I'm thinking; her long, auburn hair drawn tight in a perfect French twist; her pouting red lips so ready and wet they can only be kissed in French; all this adding to my admission, to my acknowledgment of a gnawing, corporal desire - the kind only to be found in French novels.

Being thus inspired, I'm a new man indeed when I meet Dot.Com at my stepfather's office, my offer of a chair about the only offer I'm not prepared to withdraw.

"Have a seat. Both of you," George commands cordially, my reluctance to sit broadcasting my anxiety. "Now, I don't know if Melvin has told you, or not," he begins, pausing to order us coffee over the speaker phone, "... but regardless, I'll take it from the beginning."

"That would be appreciated, Dad," I respond flippantly, "especially since I don't know what it is I may or may not have shared with Dorothy."

"Aaah, you're right," George says slowly, clasping his big hands behind his head to lean back in his tufted leather chair. "I haven't told you, have I? Well. shall we begin with a third party? and why not?" George drawing Dorothy ever so gently into the trap, "why not, indeed? For that's how this whole thing started, a third party coming to me with a proposition; a proposition that I be the one to relate his feelings regarding Dorothy, here - and you, too, Melvin, in as much as his feelings appear to conflict with certain sympathies of your own."

"Doctor Brigham, I presume?" I interject, overanxious to be done with the matter-at-hand, if not the tender manner by which it's being introduced, my well-informed guess bringing Dorothy to the edge of her chair.

"Not my shrink!" she wails, George instantly castigated by the abject disappointment in her cry, the two of us feeling guilty for even broaching the subject, let alone revealing the culprit.

"I'm afraid so," George leaning forward to rest his muscled forearms on the desk, the nuance of paternity in his deep voice calming her to a more manageable volume.

"But he promised!" Dorothy's black eyes shining with tears.

"Promised what, my dear?" I ask; a woman's tears always my certain defeat.

"That he wouldn't tell," she sobs. "And now he's gone and done it ... the one thing I asked him not to do. It was ... it was a secret I believed could prove you right, Melvin, that's all," she blubbers, "and now he's trying to turn it into some kind of magic bullet, a weapon to turn you away-"

"What the hell are you talking about?" I interrupt, regaining my earlier composure while earning a disapproving frown from George. "And when, pray tell, did you ever think I was right?"

"Your party!" she bawls, "your party, stupid!"

"Doctor Brigham and I discussed the party," George maneuvering his words between us. "He had some very definite ... no, let me rephrase that: some very intractable opinions about the ... shall we say, the effects of Melvin's party; one of which was that you, Miss Compton, came away with a false identity - a 'mistaken identity', I believe he called it - leaving you confused about your affections."

"Well!" she huffs, extracting a tissue from her purse, then shaking her head in refusal of coffee as the receptionist sets a serving tray on George's desk, "all I've got to say for him is that his memory's about as short as Melvin's member; his promise not to-"

"My what?" I break in, sloshing my coffee as I lift it from the tray.

"You heard her correctly," George interjects, a slight twitch at one corner of his mouth signaling anger. "But I'm here to tell you that rascal said nothing-"

"Oh, he didn't, did he?" Dot.Com screams. "Well, he's said worse than that to me! He's told me that nothing times nothing is a loss. My loss. And what's more, that he has the solution to my problem – even offered to prove it mathematically."

"How could he do that?" George's pall of anger fading to curiosity. "How could-"

"Knowing him," I cut in rudely, "he was probably going to demonstrate with a ruler."

"A ruler?" George echoes.

"No, silly," Dot.Com reproving me with a withering glance, "all he needed was a pencil and a blank sheet of paper."

"Oh no!" George looking away as though any shame might be his own, "what was he doing, sketching a silhouette?"

"Just figures," Dorothy replies, missing the implication. "He just wrote down ... well, here, let me show you," she says, reaching for George's ever-present legal pad, and a pen from his unruly collection protruding from a chipped pottery mug, "it's easier to demonstrate than explain," her chosen pen inscribing neatly across the pad:

0-1-2-3-4-5-6-7-8-9-0

"First, he wrote down these digits," she continues, "then he asked me to name my worst symptom."

"Symptom of what?" I ask, recalling math had never been her strong suit.

"The worst symptom of the problem he claimed ... he surmised ... of the problem he-he knew damn well I have!" she blurts. "So, I said, I-I can't sleep nights after ... after Melvin and I have ... after ... well, you know what I mean. And then he just printed what I'd told him. Wrote it out under the digits like this," Dorothy's hand at work again:

0-1-2-3-4-5-6-7-8-9-0
S-L-E-E-P-N-I-G-H-T-S

"'There', he said, 'I've printed your symptom: you can't sleep nights after ... after ... you know what I mean. And now I'm going to give you mathematical proof of the cause. It's a lack. A shortage. A deprivation - the remedy of which your Melvin is unable to provide.'"

"This, I've got to see!" George stretching over his desk to better view what Dorothy's inscribing, "a shrink with a streak of Einstein, no less. A very dangerous combination, if you ask me; a veritable formula for-"

"Will you shut up?" I cut in, well aware he'll take no offense since I'm the one about to be slaughtered. "Now," I say, employing my most command-ing tone, "Dorothy, you may continue ... but with all due restraint, please."

Which she does, accepting my directive with an atypical acquies-cence that leaves me questioning her sanity.

"Yes ... then he instructed me to choose three digits from his list. 'Any three', he said, 'and in any order. And write them down.' So I did, choosing ... oh, it really doesn't matter which three I selected-"

"It matters to me," George says earnestly, craning to read what she has on the pad.

"Not what I meant," she corrects, printing some numerals under the first row of digits and letters. "Doc told me it didn't matter which three I chose. The answer is always the same."

"That's impossible," I object, unaware as yet where she's leading us.

"The answer to my problem, Melvin, my problem," she counters, continuing her illustration. "Now, let's just take the three digits I've picked at random here, seven, six and five, and then reverse them, subtracting the lesser number from the greater like so:

765

my original choice; and now reverse it and subtract:

765
- 567
198

the remainder gives us a new three-digit number, one, nine and eight. Now, we repeat the process, reversing the new three-digit number; only this time we don't subtract. Instead, we add, like so:

198
+ 891
1089

giving us a four-digit sum; which, by the way, will always be the same unless your original three-digit choice has two zeros - a flawed formula Doc said I had already experienced by teaming up with you, Melvin. But true or not, to complete his deduction, we multiply this sum by forty:

1089
X 40
43560

giving us the digits four, three, five, six and zero; these five digits - and in this order - always the result, regardless of your original three choices.

"But now to Doc's proof," she continues, George's quick mind beating her to the dramatic conclusion, his resounding "Damn!" coming just as I, too, realize what the answer will invariably be.

"You spell out the letters under the corresponding digits, right?" I ask faintly, pointing to each letter under the numeral sequence of 4, 3, 5, 6 and 0, spelling the word before Dot.Com can do me the disservice:

0-1-2-3-4-5-6-7-8-9-0
S-L-E-E-P-N-I-G-H-T-S

George rights himself on one elbow, glancing back and forth, from the puzzle solution to my puzzled face.

"P-E-N-I-S," I spell out in a loud, oratorical tone - George shaking his head in awe of the trick - or my bravery.

"What would happen if we were trying to determine the opposite? What if we were in search of something you had too much of?" I ask, desperate for an answer other than the one now smudged in blue-brown streaks. "Just for kicks, let's use your original choice ... the digits seven, six and five. Let's skip all the trickery," I suggest, a goal firmly in mind, "let's dispense with all the reversing, the subtracting, the adding, the multiplying - the blasphemous use of the numeral forty."

"Blasphemous?" George pushing up from the desk to reclaim his chair.

"Right," I say, holding the floor. "Noah's forty days of rain, the Israelite's forty years of wandering, Christ's forty days in the desert, and forty days after His passion. That quack Brigham is attempting a miracle by association."

"You're attempting miracles, too, Melvin," George says, grinning mischievously, "going from a flood to a desert."

"Okay," I grant, "but what I'm trying to show Dorothy is that any deduction can be foisted on the unsuspecting by selecting the facts. For example, Dorothy may have selected the numerals seven, six and five subliminally."

"You mean that's all we do? Just use those three digits to find the answer?" Dorothy still sniffling from her earlier outburst.

"That's right," I say, returning the injury, "and remember what the question is, too: instead of, 'What do you lack?' it's, 'What do you have in excess?'"

"OK," she whimpers, "let's see ... seven corresponds to the letter 'G', and six to the letter 'I' -"

"Go on," I prod, my rush for revenge prompting me to finish for her, to announce with smug satisfaction, "it's the letter 'N'! The letter 'N', which gives us the word, 'GIN'! Now tell me, dear, why your brilliant doctor pal didn't smell that one when it was right under his nose?"

"I-I never have a drink before an appointment," she whines, sidestepping my assault, "so how could he smell it?"

"Could ... it ... be ...?" George muses, leaning back in his chair in a contemplative pose, "could it be that Doctor Brigham is suffering from the rigors of his curriculum? some sort of transference syndrome?"

"I don't follow," I admit.

"Well, he's a man, isn't he?" George goes on pensively, "and by all accounts, should not be subject to the malady in question; but ... could he be suffering from penis envy?"

"He shouldn't!" Dorothy's face a mottled red as she realizes her mistake.

"But whatever his problems," George leaving her slip unaddressed, "they're not why I summoned you here."

"I know," Dorothy interjects, reaching for the last tissue in her purse. "And a good man you are, too, Mr. O'Malley, to recognize that each of us has faults. I know I do," her ready admission striking me down in my pride, in my haughty, hypocritical judgment of her few and mostly harmless peccadilloes.

"So why did you ask us here?" I ask meekly; malleable, now, to most any recommended improvement.

"To reconcile," George says, the sound of Dorothy blowing her nose like a trumpet-call to repentance.

"But-but-" I can't find the words, visions of Dorothy brandishing the rod of correction - and of Miss Taylor, too, as my ministering angel – hushing me like a child; the old hymn *Trust and Obey* playing gently in the corridors of my mind, lulling me in penitent bliss, in a feeling of try-what-I-might-I-can't-alter-fate acceptance of peace; a magnanimous peace to succor my blemished esteem.

"When in doubt, sometimes it's best to do nothing," George admonishes, perceiving my confusion. "Or let me put it another way: in some situations, withdrawal would be an action ... postponement would not."

"You're suggesting a delay of our wedding, aren't you?" Dot.Com's query forcing me to stumble across his not-so-well-hidden allusion, "because if you are, now is as good a time as any for me to agree," she continues (but without the passion of the moment before, I notice), "or better yet, for me to beg your assistance in convincing my future husband to do something with his law degree besides arguing bills over his bar with every woebegone sot of a lobbyist."

"S-So ... y-you agree?" I stammer, the apparent ease with which our pressing engagement can be rescheduled, postponed, ratified, or even vetoed, almost more than my traumatized ego can comprehend.

"Happily!" Dot.Com patting my hands like a piano teacher, and smiling like one of Dickens' orphans, her tear-smudged makeup enhancing the effect. "I would sacrifice anything to help my man climb up, up, up to his highest goal," she sighs angelically, her serene remark like a leaden weight to keep me from climbing at all.

"You're a saint, my dear," George says foolishly, falling for her feminine ploys, "and a prudent one, too. His mother and I have been wishing the same ... with our firm's hard won reputation, his mother's political advantage, and - if I must say so myself - my own inestimable New England connections. Of course, Melvin's not unique among parental disappointments," George running his big-boned fingers through his graying locks. "I'm sure Mary and Joseph wanted their son to be a successful carpenter."

"And they got their wish, too," I rejoin, "Jesus ultimately built a kingdom for the entire world."

"See what I mean!" Dorothy's black eyes shining with pride instead of tears. "Melvin's quick - too quick in some areas, I'll grant you; but quick where it counts. He'll excel before the bench."

"And even more so behind it," George adds proudly, his parental prognostications not without lofty designs. "Imagine it, Melvin," he says with a genuine glow, "imagine being called 'Your Honor' by the best of your peers."

"Yeah, well, my honor's not for sale," I mutter, wishing immediately I hadn't; George redeeming me with his ever-ready wit:

"Oh, it isn't, is it? Then explain how your restaurant got its injurious moniker. Did you name it Black'N'Blue because the beef is chopped? or the breasts split? or is it more from an inherent dishonesty - serving the ribs up short?"

"All right!" I cry, "I'll think about it. But I need time."

"Would six months be enough?" Dorothy asks, her smile almost genuine now with my possible capitulation. "That would move our nuptials to the spring of next year, a more promising, if not more romantic season to wed. And your folks are busy enough with the upcoming election; and then there's Thanksgiving; and Christmas; and-"

"Don't mention it," I interrupt, regarding the previous New Year's Eve as the seed for my current crop of troubles - albeit, it was my party that attracted Miss Taylor to Vermont, her negative stance on gay marriage far less extreme than her utter denial of my much publicized past life. "One can't get much more romantic than Saint Valentine's Day," I pose pretentiously, wincing even as I say it.

"Or Saint Patrick's Day," George contributes, his Irish heritage garnering pride, "though Dorothy might deem a leprechaun-green wedding gown too extravagant for her staid, New England friends."

"But St. Pat's is in March, isn't it?" I argue, "and St. Valentine's in February?" catching my mistake before I can opt for St. Pat's.

"Yeah, and besides, I don't look good in green," Dorothy giving us the relief laughter.

"Then, Valentine's Day it is," I mumble, pleased enough to have gained the delay.

"And remember your promise," Dot.Com instructs, turning her cheek to my halfhearted kiss. "You've got six months to decide which bar you're going to march by."

"That's music to my ears," I pun; George chiming in with his own:

"Don't fall prey to syncopation, son. Staggering between bars may mar the music."

An enemy can partly ruin a man,
but it takes a good-natured injudicious
friend to complete the thing and make it perfect.
(Mark Twain)

XXX

IF THERE'S ONE THING I CHERISH ABOUT VERMONT'S bucolic charm, it's the glory of the changing seasons. October is like a birthday party for God, the whole of His botanical creation taking on a festive garb. And if October is the colorful party, September is the dress rehearsal, a lively month of preparation, of crowd-warming events for the ever swelling tide of tourists drawn north by the harvest moon -

And Vermont's World's Fair, famous since 1867.

Hosting the annual event is the quaint village of Tunbridge. Serenaded by a rock-strewn stream, the idyllic, Green Mountain setting is a cultural extravaganza as colorful as Sherman's fire-blistering march to the sea. And as if to prove the fight is "still in 'em", natives young and old wage war under barn-like pavilions in pursuit of coveted ribbons; the crackle of fire, the roar of cannon, the pop of muskets, supplanted by the bawling of home-sick cattle, the crowing of cocksure roosters, the quacking of ill-mannered ducks - all under a rippling sky of banners.   Everywhere wafts the sounds and scents of life: straw-strewn stalls and wood-chipped malls, flapjacks Bunyun and bloomin' onion, hotdog broilers and pretzel boilers, horse track dust and corn silk must all melding like a mountain mist to wet one's curiosity, to spike the nectar of Nature for a thrill not unbecoming.

Which is why I contrive to attend the fair: a crisp, sweet, satisfying quaff of cold apple cider not unlike the pleasure of my guest, the

West Virginia maiden reaching for my hand like an innocent, childhood friend; an erstwhile evangelist forgetting her mission in the light of God's greater designs.

The first exhibition sets the tone for the day: an elongated cabin of logs like a clock winding back to a time when men still held for angels. Inside, we find a stoop-shouldered, bonnet-bound organist about as old as the bellows she pumps; her withered hands, yellowed as the ivories, playing the haunting *Amazing Grace*; her smile as serene as the timeless refrain. Nearby, a grandmother hums approval, spinning wool into yarn, while another weaves yarn on a loom; and a rosy-cheeked lass baking biscuits over the fieldstone hearth, while another dips wicks into hot molten wax.

"Fifty dips, miss, and a lot of patience 'fore it grows to an inch in diameter," she explains, fashioning Miss Taylor a pearlescent taper to brighten some darksome night. Next, we watch a round-faced mother, with a sleeping child, happy to be counted among the privileged as she quilts from a colonial original. And just outside, a two-seater, double-spring sleigh becomes the dais for a gray-bearded, suspender-clad senator; the old gentleman soliciting support, declaiming more convincingly than he presumes, "I'm not a radical ... I just wanna take Vermont back a little ways, that's all."

As do I - far enough to predate my engagement to Dorothy - my dilemma soon forgotten, lost in the softness of Miss Taylor's hand, her genuine awe of the animals somehow a license to hold, to squeeze my fingers, as I give thanks to the magical beasts: the Red Holstein ox, its massive bulk weighing in at over 2,500 pounds; the Yorkshire sow, larger than life at a whopping 810.

And on to the hay-munching goats, their short tails at constant attention; the helter-skelter of baby chicks scurrying to the giggles of children; the worried peck of nervous bantams scratching a bed of chips – the rabbits at peace with it all, amazingly asleep in their cages. And then the amusement of a Jersey heifer enjoying a bath as though she has plans for the evening. Outside, a happy gang of tow-headed boys splash in the clear water stream - Tom Sawyers, all, grappling for a retreating crayfish.

The boys make me recall my own rustic youth, my happy-go-lucky, long summer days forgone to a fretting world. (With Miss Taylor at my side, perhaps she'll wield Becky Thatcher's magic, reclaim my fairytale world of the dashing and brave, the occult and the odd.)

Just ahead, a bright carousel dances gaily around a path leading nowhere, as the click-clack of a high coaster car plummets to screams of delight. Behind the roller coaster, and beneath an elm festooned for fall, hides the "hair wrapping" booth of an old Ecuadorian, the wizened woman weaving threads of small colored beads into strands of her customers' hair, practicing for profit some high priestly rite long borrowed from lost beliefs - a designer bag stashed by her moccasins as misplaced as her ancient trade. Down the path, a "Pearls in the Oyster" jewelry cart plays host to a gem-colored fly, a bedazzling beauty on its delicate perch on strands of slim silver chains. Next, a card-table topped by a turquoise blanket with the latest in Peruvian tunes, CD's interlarded with a fad from the past: an astounding array of mood rings.

Nearby, a county coterie under a silver maple: old codgers catching naps behind snores, snorts and corncob pipes while their wives lick creamees over a stump - the ladies, too, a side-show to see, all dexterously agossip twixt milk canned mums and dahlias - the cozy scene like a slow-burning fire casting comfort over all who pass, warm shadows of the way things were.

Miss Taylor opines how she wishes she'd been born in some past and sweeter time ... or perhaps in some gentler place. I take full advantage by agreeing, sharing my experience in both ... only to be rudely interrupted by the deep rumbling burp of an emu.

But if earlier seems better, then bigger is best, the next pavilion dedicated to proving it: a 12' sunflower as tall as a fairytale stalk; a 100-pound squash, a half-ton pumpkin, both round as the fifties Ford pickup from which they bulge. The pavilion displays the best from the farm and the pick of the garden, each winner arrayed with a ribbon: yellow peppers, golden shallots, cherry tomatoes, green slicing tomatoes, ripe pickling cucumbers, perfectly symmetrical sweet corn-on-the-cob next a first-prize flat Dutch cabbage. The best of the henhouses, too, up for grading by discriminating judges: brown eggs, white eggs, gray-blue eggs, yellow-green eggs, even the olive-green giants of the gangly emu in line for awards of their own – the lot being admired by Miss Minnie Ruth Taylor as I stand admiring her, the attention-grabbing noise of a public announcer distracting us from the open end doors.

"Harness racing," I explain, my arm dropping casually to her waist, the rush of the throng to crowd round the track excuse enough for protection - a pistol shot, and "There off!" signaling the event underway.

"And, it's F-i-r-s-t T-i-m-e," the loudspeakers blare. "After a late scratch of Rash Judgment, it's First Time taking the lead inside, with Dewey, Cheatem and Howe battling for second. Dead Eye Dick's on the outside - closing in - with Tailor Made running last," the similarity to my charge's name bringing a squeal of delight.

"Look at them go!" she cries, bouncing on the balls of her feet like a Southern Baptist camp meeting song leader, "and their little chariots, too! They remind me of Pharaoh and his generals running hard after dear old Moses!"

"Except there's no Red Sea to swallow 'em," I add, my arm not relinquishing its hold, "which means Pharaoh has a chance this time-" the speakers overhead interrupting:

"It's Dead Eye Dick and Tailor Made now neck and neck with Cheatem ... and into the first turn they come ... Tailor Made finding the rail as First Time falls back with Cheatem ... then it's Dead Eye Dick with Dewey and Howe close behind-"

"Oooh!" Miss Taylor bubbles, looking up into my eyes with a pleasure I've only imagined, "do you think she'll win?"

"She's tailor made for it, if you ask me," I say, thrilling to her worldly enjoyment, the race changing as the announcer calls out the order:

"And through the far turn, it's still Tailor Made, but with Dead Eye Dick on her tail ... and Howe-"

"She's still ahead!" Miss Taylor shrills, jumping up to bestow a kiss on my blushing cheek, a kiss that leaves me numb for the finish. "And I can see her now ... her purple colors streaking by ... her number the same as mine-"

"Yours?" I manage, hoping her horse - her abandon - will both post a win today.

"Number eight," she says, craning to see the finish, "the number of power, of money, of-"

"I-i-i-t's Tailor Made by a nose!" yells the announcer, "with Dead Eye Dick, by a length, finishing strong over a winded First Time," the roar of the crowd suspending my inquiries, and Miss Taylor's asides, on the mystic meaning of numbers.

"I won! I won!" Minnie Ruth Taylor effusive, the race becoming a personal triumph. "It's the number, eight, I tell you. It'll win every time!"

"Eight's my number, too," I assure her, wishing I had something to measure up, "... or at least, it's a number I've always envied."

But Miss Taylor seems not to hear, exuberance deafening her ear; my suggestion to watch the pig race down by the stream setting her off on another foot-bouncing, song-leading dance; her syncopated versing of *Take Me To The River* unlike anything I've ever heard. Her jubilance leaves me wanting more; her toe-tapping, knee-slapping, hand-clapping rhythm arousing a response in my own lithesome frame that brings a blush with the thought it accompanies: a grass-skirted, hip-swishing Swahili temptress closing in on my naked readiness, her breast-swinging, lip-licking, moan-making motions too much for the vision to hold, my randy roar of, "Take me to the river! Take me!" cracking my decorum; her, "My, oh, my! We should go dancing sometime!" suggesting her religion is cracking, as well – the husky bark of the pig race caller drawing us down in the dirt:

"I-i-i-t's Shaken' Bacon, folks ... shakin' it out early ahead of Swine-before-Pearls, with Noah's Arse givin' a'hell-of-a chase. Shem-Sham and Ham-Bone closing fast at the turn, with little Japheth squealing in the rear."

"I love it!" comes a cry from my side – whether to my searching hand or the call of the race, I can't be sure, Miss Taylor responding to both. "Noah's sons are still in the running!" she exclaims, "and I'll bet you anything Ham's going to be the winner!"

"What's good for the goose is good for the-" I start to say, a sudden perplexity stopping me short. "Damn," I mutter, shaking my head, "those civil union provisions are starting to show up everywhere, what with sows being named after sons."

"And Ham-Bone it is, ladies and gentlemen!" calls the announcer, Miss Taylor looking as smart as her bet, her biblical commentary proving it:

"Legend has it, you know, that Ham was the father of our dark-skinned people on the great continent of-"

"I won my share of little gold stars in Sunday School," I quip, cutting her off before color can shade our morning. "Not to imply," I add quickly, "that I'm not eager to win another!" a palmist's tent, but a few steps away, seeming timely for a needed diversion; my "want to?" as understood and accepted as my hand tracing the curves below the pinch of her waist.

"I've never done anything like this before," she says, the excitement in her eyes, her voice, revealing an eagerness to explore. "But ..." she appends, and with a touch of her old evangelism, "I'm only doing it because a fair is the stage for amusement, right?" a quick glance at the adjacent entertainment apparently justifying her choice, a toy-gun shooting gallery and a teddy-bear for tiddlywinks not up to her height of interest. Instead, a geranium-red bandanna catches her eye, its octogenarian owner - if not a direct descendent of Ham, a very close relative - beckoning us in; the whites of her twinkling eyes, of her gleaming teeth behind an approving smile, making friendly our escape from the crowd.

"Ca-moan-in," the decrepit old woman calls over the stoop of her shoulder, hobbling round to a splint-bottomed rocker behind an unpainted table. The poverty of a melmac ashtray, and a milk carton of daisies wilting over a tattered cigar box, decorate the pine-board top. "Y'all pull up a cheah deah 'n make y'allselfs comfey," she rasps, a chest-rattling cough dropping her roughly into the rocker. "I jist luvs readin' young folksez life-lines," she professes, a trembling hand reaching for the familiarity of the dingy, pollen-dusted cigar box. "Da mysteries of da magnet," she rattles on, finding a stogie stashed in the box, one wholly inferior to the brand still faintly discernible, "... sweet Jesus ... sweet Jesus behind 'em all, too ... every one of 'em, yessiree. Da kind of magnet dat's attractin' da bees to da flowers, da fishes to da rivers, da sailor mens to da seven seas," the strike of a match momentarily obscuring her behind a pall of smoke, "... and mostest of all," she continues, "da hansom boys to da purdy girls."

I'm standing behind Minnie's chair, unnoticed by the drooping oracle; her attention elsewhere, her eyes closed, her next statement barely audible: "I charges twenty dollahs for a readin' ... thirty-five, if'n I reads fer two."

"It'll be forty if it's a nickel," I reply, drawing up a folding chair to sit beside Minnie, Miss Taylor's smile at my easy charity brightening the old woman's dim canvas salon even more than the coal oil lamp she's lighting.

"God bless ya, chile ... 'n, me, too, considerin'," our host snuffing a match between a gnarled finger and thumb as though feeling is restricted to her heart.

"Considering what?" I ask, before I can think better not to; Minnie sliding me a look of chagrin.

"Considerin' I owes da boss man a sawbuck fer ebery hand I reads," she explains, taking a long drag on her stogie; the thought of a gratuitous five dollars apparently worth the reflection. "But what 'e don't knows don't hurt 'im," she adds, suggesting her "two for less" offer is worth an extra fifteen if the boss isn't counting the bodies.

"Read hers first," I say, producing two twenties and nodding at Minnie as I draw closer to the pine-board table so as not to miss what her hand might reveal. "That is, if you can find any creases in that perfect little hand!"

"I knowed you's a charmer soon's I seen ya a'strollin' my way," the old lady chortles, stuffing the bills down the front of her gray cotton dress and winking a round, dark eye. "I could tell by da way you's a'lookin' round fer da chance to go a'pattin' your sweetie on da bee-hind wid no one else a'noticin'"

"You didn't!" Miss Taylor gasps, pretending ignorance of pleasures unspoken, "why, you naughty, naughty boy," she finishes, trailing off in the guilt of pretense.

"Maybe 'e couldn't hep it," the delighted old woman teases, reaching for Minnie's hand, "maybe you's a witchin' 'im all da way!"

But if Minnie is about to admit to something, it isn't a spell, her fluttering of heart, her flirting with sin, all allowed within the context of "fair-going", this amazing venture into the "devil's den" proof enough it's all in fun.

"Well?" I ask expectantly, watching the old woman's eyes for any sign of revelation, the arthritic hand tracing over Minnie's palm as slow as the stogie burning away in the other. "Any major indications there regarding Miss Tay---, regarding my sweetie's career?" I amend, taking the opportunity.

"Lawd-a-mercy!" comes the sudden reply, her intensity causing Minnie to jerk her hand back in freight. "Why don't ya warns me dat you's a man o'da'cloth 'fo'e dis po ol' body cuts out wid su'prise?"

"You mean a lady of the cloth, don't you?" I correct, taking Minnie's hand to offer it anew.

"Now she is," the superstitious old creature cries, snuffing her stogie on the near edge of the table with a vigor making graphic her fear. "Now she is ... but da misses, she was a mistah befo'e!"

"We're not going to be angry with you if you make some mistakes," I reply, patting the top of her hand to underscore my assurance, "but I've got to tell you, ma'am, taking Miss Taylor for a man is one mistake no good pair of eyes is ever going to make!" Minnie's eyes lowering in a look of surrender for which Madison Avenue would gladly pay millions.

"Ya not a'understandin' my p'int," she replies, exasperation diminishing her fear, "da misses, heah, she done lived befo'e; a'preachin' in dat life, too!"

"Aaahhh," I sigh, sitting back in a quandary, trying to decide whether it would be advantageous to admit this unexpected support for my past life theories or proscribe it for its primitive source.

"And I'll giv da misses all da proof she needs," the old woman insists, her red bandanna nodding affirmatively, bringing Minnie and me to head-touching, body-leaning attention over Minnie's tentative, outstretched palm - a toothy, "but it sho'nuf ain't in da hand, deah," setting us back hard against the rust of our metal chairs. "It's dat dad-blamed birthmark," the old woman's belief in "impressions" appeasing what fear remains, "dat dark spot on da misses' right hip deah dat looks like a good deacon's medicine bottle; da kind dat poahs out dat lite'o'd'moon fer what ails ya in da deep o'da night."

"A flask?" I query, putting words in her mouth, "because if that's what you mean, you've got us confused. I'm the one with the birthmark, not Miss...not my sweetie; although it is in the place you indicated," the excitement of such a direct hit bringing me to my feet; the wag of a gnarled finger alerting me she isn't finished – Minnie's cry, "But it's true! I do have such a mark on my hip!" forcing a momentary pause as she twists in her chair for the pleasure of surprise in my eyes.

"You do?" I mouth incredulously, smitten by the infinity of odds that would produce such a likeness. "And your ministry?" you-you were once a-"

"And just when I thought I had you convinced!" Minnie retorts, convulsing in laughter. "Of course not. I've never been a man," she goes on. "But let's keep the sweet lady going here. I'm having fun ... the while proving what I've suspected all along."

"And that is?" I ask, confounded by her claim of an identical birthmark.

"Well, first, that the same man who would so nonchalantly drop forty dollars on the nonsensical, would even more readily wager a fortune on his creed," she answers, turning back to solicit the old woman's support, "and second, that I want to be that creed," her unabashed admission driving me deeper into bewilderment.

"Must be the number eight," I say, "must be that power thing you were telling me about. I've been thinking about it ever since - and this is the eighth tent, counting those on the right, since we left the pig race; and-and just a moment ago, I held your hand for the eighth time this morning; and now you're the eighth customer this dear lady has read for today-"

"How-how can you know that?" a flummoxed Minnie breaks in, giving the old lady a questioning look, as well, "explain how you've counted her customers when we haven't-"

"The ashtray," I say, pointing to the melmac monstrosity in front of us, "count the burned match stems in the ashtray. Allowing one for the lamp and one for her stogie each time she begins a reading, sixteen matches would suggest eight customers."

"Da boy's right," the palmist offers, "an'a keepah, too, Miss Minnie, I do decla-ah!"

"Now that's good!" I shout, beginning a nervous pace behind our chairs, "damn good! Reading the name of your customer from a crease in her hand!"

"T'ain't dat," she explains, giving Minnie's open palm a motherly pat, "it's on account o'me a'hearin' 'er on da radio, dat's why. I'd ne'er fergit a voice like dat. Like an angel's, i'tis, yessiree. I listens to ya ebery Sunday, Miss Taylah, when e'er I's down home."

"And where's home?" Minnie beaming with pride to have a fan.

"Macon," she answers, her smile broadening. "Macon, Gee-ah-gia."

"Otis Redding," I follow unwittingly, still stung by Minnie's affirmation of creed.

"Lawd, yes!" the old Georgian seconds me, her dark face aglow, "I use ta he'ah his daddy preach down da Vineville Baptist Chu-ich, n'da boy would be a'singin' in da choi'ah, 'e would. An den when 'e was growed to a hansom man, I seen 'im at da Douglass Theatah theah in Macon, jist a rockin' da house, he was."

"These arms of mine," half talking, half singing, I mimic the tragic author's soulful voice; Minnie and the old woman melting to his sensual verse as I begin pouring out my heart in earnest, singing about loneliness, feeling blue, yearning, and how grateful I would be if Minnie would let me hold her in my lonesome arms.

The fortune teller joining in, swaying to the heart-tugging beat. Minnie, too, humming harmony to a song she's never heard, accepting my offer to dance - the dark old tent becoming a lover's lair, as the old woman trims the lamp, then hobbles under the flap of her canvas den to leave us alone, sheltered from the clamoring world.

A mystical world, as we dance, as I sing about Minnie being my woman, treating me right, holding me tight ... how I need her tender lips -

Our kiss an unwritten verse Big O would have blushed to sing.

To be great is to be misunderstood.
(Emerson)

XXXI

ENTREPRENEUR OR NO, SIMON FARLEY, JR. HAS NEVER
evolved into a man about town, his social life restricted to the pleasantries
exchanged with his patrons; so it isn't unusual for him to be conversing
with the saucy Dorothy Compton while she culls and mulls over his psych
section. Not unusual, that is, until he asks her to accompany him on a spur-
of-the-moment whim, a sudden urge to close his store and motor south for
the unplanned insouciance of a day at the Tunbridge Fair.

Dorothy has no conscious aversion to the tall, graying, sixty-some-
thing wisp of a man; their sparkling discourse, over a common interest,
like an excellent wine redeeming a poorly prepared dinner. But were it
not for Melvin's absence, she wouldn't accept; the would-be-restaurateur
unexpectedly making excuses for the day: meditating on his pending decision, he tells her; a pondering that requires the changing of leaves on some
quiet and bowered lane meandering through the riverside uplifts. With
Dorothy's idea of meditation falling closer to the flash of strobe lights than
the temple of falling leaves, it's uncomfortably obvious how Melvin's pother
gains him the woods - like he's given thought to her greatest dislike, opting
to spend a day in Nature's silence because he knows she'll refuse his offer
to accompany him.

The Tunbridge World's Fair, on the other hand, is more to her liking
- even if it means an hour's drive through the woods with a small-talking

Simon. With her "Darn tootin'" understood as a "Yep", and her flash of a smile an acquiescence to most anything else the friendless Simon might wish to throw in, they're off on a back roads jaunt.

Desert yellows, sunset golds and burnt oranges highlight the deep forest greens - recalling her meditating Melvin. He would be discoursing on the colors, if she were with him. She'd have to think of something else to say, something more pertinent than nature - Simon intruding with a query she's heard dozens, even hundreds of times:

"What did you think of Melvin's party? did you believe any of that stuff he was mumbling?"

"Some," she replies, setting a trap inquisitors invariably spring, "... some."

"I think it's all true," he ventures, taking her bait, "all but the part about Thelma hiding an art gallery in her basement."

"Oh? and how is that?" Dorothy keen for the seamier side of the saga.

"Because, I was nosing around her cellar a few months after my dad and Thelma married, and I didn't see anything resembling an anatomical collection. Nothing. Nothing at all. Well ... nothing except a couple of sticky mason quarts lying smashed on the earthen floor."

"Thelma may have cleaned up her exhibit before she got hitched," Dorothy conjectures - dispute being something she holds dear.

"That's what I thought, too, at first. Then, I began asking myself, why wouldn't she clean up everything down there? I mean, why remove the salacious centerfolds and leave the jam spoiling all over the floor?"

"Dunno. Tunnel vision, maybe?" she retorts, looking for a crack in his logic.

"Aaah! Same thing Melvin said - except we were talking about his folks when he said it."

"His folks?" she shoots back, irritated with his abandonment of a contested point.

"That's right. Melvin told me that George, especially, puts no credence in his so-called recollections. And though his mom is less overt, she, too, merely placates him with a sweet silence on the subject, her love prevailing over any wish to tout her disbelief."

"Well, he told you the truth," she laments. "They believe most of what Melvin recollected came from, and I quote, 'The fertile fields of childhood, a childhood fostered around his grandmother's hearth, her fireside stories but seeds for his reaping."

"And you?" Simon prods, braking his dilapidated Dodge on a mountain crest, the cascading expanse of crimson and gold a celebration he doesn't want to miss, the higher elevations ahead of the valleys in their enthusiastic embrace of fall.

"W-e-1-l," she stalls, surprised this docile, village bachelor has the aplomb to press her opinion. "There is the theory of the collective unconscious, you know."

"Carl Jung? Yes, I know," Simon answers curtly, as though the name of the great man is agitating. "Your interest in psychology is what prompted me to invite you along," a heretofore unnoticed urgency in his voice, like a compulsion to go screaming down the side of the mountain. "Jung is my bedside companion; my father confessor; my-"

"You? a psyche student?" she interrupts, amazed at his unfolding ... perhaps his unraveling. "I would've never guessed!"

"Part of my problem," Simon accelerating through a precarious curve. "Just a part, you understand; but still a part I need to address."

"You've lost me," a bewildered Dorothy sensing a direction away from herself, away from the party.

"What has Little George told you about it?" Simon offering no clues to his bearing.

"About-about Jung?" she stutters; wishing, suddenly, she were in the woods with Melvin, silence becoming synonymous with safety.

"No, about the party ... about his beliefs, or disbeliefs, in what the tapes put forth as truth."

"The-the party?" she screams, Simon careening within inches of the narrow, leaf slick shoulder.

"Sorry," he mumbles, redirecting his car, and her attention, as though nothing happened. "The reason I ask – about Little George, I mean – is because we've been sharing some common concerns; or more accurately, some personal dilemmas; something we each have to face, to work out-"

"Little George?" Dorothy green-faced, Simon's discourse as crooked as the twisting road.

"You know what a bookworm he is ... in my store most every day, looking for that-that 'authority', as he calls it, on some subject or other that's caught his expansive fancy."

"So ... what's his problem?" Dorothy keeping one eye on the perilous curve ahead and both hands on the hard metal dash.

"Let's just say that his parent's ambivalence over the recent civil union legislation seals his lips at family discussions, keeps his problem a secret; one he's shared with me."

"His problem? shared with you? not George? not Melody?" Dorothy gasping as they skid through the bottom of the curve.

"The most compelling reason being that his parents refuse to believe the tapes," Simon says, "and he wanted my opinion as to whether I thought there was anything in the tapes that might allude to his-his condition. He's aware, you see, of my predilection for Jung; how I've struggled to analyze, to understand-"

"His condition?" Dorothy echoes, "his problem? Simon Farley! enough of your vagaries!" that Simon's her elder no longer a consideration; both his driving and his conversation in dire need of direction. "Be specific," she demands. "What problem does Little George have?"

"None. None whatsoever," the ever evasive Simon parries, gunning his Dodge in jerky spurts along the stream-bordered road at the mountain's base. "None, that is, since the civil union bill literally legislated the problem out of existence."

"But that's about gays marrying gays," Dorothy shouts, confused, impatient, "about their rights as partners; like being the responsible party in medical emergencies; like ... hey! what are you saying?" Dorothy abruptly removing one hand from the dash to pass through her raven hair and trail down the side of her neck as though the effort can clear her thoughts. "Are you saying Little George has a medical problem?"

"Specifically, no. But back to the civil union law, it implies a great deal more than the obvious; more than the rights of a partnership," a nervous Simon postures, "in fact, it moves the problem of-of ... the problem, well ... the problem is transferred to the public at large. Out of the closet, you might say, to be carried on the back of society – or at least by those who still regard it as a problem. Their own cross to bear, I suppose; though to be sure, it's one of their choosing, thanks to the bill."

"Then-"

"Yes?" a shaking Simon prompts, his high voice no more than a squeak, "you were saying?"

"Then you are gay?" an incredulous Dorothy mouths. Still on the flat stretch of road, her thoughts are free to postulate, to deduce, to think the unthinkable, to accept the unacceptable-

"And free," a relieved Simon follows; that she has voiced the difficult word making it easier to express its partner.

"And Little George?" she mutters, moving gingerly towards the light of the thing as though it holds harm in abeyance; as though at any moment it might reach out to include her, to diffuse her with love and warmth, with acceptance of all things mortal. "... Little George?"

"Not so little anymore, is he?" Simon whispers, the large thing he has said like the stream running clear and determined beside the road, its purpose as natural, as beneficial, as the rain that gave it birth.

"No, he isn't." A cleansing pride in Little George flowing over her shock, washing away what bias she's acquired, her empathy with his suffering more than she can hide; his pain, his fear, his love of family all at odds with who he is. The thought of pain bringing her back to Simon. "But you, too," she says softly; her eyes aglow with resolution. "We've got to do something. Make it right for Little George. For you. For all those-"

"I'm older now," he interjects, "my habits are deep; self-protecting. And I would just as soon not change anything for myself. But Little George?" the strain in his voice, his actions, all gone; his driving now a thing to be admired. "He needs to feel it's okay to be himself; to make the most of his talents; to fully enjoy his career as a teacher - a college professor - and to know his family, his friends, his students, will be all the more proud for his honesty."

"Yes, and a brave honesty it is, isn't it?" she adds, searching his face for admission, for any sign he might yet wish to join the realm of the free.

But his wall is too high, his defense too entrenched; all the years of secrecy, of pretense, the very bricks in his reclusive tower. "What's this I hear about your engagement?" he asks, his change of subject as refreshing as the cold mountain air Dorothy introduces, cracking her window with a suddenness and force suggesting suffocation.

"Change of date, that's all," she offers, her terseness exposing the lie.

"Melvin thinking of joining the firm?" he continues; relief from cracking his closet door leaving him unresponsive to Dorothy's cues. "Little George told me about it."

"Then, you know," she says, a flip of her lustrous black hair catching the sun - and Simon's eye.

"So, where did you get your eyes? your hair?" Simon blind to her resistance, her stubbornness when an issue remains unresolved.

"Same place Little George got his sexual persuasion," she answers, flashing a smile that's more from satisfaction with her ready reply than any change in her curious mood. "Hidden in the family genes, I guess."

"Wait till I tell Little George!" Simon wails, laughing wickedly. "'Hidden in the family jeans', she says!" The Tunbridge general store coming into view as he guffaws; Dorothy suggesting a late morning snack before their trek through the bustling fair - and getting it, too, at Simon's expense: a couple of horseshoe kielbasas and a block of Cabot habanera cheese funding their drive through the old covered bridge, two explorers ravenous with anticipation as they pull within sight of the barns.

"Shall we tackle the rides first?" Dorothy wiping the last trace of mustard from her lips as Simon parks.

"Be my guest," the generous Simon obliges, taking the unnecessary precaution of locking his battered old Dodge. And striking out across a narrow, wooden-rail bridge - its bird's-eye view of the Tunbridge stream not unlike what lies ahead - the fair seems a span over the passing world, each year bringing something new.

Yes, now here are the real colors, Dorothy muses, feeling for the rail as she peers up the hillside ahead, the colors one should drive out to see, a myriad bright banners beckoning in the Green Mountain breeze. Melvin doesn't know what he's missing! The hot pepper yellows, the hard candy purples, the hotdog reds all streaking like Vincent's life-vibrant oils over a canvas of seawater blue.

And the characters, too, no less colorful: the Ferris wheel spun by a tale in the making, the operator assuring those waiting to ride that he was once an attorney at law (Simon whispering that if this swaggerer was ever before the bench, it was probably at the arm of the law). All this overlooked by Dorothy, the thrill of the wheel more excitement than caution can stem.

But when she disembarks, a dizzy survivor of Simon's "circle of death", she joins him on the ground, a bit of personal puffery in her friendly taunts and dares:

"Come on old fellow," she teases, "if a frail little thing like me can face these frightening machines, a man of your stature can bring them down to their rusted knees!"

Which is exactly what he fears, Simon's excitement running more towards the absolute, the certain - the risk of a bee escaping a glass encased hive, the apogee of his orbit with danger. His fascination with safety gives him pause before each mechanical amusement, Simon deducing mystic meanings hard taught in the twisted steel.

"I wager you're beyond the attraction of that monstrosity," he says, pointing to a towering platform from which ticket holders are plunging like seals off an Artic berg to slide down a roiling trough of water.

"I am," Dorothy agrees - after trying not to. "But why do you say so?" she asks, chancing an argument.

"Because life has taught you better," Simon giving her shoulder a little pat - half affection, half compliment. "Taught you the value of effort, of time; and of what you should expect in return. Just look at those kids, their arduous climb up the long flights of stairs, the time-wasting line for a turn at the trough - and all for the five-second thrill of sliding down. You would think the unfair exchange would eventually be recognized for what it is," he laments. "And yet, year after year, I see them climbing, see them panting in line to slide back down to where they worked so hard to escape."

"Wow!" Dorothy exclaims with exasperation, "you're worse than Melvin! Always looking for that deeper meaning, that higher design. What's wrong with just living it up while we still have a chance?"

"W-What's wrong?" he stammers, backing away to take her fully into view, "it's me that should be asking you that question, my dear! You're the one who's had the benefit of a guide, a rare insight into the past, reviewed the lessons it has for the present. Take, for example," he scolds, and with a sweeping motion of his arm, "... take all these people round us here. Just look at what they're doing: paying their hard earned cash for a chance – a chance to make some impossible shot, some improbable toss; one that, if successful, only wins them an impractical toy."

"Yeah? so what's your point?" a petulant Dorothy fusses; that her benefactor has become a lecturer – and with the bad timing of doing it at the very feet of Mother Pleasure - more than she's bargained for; more, even, than the disparity in his little "unfair exchange" illustration; a retaliatory thought finding her impertinent tongue:

"Maybe you're not gay at all, Simon Farley. Maybe you're just so damn unhappy to be stuck here on earth that you can't handle anything that might make you want to stay," she declaims, defiantly flipping her shoulder-length hair – Simon ignoring her barb to address her question:

"My point is this, my scared little girl – for I think you are frightened; afraid that what Melvin recalled about you might actually be true – I think you know life is not a chance. In fact, it's anything but a chance, what you learned at the party bearing down on your conscience like Damocles' sword. And unlike these scatty pleasure seekers chancing the toss of a ring peradventure it loops the neck of a bottle, you know from experience – remembered experience – that the real challenge is yourself. Grab yourself around the neck, and the prizes will follow - come tumbling down from the skies, if you will - if only you stick out your neck, take a chance on what your heart already knows you should do."

"I-I'm sorry," Dorothy drawing closer to take his arm, "I'm sorry I said that awful thing, that slur about you being-"

"Honey, I've heard worse things said on the subject," he interposes, easing her contrition with a nervous titter. "But what about you? do you agree with what I said? that what's really bothering you is Melvin's recollections?"

"I need time, Simon," she replies, after a moment's consideration, and after they walk past a crowd - a crowd rooting for favorites in a pig race. "I need time to reflect, time to analyze, time ... time to know my own heart, as you said. And to help me do that, I've been seeing a psychiatrist," Dorothy noting the comment seems to please him. "So there," she adds, "now you know why I was in your store this morning looking for material on Jung."

"And thrilled to know it, too," Simon looking about for anything not billed as a threat; for anything which this troubled young lady and he might share without fear. "And would you look at this!" Simon pointing at a palm reader's tent, its sign the mere symbol of an open hand. "This is the very thing we need! You see?" he goes on excitedly, "there's no chance, no so-called luck in our lives. What we need is always there if we'll but recognize its form! And in this case, it's a fortune teller!"

"Since when did palmistry become an essential?" she queries, laughing at Simon's childish delight, his sudden reversal – the same man, who, decrying the fair's entertainments as frivolous only moments before, is now eager to partake.

"Since it occurred to me that this could be your litmus test," he answers - Dorothy's laugh subdued to a smile. "We can check out Melvin's party, see if anything turns up to validate what he said," he continues, taking her hand and playfully tugging her to the tent, to the flap hanging loose over its entrance.

"Should we just go in like this?" she asks, as Simon reaches to pull back the flap, "... unannounced? What if someone is in the middle of a-?"

Dorothy's objection quashed by the lingering kiss of two lovers - Melvin's betrayal cutting deeper than forgiveness can heal.

Man will become better only when you
make him see what he is like.
(Chekhov)

XXXII

FOR A DAY BORN TO SUCH HIGH FLYING HOPES, THE
war between my heart and my head is a sudden and crushing blow, the
kind of defeat that can only find solace in a cemetery. Collapsed under the
yellow moon - my father's gravestone like a shard of my shattered heart
- I recall my sweet Minnie's whisper, feel her breath on my neck as the
blinding shaft of sunlight stabs like an accusing finger through the flap of
the tent.

"No one has ever waited for me under my window," she whispers,
pulling back from my hungry arms, searching my eyes for hope, for promise, for anything to consecrate what she regards as sin - my commitment
written in the shine of my tears. Yes, my tears; for I'm overwhelmed by a
glimpse through the portals of bliss, my tears spilling forth like a fountain
to wash from my mind the stains of a troubled past; the dull, leaden drag
on my heart that's long held me back from such heights, a weight suddenly
crashing through the tent to pull me down anew.

Moments later, Simon departs with Minnie, escorting her to her
lodgings in Montpelier. I'm the odd man out; a man with a banshee on his
back. For death seems my only escape; and one most welcomed, too, with
Dorothy playing the torturing roles of good guy, bad guy, cajoling and cud-
geling to compel my carnal confession.

But what can I say? what can anyone say in such bewilderment? I feel at once guileless and guilty, saintly and sinful; Dorothy's distress, I tell myself, no more painful than my hurt to have caused it – except, I'm innocent of the charge. After all, there was nothing amiss with my intentions, playing cicerone to an out-of-state guest a kind of charitable deed, the venerable cloak of the Good Samaritan even now to be seen on my back, if Dorothy will but trouble herself to look – the kiss notwithstanding.

One must consider the circumstance of that kiss, I reason; most any red-blooded male, regardless of his pigmentation situation, prey to thrilling lips when accompanied by Otis Redding – the dance notwithstanding.

One must consider the circumstance of that dance, I venture; most any high-spirited male, regardless of his fermentation situation, prey to willing arms when accompanied by-

But I hadn't consumed a drink! And furthermore, I am the man who turned to that tent of temptation, not Otis. Again I succumb to bewilderment, feeling at once both guileless and guilty, saintly and sinful; the entire delightful morning replaying in my mind, only to end with Dorothy at my bar, in the dregs of her gin, while I climb a stone-strewn hill, the grave of the man who gave me my name now a pedestal to hold my hurt.

"My father told me I'd find you here," an unmistakable voice announces, Simon's long, thin shadow like a diaphanous calling card falling across my knees, "told me you needed the poet's eye; needed to peer through the dismal mist; to recognize advantage when cloaked in the guise of failure."

"What calls you up to cemetery hill on this cold and friendless night?" I ask, unperturbed by his nocturnal rambling.

"I told you. I'm here as an emissary. My dad-"

"I appreciate what you did today, Simon," I break in, any credit due his dad not on my list of obligations. "What happened there in the tent ... let's just say it was misunderstood." Simon taking a seat on the edge of my great-grandfather's grave, its headstone reading:

Manassas Melvin Morrison, minister, husband, father - and in that order - rest in peace

the inscription in dreadful disagreement with my present predicament. Meriting not one of my great-grandfather's titles, I can't imagine resting in peace.

240

"Never noticed your grandpa's tombstone before," Simon straining to read through the wreathes of mist collecting about our feet, our legs, the chill crawling up from the river below like the icicle breath of death. "Minister, husband, father," he says as though reciting an incantation, "... now, where have I heard those words before?"

"Common enough," I respond. "And not that it matters, but that's my great-grandfather's resting place, not my grandfather's." Anxious to inquire of Minnie, of what she may have related after their unexpected pairing at the fair, I redirect. "Common enough as words, I mean; but what I was going to ask-"

"Church!" he exclaims, "I heard them at church! Well, almost-"

"Almost?" I quiz, amused by his interest in epigrams; especially one as terse as my great-grandfather's.

"Yes, yes, it was your lady friend," Simon referencing Minnie with cheerful delicacy, "she said a similar thing in church. Remember?"

I do not - a firm wag of my head conveying my denial.

"Yes. Her exact words were 'Minister, helpmate, mother – and in that order', just like your grandpa – I-I mean, your great-grandpa. And I'll tell you what else she said," he continues, brandishing his skeletal arms as though the rising mist were a monster, "she told me the fortuneteller revealed the two of you have matching birthmarks. And I told her about one of your tapes – one she hadn't read about in the press – the one about Little George being born with the same mark, the mark he shared with Melvin Senior. In the same place, too; and-"

"Judicious of you," I interject, pleased to be a part of their discussion, and hoping her heart is not yet in touch with her head. "What was her response?"

"Keenly interested, I'd have to say. Intrigued."

"Are you certain?" I press, hope building.

"She told me as much," he avers, challenging any doubt of his opinion, "said she had a lot of reading to do. Said she'd see me in my store tomorrow morning – which is why my dad sent me up here to find you."

"Your dad?" I query, elation obscuring my memory.

"Sure, like I told you: I communicate with Dad all the time," his matter-of-fact assurance convincing, save for his frantic eyes; his fixation with the disappearing stars a trance I'm compelled to disrupt.

"Look at me, Simon," I demand, getting up from my father's grave, "it's Melvin Morrison you're talking to here; Melvin, Jr.; the same Melvin who's been the target of ridicule over what some consider to be my fraternizing with ghosts. So take my advice," I counsel, returning to my granite slab, "don't be telling people you talk with the dead! Reclining across my father's tomb, my hands clasped behind my head, I continue, "Now, tell me ... what did he say?"

"Came to me in his usual way; just an impression I get sometimes - like when I rest in the old rocker by the stove," Simon's face upturned, his eyes now as closed as Sunday. "Said you need to recall some things ... figure them out from the evidence provided you thus far."

"Evidence?" Simon the soothsayer beginning to sound like Simon the detective. "Evidence of what, for God's-"

"Says you need to watch your mouth," he scolds, shiver-twitching, "pay homage where homage is due. And right now your account's in dire arrears."

"I don't know about this-this impression business," I reply, turning my head in my hands to keep him in view, "it's too vague ... leaves too much to our biased interpretation – that is, if we can decipher what it is that needs interpreting."

"Try fidelity," he returns, the word clambering up my spine like ice-cold fingers; my recollections, on those damning tapes, looming as ghosts in the moonlit mist.

"But it's only now that I ... that I suspect ... that I think ... that-that I know I'm in love," I protest, all the guilt I'd laid down on those party tracks coming back to haunt my admission.

"Says there's more to fidelity than romance. Says you should consider your destiny, your chosen work ... the plan you were given before you returned. Says your work demands fidelity, too."

"Aaah," I sigh, turning back to what stars still burn through the mist, "sort of a 'be true to yourself' admonishment, is it? Like maybe I shouldn't be dabbling in the restaurant business if it robs my time, my attention, my will to achieve in my chosen profession. Is that it?"

"Says that's part of it. But you know that already. Says you discovered long ago that an attorney could do more than just practice law. A profession that wastes an entire career by 'practicing' lacks direction. But you have direction. Says you shared it with him as a teenager - and it wasn't to turn a spit on the banks of the river."

"But I've been progressing on an as needed basis," I argue; recalling the winter's night old Simon let me spin my dreams round his wood-burning stove, the old man wafting along in my aerial flights as though he, too, were a youth this side of adventure.

"As needed, you say? Well, you need to know ... need to do ... need to proceed with the plan," Simon says, slipping insubstantially off my ancestor's tomb like the shadow he'd cast at his entrance, the thump of his boney frame on the mist-moistened ground jolting him back to our mountain; his, "Holy Moses!" as harmless as his crumpling fall.

"Drift off to sleep?" I ask; curious to know if his impressions are as unremembered as my regressions.

"Must have," he mumbles, unscrambling his limbs to sit upright on the granite, "... must have. I was in the middle of a dream when I fell."

"What were you dreaming?" I ask nonchalantly, masquerading my investigative purpose.

"I-I think it was about my father. Must have been the suggestion of your grandpa's grave."

"My great-grandfather," I correct, sitting up in the throes of a shiver, "but do you remember any part of the dream?"

"No ... yes ... well, maybe," he struggles, fumbling with the collar of his jacket in search of warmth. "I think I recall a scene ... a little vignette. .. and-and you ... yes, you were there, Melvin ... there with my dad, the two of you sitting by the old wood stove."

"What happened next?" I prompt, eager to hear his rendition of what I assume is my memory of a night with his father.

"What happened next was I fell off the tombstone," he blurts, disappointing me, rubbing his hands, his legs, his upper arms with a vigor that warms even me. "But I do remember what we were talking about before I dozed off," he pipes, a return to Minnie Ruth Taylor apparently forthcoming, "Your brother's chair at Godhard College," dashing my expectation.

"We were not!" I object. "We hadn't mentioned Little George; nor, for that matter, his English chair at Godhard."

"Then, I suppose I was about to," Simon disarming my objection; "for Little George was much on Miss Taylor's mind."

"He was?" I rejoin, giving Simon a prosecutorial stare to be certain he's awake. "Little George, and not me?" I question, broadcasting my alarm.

"Yes; because I told her about your brother's problem ... his reticence to admit his sexual bent; and she-"

"You what?" I bellow, coming up from my father's grave as though Gabriel just blew his horn. "Tell me you didn't!" I cry, taking a belligerent stance before his faint and folded figure. "Tell me you didn't break my brother's trust!"

"Okay, okay," Simon cowering, waving his attenuated arms to the vestige of stars disappearing in the blanket sky, "okay, I didn't."

"That's better," I say, lowering my voice, though still holding him suspect for entertaining the thought.

"Little George told me I could discuss it with her," he vacillates, shivering me back to my grave, to my raft on the sea of the dead. "Said I could see if she'd be willing to talk with him about it; to explore his options."

"His options?" I echo, dumbfounded that we are having this conversation; that this issue - of all issues - should have been broached on such a day of discovery for Minnie. "You know, Simon," I whisper, the hushed effect more virulent than a scream in the pregnant dark, "... you know, I suppose, that the Supreme Court recently ruled on the Boy Scouts issue - ruled that the Scouts can ban homosexuals from acting as Scoutmasters. And when one couples this finding with our own state's obsession with our private lives, our private parts ... there's nothing civil about it. We appear to be at war with the national majority."

"So?" a seemingly complacent Simon mutters.

"So, I can't hold Miss Taylor accountable for her opinions," I argue, "at least, not in the light of their origin."

"And Little George?" Simon cutting to the heart of my distress.

"Has my total support," I parry, and quickly; my brother and I having years before found a mutual strength in our difference. "I think – and he knows it – that he should live his life with the same enjoyments as his peers; and that includes his-his-" I falter, recalling what Simon just said, "his chair at Godhard. Were you suggesting-"

"I was about to say your brother is considering a change, his love of literature, of poetry - in fact, of everything beautiful – suggesting a broader path, one more accommodating than his local professorship."

"And this is why you were seeking Miss Taylor's advise?" I ask, "a career counseling session couched in the guise of gay rights?"

"Of course not," Simon's tone indignant. "Your personal fascination with the very lovely Miss Taylor is most warranted; but I dare say you would agree that her credentials as a guidance counselor are somewhat lacking."

"Then how do you explain your attempt to arrange, on behalf of my dear brother, what appears to be just that: a counseling session?"

"I'm surprised you don't admit to the reason yourself," an adversarial Simon poses. "After all, he is your brother."

"And what's that supposed to infer?" I quip, our impromptu powwow taking on the ominous aspects of a war council, my gentle visitor bristling at every turn.

"That your brother loves you ... perhaps even more than himself ... and in consequence, is fully aware of your burgeoning feelings for Miss Taylor – something he supports, if for no other reason than she appears to inspire in you a new vigor for life; 'an awakening', as he puts it."

"But-"

"I'm not finished," Simon cutting me off; his ire now up to his task. "Returning to your comment but a moment ago - the one where you compared the Boy Scouts finding with Vermont's civil union law – I'm shocked by your blindness, Melvin; by your failure to discern, as a man of the bar, what's really at issue here. This ruling, and this law, is not about gays at all – no matter your views on that subject - but about the rights of a private organization, and of private citizens, respectively."

"I surrender," I reply, not wishing to engage his umbrage. "But the question remains: how did Miss Taylor respond to your portrayal of Little George? to his request for a private meeting?"

"Most agreeably," he says, and with a force I take as honesty. "She told me her morning with you had been like a heavenly visitation ... like Saint Peter's dream."

"Afraid I'm not familiar with that one," I admit, suddenly much enamored with Simon and his winsome way with the object of my affections, "but I'm sure you'll enlighten me."

"Saint Peter dreamed of foods being offered him from heaven; foods judged unclean by the old Hebrew law," he explains. "But with the heavenly offering came a heavenly voice overruling the law to make all foods acceptable."

"Never thought of it that way, but I doubt any of the food she saw at the fair was kosher," I muse, smiling over Minnie's 'heavenly visitation', imagining my high and honored place among her angels.

"Remind me never to retain your services, my dear boy," a laughing Simon retorts. "You've missed her import entirely! Your little lady was implying an ordered change in her beliefs; an acceptance of certain worldly goings-on she'd heretofore deemed immoral." The word 'immoral' key to my understanding, Big O descending from heaven in a vision akin to Saint Peter's - only food isn't the pleasure so blessed.

"Going shopping tomorrow, is she?" I ask, giving my limbs a regenerative stretch before standing up. "Perhaps we should get some sleep ... you know, be bright and alert at tomorrow's call, our duty a supreme demand."

"Ours?" Simon queries, joining me above the mist, "I guess I hadn't mentioned it, Melvin, but Miss Taylor is expecting the benefit of your brother's knowledge, Little George's untrammeled familiarity with books ... such anticipation a constructive force we shouldn't toy with."

"Untrammeled familiarity?" I repeat, my salacious smile going unnoticed in the dark. "Untried familiarity is closer to the mark."

Wear a smile and have friends;
wear a scowl and have wrinkles.
(George Eliot)

XXXIII

SIMON HAS NO PATIENCE FOR AN OBDURATE MIND;
and with Dorothy storming into his store under the steam of his first pour
of coffee - his morning ritual of fresh-ground hazelnut-mocha - he is sorely
unprepared to disguise his displeasure. The immediacy of her attack, the
asperity of her manner, are more than civility can manage; what modest
satisfaction he admits for arranging a meeting between Little George and
Miss Taylor, smoldering in fiery aspersions, a volatile Dorothy shouting
him into a fray.

"How could you do such a thing?" she screams, slamming her
sequined clutch on his book-cluttered desk. "How could you be so
thoughtless, so cruel as to set me up like that? knowing all along Melvin
was trapped, was stupefied by that-that Jesus junkie, that-that-"

"We reserve the right to refuse service to anyone," Simon screeches,
pointing to a faded wall placard Artie had nailed, years before, over a hole
in the plaster, Simon's sudden whirl to point at the sign-cum-patch spilling
his coffee.

"You and your moralizing," Dot.Com sneers, ignoring his attempt
at expulsion, "your song and dance about Little George - about me, about
my advantages gained through the tapes - it was all a smoke screen wasn't
it? an attempt to soften me up for the punch you were planning to deliver."

"Young lady, you do need Jung - and how!" a shaking Simon rebuts, fumbling in a desk drawer for a cloth to wipe up his spill.

"Like hell I do! It's you and Little George who could do with some therapy!" she snarls - as behind her, the thunder of books crashing to the floor halts her barrage; a groaning morass of sprawling limbs causing her to turn and gasp:

"Little George! W-What happened?"

"I heard you screaming from across the street," he grumbles, getting gingerly to his feet. "Thought you were being attacked. Raped, maybe. So I came running to save you; and this is my singular reward: a pile of two dollar, third-hand hardbacks, and a four-alarm fake from you."

"Never mind the hardbacks," Simon sighs, daubing the front of his trousers with a dust cloth he'd found in the drawer, "just help me with this hardheaded woman, would you? The books I can manage, but I haven't a shelf small enough to handle her piece of mind."

"I'll see you in court for that wisecrack," Dorothy steams. "And with George as my witness. And Melvin, to boot – my attorney to boot your ass, that is!"

"She'll cool off," Little George advises, Dorothy's hand now firmly in his, the big man backing towards the door, half dragging his fuming charge - that the door is opening as they approach, seen only by Simon, his brisk, "Good morning, Miss Taylor!" serving as both a greeting and a warning.

"Your timing couldn't be better," Simon avers, pouring a much-needed brew. "Hazelnut-mocha," he says, rolling his eyes in pleasure. "Care to savor its ecstasy?"

"Try it before you say no," Little George interposes, his grimacing companion on her knees from the crush of his hard-gripping hand, "it's better than you-know-what."

"My goodness! How can one say no to that?" Miss Taylor replies, her cheerful acceptance mistaken by Dorothy as the wiles of a wanton woman.

"That depends on just who your 'you-know-what' is with," Dorothy manages between writhes under George's hand, "but I wouldn't count on a comparison from either of these gentlemen - the emphasis being on the 'gentle', if you get my drift. They're just happy, happy, happy, these two; just gay, gay-" little George pulling her through the door before she can further tarnish the morning.

"Was she-"

"The girl in the tent?" Simon finishes for her; Miss Taylor's smile shrinking like her cheeks hurt with the effort. "The girl in question? the girl in trouble? the girl in my hair?" he continues, diffusing the tension, "... and now the girl not in my store, thank heavens - but what do you take in your coffee?"

"The blacker the better," Minnie gushes - images of the man Miss Taylor was with in the tent coming instantly to Simon's mind.

"Saw Melvin last night," Simon making conversation about as clumsily as he pours the coffee, her saucer catching more than her cup – Miss Taylor unaware of either.

"Melvin?" she repeats wistfully, her blush becoming a permanent feature, her cheeks as red as her half-opened lips. "My Melvin?" she whispers, taking Simon's offered chair, then leaning across his desk as though the very name requires intimacy.

"Your Melvin, my Melvin, his Melvin," Simon rattles on, lost in the aroma of hazelnut-mocha. "Met him on the grave of his grandpa - his great-grandpa - had a nice little chat under the moon."

"You and his great-grandpa?" Minnie drawing in her breath, sitting back in her chair as though the revelation requires a more formal distance.

"Funny you should put it that way," Simon failing to satisfy her query. "His tombstone has an inscription very much like something you said in church the other night, his epitaph reading, 'minister, husband, father - and in that order'; compared to your statement of, 'minister, helpmate, mother – and in that order'. Very strange. Very strange, indeed. It's like you had read his akashic record or something."

"His-his what?" she falters, clasping her hands around her steaming cup to borrow its warmth, "some sort of record, you say?"

"Edgar. Edgar Casey," Simon explains, between sips of his morning magic, "America's most documented mystic; and one I'm sure Little George will suggest for your study. At any rate, Edgar claimed to read - while in a trance, or sleep state - from the akashic records; this to the benefit of his clients, gleaning advice on everything from careers to health - or the lack thereof, as was usually the case."

"And Melvin's ancestor has access to this akah ... this record thing, as well?" Minnie's effort to hide a shiver unsuccessful.

"Maybe. I don't know. How could I know?" Simon giving her a curious look. "Why do you ask?" he appends, wondering if she's misunderstood him from the outset.

"For Melvin's sake," Minnie raising her cup as though taking the Sacrament, drips of hazelnut-mocha leaving a zippered trail between her lips and her brimming saucer.

"Sounds serious," a comforting male voice announces, Little George making his hurried return through the back door. "Anything done on behalf of my brother must be grave indeed."

"How close you shave the subject, my friend," Simon shoving the last of his chairs in the direction of George. "An amazing feat, too, with no help from ourselves. We were on the subject of death, of graves - and of records both here and beyond."

"Your family plot," Minnie adds, accepting his handshake before he sits down.

"And which act are we in at the moment?" George queries, declining Simon's offer of coffee. "Act one? Act two? Act three?" the drop of Miss Taylor's chin signaling her state of wonderment.

"I-I guess I'm lost," she stammers, reaching for Simon's dust cloth, drops of coffee clinging like translucent pearls to the nap of her pink wool sweater." I thought we were talking about Simon's visitation," she says hesitantly, "about Melvin's great-grandfather reading from the ah-kah-chak records."

"Which only proves what a poor communicator I am," Simon apologizes "I was talking with Melvin up in the cemetery, last night; the happenstance of my granite seat the tomb of Melvin's great-grandfather, the same tomb from which I read the inscription I recounted a moment ago. And as for akashic, allow me to spell that troublesome word, since it seems foreign to your religious persuasion-"

"She'll see it soon enough," George enjoins, easing her embarrassment with a disarming smile. "I'm here to supply a reading list, am I not? And if so, that word will be among the creeds in the list. It's a theosophical term for a kind of universal filing system, one that records every thought, word and deed. The records are supposed to be on a substance called 'akasha' - hence the name 'akashic records' – a substance believed by the Hindus to be the primary principle of nature. In fact, it's from this principle, they hold, that the other four were created - namely: earth, water, fire and air – these five, in toto, corresponding to our own five senses. And from this it follows naturally that the akashic records are akin to a cosmic, or collective consciousness; an ancient belief held long before our late great Dr. Jung postulated his 'collective unconscious.'"

"What did I tell you? See how simple he makes it all seem?" an admiring Simon contributes, giving his guest a moment to recover; to ponder this new beast of thought, an idea poking holes in the thick old hide of tradition. "It's the teacher in him," he adds, stretching for his trusty pot.

"Really?" a modest Little George inquires, "then please forgive me if I seemed didactic. I was only-"

"No apology needed," Miss Taylor braving another of Simon's pours. "I'm the one who stands accused, my excessive moralizing too long my heart's tyrant, my head and my heart in secret disagreement all along."

"But your sermons are so sincere; so-so heart-felt, if you will," a surprised George contends, "which is one of the reasons I shared with Simon my desire to have a talk with you."

"And the other?" Minnie wiping the bottom of her cup before hazarding another sip.

"My brother Melvin," George answers, noting her telltale blush, the sudden light in her hazel eyes. "I want to be of any help possible in furthering your ... your friendship with Melvin. He's too happy of late to watch joy disappear – joy touching on the other reason I sought your ear."

"Perhaps we can help each other on that 'other reason', as you so delicately phrase it," she replies. "For as you probably know, I came up here to do battle for the cause of Christ; to rattle my righteous sabers on the capitol steps in defense of traditional marriage, in defense of the sacred duty of man and wife."

"And I don't take issue with that," Little George soothes, "with the possible exception of your phrase, 'the cause of Christ'. It's my understanding that Saint Paul was the one who preached most radically against the sexual practices of his day, not Jesus; some scholars even postulating that his oft quoted 'thorn in the side' was nothing more than a shaded reference to his own suppressed homosexuality."

"What Sunday School did you attend?" a laughing Simon asks. "My stepmother would have killed to have a student like you; if only to whip you into the fold!"

"So I've heard," George acknowledges passively; a wink for Minnie signaling his shrug of Simon's humor. "But tell me, Miss Taylor, what did you mean by us helping each other?"

"Well," she begins, returning his wink, "you're to help me with a reading list, I believe; and you've just offered to help me with Melvin - whatever that means-"

"He means with that screaming Neanderthal he dragged from my store this morning," Simon interjects, earning a quick glance of disapproval from Little George, his idea of help excepting Simon's graphic disclosures.

"It's the coffee, Miss Taylor; you'll have to excuse him," George intervenes, avoiding mention of Dorothy.

"Minnie," she says, becoming more at ease with this suave young man beside her, with his persona of unvarnished charm, "call me Minnie. Miss Taylor's far too formal for the kind of help we're about to exchange," her cheeks once more a brilliant red for an inference she hasn't intended.

"Okay, Minnie," George agrees, and readily enough, "but before we continue, I think we'd do well to retire to my brother's bar. There's no one there this time of morning; and our absence here will assist Mr. Farley in promoting his own business, instead of ours," the remark prompting laughter. "We can return at your leisure," he adds, "for if there's one thing at which Simon is expert, it's what I call 'book battling': the collecting of 'authorities' on a given subject until all sides are covered, all positions entrenched. That way, you can play God Himself, looking down on the skirmish with a compassionate eye for the warring ill-informed."

"Well, I don't know much about your war of words," Minnie following his lead and standing up, "but I do know this: you have a minister's flair for the illustration."

"Is that what they call it where you come from?" Simon jokes, shoving back his chair to follow them to the back door - George on the lookout for trouble. "Around here, we call it lying!"

"Like I said," George parries, peering through the small square of glass in the door to be sure they're still alone, "if there is one thing at which Simon is expert ... it isn't flattery!"

We are not endowed with real life till the heart be touched.
(Hawthorne)

XXXIV

My Plainfield food emporium hangs from a pre-cipitous rock over our babbling river. Once a thriving gristmill, the unpainted, wooden structure was an enterprise, no doubt, prospering cartloads beyond what my restaurant and bar can aspire to, the gristmill's great dripping buckets driving a veritable wheel of fortune compared to the squeaking turn of my spit. But with the natural occurrence of rapids attendant to such drops in the river, the waterside deck of my smokehouse bar can be spirited. Especially when Spring starts nursing the mother mountains, their snow-swollen slopes feeding the newborn stream its life-giving rivulets; the writhing, untrained river kicking up a maddening spray, dousing my alfresco imbibers with occasional sobering showers – the sousing effect of the river's awakening effectively awaking the soused.

This September morn has other delights to share, my perch over the water like a painter's palette to daub the forested hills: locust and maple, sumac and birch, all wet from the press of the artist's brush – a work I would dally to admire were it not for the footsteps approaching my deck with ever-increasing urgency.

"Melvin?"

From somewhere inside booms the voice of my brilliant sibling; that he would be here so soon after his meeting with Minnie, curbing my expectations.

"On the deck" I yell over the river's music; reluctant to turn from the vibrant Van Gogh now fading to an Ansel Adams, the eerie emptiness of a Moon and Half Dome done up in silver-gelatin - nature, too, a spirit haunting swathed in the spectral past. "Out here on the deck!" I shout again; the weight in my heart becoming as heavy as the double, iron-hinged doors about to spill Little George from the bar.

"I take it you haven't been here before," I hear him say, alerting me to another's presence - to my shock and immediate revival, Minnie breezing through the double doors, my delight overwhelming restraint.

"We meet again!" I cry, my arms outstretched as though to continue our dance, our embrace - our life changing kiss.

George's unabashed smile forgiving my absurdity, his hand a guide on Minnie's shoulder. "And the joy continues," he mutters entre nous, a sunny secret with which Minnie concurs, her easy smile, and quickened step to be in my arms, so natural it seems she's never left.

"You've missed your calling, Melvin," she bubbles, her soft cheek a feather against mine. "You should be a performer, employ your talent for music."

"Darling," I whisper in her ear, emboldened by her nearness, "you are my music, my heart's abiding refrain; any one else but a toneless, clashing cymbal."

My arms are reluctant to let her go; George giving them every opportunity not to:

"I have exams to write, essays to grade ... a thousand other things to do besides be in your way," he offers politely, stepping for the open doors to prove his intent.

"Nooo," I falter, my hesitance but a small indication of the larger favor I'm granting. "I ... we want you to stay-" Minnie coming to my aid:

"That's right, George. We've yet to address that 'other reason'. Remember?"

"You mean his wanderlust?" I tease, "his daydreams of greener pastures? Simon told me, big brother," I add, addressing George, "told me what you should've told me yourself."

"Poppycock!" he chortles, shutting the old mill doors before joining us at the railing. "There's no truth to that, Melvin. I was just planting seeds, irrigating the field; the certainty of Simon relaying my feigned discontent to the Godhard dean as certain as the dean's recurring visits. The old fellow's a fixture in Simon's store every Saturday."

"And this for what gain?" I ask, relieved by his explanation.

"The same as any good farmer's," George's eyes cast down with boyish mortification, "for a bumper crop; for a raise come next month's meeting of the trustees," his voice strengthening with conviction. "Somebody's got to keep you from drowning in the river of debt you've dug for yourself. Even your peppercorns aren't what they're cracked up to be, your vision of Black-N-Blue Bar-B-Q more a nightmare than a-"

"Financial woes?" Minnie breaks in, her solicitous eyes worth more than the national debt. "Maybe what you need is a mission," she suggests, glancing appreciatively at nature's bounty surrounding us, "an agenda ... an inspiration ... one like Jesus gave Peter when He said, 'Feed my sheep.'"

My thoughts return immediately to Peter's vision - to Otis Redding; George's agreement with Minnie so ready and rash he stumbles over his words:

"Maybe - maybe you can talk some sense into his stubborn head, Minnie; succeed where another woman failed," Minnie leaving his blunder unaddressed.

"I've been thinking of selling," I venture, "putting my finger to the wind."

"With your family's Harvard polish, and my evangelical bent," Minnie exclaims, "we could revive the Yankee's appetite for southern spoils, host a gala event; a Plantation Party, maybe; a Savannah Soiree, or a Richmond Roast; one where carpetbaggers will have the rugs pulled out from under them!"

"Selling, and selling out, are two different things," my brother notes, perplexity creasing his brow. "Why would we want to hark back to such unsettling times? why regress from minister to minstrel? from nabbing souls to tapping soles-?"

"That's it!" a jubilant Minnie cries. "That's it! You've smitten the rock! Parted the waters!"

"What do you mean?" I query - George too astonished to respond.

"The harking back!" she rhapsodizes. "The unsettling times! Your Onion River gristmill could be the ferryman's dock on the River Styx!

Charon's dock! Think about it - the veritable prow from which to hail the dead!"

"The most enchanting idea I've ever heard!" my excitement building, "... assuming you're willing to hazard your ministry by berating our deviltry here; to broadcast our goings-on like we're the very keepers of hell's gates. You know, stir up a backlash, get Black-N-Blue some national attention, some hungry protestors to order sandwiches while they're picketing."

George is thunderstruck, his furrowed brow putting Rodin to shame, *The Thinker* cogitating, choosing, from among the furniture of his mind, a sturdy bench from our New England past:

"'The quality of the imagination is to flow and not to freeze,'" George's scholarly Emerson quote halting our errant imagination. "You can take any trip you wish, so long as its name isn't guilt," he lectures, "you can even hope for the surprise of success. Why? Because, 'All men live by truth, and stand in need of expression' ... yet another Emerson adage."

"Your kind monition notwithstanding," I retort, "we're only toying with ideas, George. Sometimes a bad idea can lead to a good one, you know."

"Granted," George nodding furtively at Minnie, "but when a good idea is also a beauty, one had best claim it before Fate has time to measure it untenable-"

"Fate?" I interrupt, Minnie shooting a glance from me to George, then back again. "Should there be such a measurement, George, I dare say it would be by one of your swingers of philosophical yardsticks, by one or your long dead but oft quoted authors-"

Minnie taking both of my hands in hers, peering into my eyes for the truth she presumes I'm avoiding. "Which is not to imply that George is anything but your touchstone, Melvin; your brother in more than the literal sense. He cares for you. Loves you, in fact; the very word bringing to bear my own heart's cry for expression!" her eyes closing for my expected kiss.

"Aaaah," George's restrained tone a gesture of respect, "for some of us, a library isn't big enough to hold what our hearts wish to expound; your kiss expressing with ease what no author could hope to phrase. And yet ... well, yes," he goes on, after a pause, "yes, I deem it proper to bring this up in Miss Taylor's presence-"

"Bring what up?" I ask, any subject other than Minnie unwelcome.

"Your dream, Melvin ... your ideal life ... your-" Minnie murmuring:

"Is it a dream with room for me?"

"You are my dream," I promise, turning my brother's comment to benefit.

"I agree," George too near to miss our exchange. "Minnie could well be the unseen wind in your sails, the inspiration she was alluding to earlier."

"I've been called a lot of things," Minnie coos, cuddling close in my arms, "but never 'the unseen wind.'"

"That's because 'unseen' is not applicable to you, my sweet," I say, hoping my dream forgotten – George unrelenting:

"Nor is failure, if I read her right. No, Minnie could be the magic that turns the dream to reality, the faith that inspires its achievement; all this but a metaphor for Melvin's wish to be an artist."

"You don't say!" Minnie gasps, pushing away to regard me with awe – George augmenting the effect with another of his ever-ready quotes:

"'The experience of each new age requires a new confession, and the world seems always waiting for its poet.' Emerson again," he appends glee-fully. "Can't go wrong by the man. And a poet, too."

"So, is poetry your art?" Minnie questions, askew in my arms, staring up me like I'm a bronze to be admired.

"Poetry?" George erupting in laughter. "No, but I should like to review what Melvin might verse ... the effort could be worth its entertainment!"

"Then, what is your medium?" Minnie persists. "Is it-"

"Watercolors, my dear," George capitulates, "watercolors; and with an emphasis on Titanium White!" Minnie turning Ruby Red. "You should see him with a set of brushes. A one-man gallery, he is; and especially if he's strokin' to music."

"To music?" her stare softening to an appreciative gaze.

"Yep! His favorite's a gospel quartet called White Soul ... ever hear of them?" Minnie realizing she's been duped.

"Sure have; but I won't buy an album because the bass is rumored to be gay," she shoots back - George protesting:

"I was just having some fun. Melvin and I tease each other all the time. We don't mean anything by it."

"Nor do I," she says, "and just as White Soul is fictitious, so is my bias for gays - since meeting you."

"Yes," I interrupt, and with a tinge of shame at her rebuke, "but we only tease privately. Never would we dishonor one another by allowing a stranger to think we ... I guess what we're really making fun of is the world at large. Bigotry at large-"

"Which, in my opinion, is just another form of bigotry," she counters, her eyes losing their approbatory glow. "If you're going to address the world, fellows, spend your energy on its needs, not its-"

"Are you the same reverend Taylor I've heard on the radio?" George interjects mischievously. "The minister who consigns homosexuals to the darkest cellars of hell?"

"No, as a matter-of-fact," Minnie punctuating her denial with another kiss, "I am not the same reverend Taylor, thanks to the two of you. I am Miss Minnie Ruth Taylor, late of ignorance and currently on the mend. And who knows? Perhaps soon to be late of the airways, too, if my reformation isn't well received."

They are slaves who dare not be
In the right with two or three.
(Lowell)

XXXV

MINNIE HAS BEEN GONE FOR MORE THAN A MONTH, and still her broadcasts make no reference to my restaurant; only the inclusion of my name on her radio ministry prayer list - a kind of long distance fondle, one even Marconi would sanction since Italians believe "love is in the air". But I'm not Italian, and my Black-N-Blue B-B-Q needs something more substantial than fondling, my temporary salvation the busloads of southerners up to video the Green Mountain colors. "Leaf-peepers" the locals label them, Vermont happily accepting their dollars, the annual pilgrimage of drive-by viewers a welcomed windfall making money growing on trees a fairytale come true.

But somehow, a good New England stout and an Appalachian prayer list aren't the party mixers my customers crave. Local patronage is falling off faster than the pork on my sizzling ribs. Miss Taylor's taped sermons, repeating over my establishment's sound system, are received less favorably than tepid beer, the evangelist's lilting lectures on celestial tranquility eerily amiss amidst the smoke of mesquite and the aroma of bubbling cobblers. Such earthy enjoyments are more akin to B B King's Lucille, or the wailing rasp of Muddy Waters. My last hope is my own one-man show behind the bar: my song and dance about Black-N-Blue being a lucrative retirement for some swaggering Texan, industrious Okie or embarrassed Arkansan, producing sparks of interest most every night - said sparks the brighter, I've noticed, the stronger I make the drinks.

Long convinced the absence of something merely begs its introduction, I began my business on impulse, discovering too late that if anything is to go begging it will soon be me. But if my dream is false, my hope is not; a bold young man at my bar, several weeks back, proving to be the very solution my faith imagined.

Bunker is his name. Bunker Hill. (Just his historical handle enough to provoke conversation.) Within minutes of swapping names, I learn the young man's father is a Godhard alumnus. For this, I keep our discourse alive, the surname Tenklei coming round at last (Bunker only using it formally). I share with Bunker my saga of past lives, including tales of his father. Two days later, Bunker is checking into Godhard while I'm banking his check, both the son and his money finding a home.

Because no house is a home absent romance, Bunker is soon playing the knight to Pamela, spanning the moat to her attention - a simple endeavor, indeed, given her attention span. But brief or no, the jump is made (or the "step taken", to avoid that connotation). And tonight, I'm sitting with Dorothy and my mother at my former bar, celebrating Bunker's timely investment (and his skill at making time). Bunker's engagement to Pamela is a cause célèbre, not a few of the locals either a-gag or agog over yet another romance in black and white.

From the leisure side of the bar, I ogle the new barkeep, her liquid eyes hinting reptilian, her rainbow cosmetics chameleon. I haven't the faintest interest in the bumbling girl – my mind on an angel writing sermons in Appalachia – but my mother is intrigued by the red-haired trainee.

"The brash young lady could well be Thelma's daughter, had the old firebrand ever claimed one. Her flip asides," Mother observes quietly, "her curses if crossed, her torrent of adjectives for most anything catching her eye, all attributes of Thelma Peabody."

I whisper to Mother that the barkeep's birth date most likely postdates Thelma's death; a supposition with disturbing potential, if Mother will accept reincarnation. But a sudden disturbance prevents developing the theme:

"It's a wonderful day in the neighborhood!" my sister cries from the entryway, Pamela announcing her own bumbling presence - her cleavage announcing a pendant, heart-shaped diamond.

"Look what Mom gave me!" she boasts, her auditors aghast at Mother's overt generosity, my sister's trio of gifts in provocative display as she swishes by, thrusting between the bar and the barkeep to preen before the backbar mirror. "Bunker's daddy gave it to Momma before I was even born, and-and now she's giving it to me! Isn't it grand!" the diamond's history, and Pamela's bumptious telling of it, piquing Dot.Com. to go live and viral.

"Grand!" Dorothy shrills, a whirl on her stool punctuated with breaking glass - with my groan, as I grab my gin-doused crotch. "Grand, indeed!" she rants, unaware of peripheral casualties. "I always wondered who had the family jewels. You can take my word for it: Melvin doesn't!"

Little George appearing magically at the door, as if summoned by Dorothy's screams – that I'm blotting down the front of my trousers, completing the illusion.

"I could hear you yelling from the parking lot," George grumbles, "but this time I knew better."

"You knew Better?" I echo, extracting a twist of lime from my fly.

"I knew if trouble were brewing, Dorothy would be the instigator, not the victim," Little George selecting a stool at the safe end of the bar. "Dad's right behind me, if you need to straighten up a bit. You know, get tempers under control - pretend you're happy to be here tonight."

"I am," I protest, wiping my stool, "I'm happy to be on this side of the bar. I'm happy for Dorothy, too. Drinks aren't free anymore."

"Oh yeah," Pamela breaks in, employing the mirror to flash a supercilious glance, "I'm not supposed to tell, but Mom and Dad had a call from Miss Taylor this afternoon; something about a secret."

"Well?" the redhead prods, the rest of us having reasons to pretend disinterest.

"W-e-l-l?" Pamela mimics with a contemptuous smirk, " ... that's it. Like I told you: it's secret."

"Meaning, you don't know," Little George quips. "As far as you're concerned the call was cryptic, mystifying; its purpose-"

"Yeah ... that's it," Pamela chimes. "You guessed it. I heard Momma say something about crib ticks - or was it bed bugs? No. Cradles. Yeah, cradles and thieves."

"I know your cradle was robbed, missy," Dorothy steams, pounding her fist on the bar for a drink. "In fact, your entire family's been robbed. All of you: what with you missing your sense, Little George's senses amiss, and Melvin not having the sense to miss anything."

"Am not!" Pamela objects, coming round to take a stool by Little George. "Well ... all right, if you must know, I have missed once since Booker's been-" Little George clamping his hand over Pamela's mouth as the youngster behind the bar lets go a cry:

"Mr. O'Mal-leeee!" A beatific George Senior standing in the doorway's aura of light like an immortal just down to share joy.

"Your powers of observation are inscrutable!" teases Little George - and with real relief, too, Dorothy a hungry tigress in pursuit of a kill.

"Shall we stay at the bar until Booker arrives?" our father asks, towering behind Little George, "or find our table? Has Melvin said anything to-?" he inquires soto voce, bending for my brother's ear. "You know what I mean. The restaurant ambiance might be more congenial."

"He hasn't, Dad," Little George assures under his breath, "I think he's waiting for Dorothy to tell him what she knows he should be telling her – not that it matters. Melvin and Minnie are the talk of the village; and Dorothy's usually the first to know most anything around here. You can bet she's just waiting for that special moment, one pregnant with-"

"Shush!" George warns, bending closer, "the word frightens me, son. Your brother could be so easily trapped."

"Now there's an advantage I have over Melvin!" Little George mumbles - our father stepping over to stand behind Dorothy, his big arm weighting my shoulder like the problem vibrating beside me.

"Drop your drink, son?" he asks, feeling the glass crunch under his feet.

"He's dropped everything, Mr. O'Malley," Dorothy interjects, giving me a fiendish wink, "... even me!" Dad turning to Mother, avoiding the challenge, leaving me to play the victim - or fight:

"Going in, or staying here?" he asks as nonchalantly as any happily married man might do.

"Here, I suppose," my saintly mother decides. "The night is young ... no need to hurry; and Booker has yet to join us. Probably still working on his speech, his presentation."

"Oh yes, I forgot," Dad claiming the stool at Mother's side, leaving me alone with my plight. "And isn't she going to be surprised, too? Both stones from the same-"

"George!" Mother's index finger at his lips, "... you're going to spoil the moment! The moment a girl dreams of, darling; the moment-"

"Aw, go on Dad," Pamela butts in, presuming she's the dreamer in question, "because if it's about that moment, well ... what can I say? 'He that is without sin cast the first stone'?"

"Or better yet," contributes Dorothy, giving a kick to my shin, "for our present little drama we could say, 'He that is without sin stone the cast first.'"

"But that's not fair, Dot.Com," Pamela pouts, "you're always the first to get stoned."

"No doubt about that!" I crack, returning the shin kick under the bar.

"'If a man will begin with certainties he shall end in doubts,'" Little George philosophies, my grimace bringing him up short; though I'm grateful for his ready aid.

"Thanks, brother," I retort, "but we need something stronger than the old Sage of Concord to season this barroom drivel. We need younger spirits, like an eighteen-year-old single malt; or a three-fingered whiskey with a-"

"Ah! Mr. Emerson, you thought, eh?" Little George counters. "Fooled you this time, Melvin. Francis Bacon, it was; and a quote for the occasion if ever I conjured one."

"You mean for Bunker, I presume ... for Bunker's occasion."

"With certainty!" Little George puns, "but one could draw other allusions, as well - that is, if one began something with certainty once upon a time, only to end up in-"

"Say no more," I interrupt; words to finish the line flashing before my eyes, "divorce court", "insane asylum", "funeral home", the mental montage frightening me into a martini - into two martini's: one each for Dorothy and Minnie.

"Another twist?" the redhead asks; the annoyance of Dorothy's empty glass, twirling on the hardwood bar, begging intervention as a muffled cry is heard from behind the coatrack in the entryway:

"Chubby Checker, eat your heart out!"

Booker appearing out of nowhere, a monstrous grin announcing his pleasure: one hand, raised aloft, waving a solitaire of disturbing size.

"The only twist allowed in here tonight," he declares, rushing proudly to Pamela's side, "is the one that will put this on my sweet love's finger; and her love forever in my care!"

So saying, he reaches for her hand, bestowing on her ring finger the pendant's twin: a three-carat, heart-shaped diamond.

"And what do you say, dear?" Mother coos, the rest of us in stunned silence.

"Th-thank you?" Pamela stammers, ogling the mirror in frantic awe.

"No, no, no," Mother blushing for this dense child of hers. "I mean, do you say 'I will', or 'Yes, darling', or-?"

"Oh, I say that every night, Mamma!" Pamela gushes, flashing the ring and the pendant under Dorothy's envious eyes. "Booker has this sweet way of asking ... a look in his eyes ... a pitiful 'Please help me' look, like a little boy caught with his pants down-"

"Pamela!" the two Georges object in chorus, her theme a counter-point to propriety – Dorothy striking up a variation:

"At least Booker has a peg to hang 'em on," she snipes, "a reason to take off his pants."

"Another remark like that and Melvin might surprise you," Little George contends, warming to her fiery tongue.

"Another gin, and I can guarantee it," the redhead shaking the bloom off a Tangueray in her zeal to make it happen.

"One would do better to have reasons to keep them on," my ever-proper mother responds, "even more so in winter weather."

"Thank you," I chime, reaching past Dorothy to give Mother's hand a pat – simultaneously realizing my own conception may have required a dropped pair of pants. "Dot.Com was just having her usual."

"Another gin?" Dorothy asks, brightening to my darkening scowl.

"No," I grouse, withdrawing my arm before she can mistake my reach for a hug. "By 'usual' I mean your fun at my expense."

The r-r-r-ring of the backbar phone is almost lost in the rousing refrain of *Whiskey River take my Mind*, the redhead feeding the jukebox in hopes a dance might reveal what the gin has not. Stumbling round the end of the bar, I answer:

"Bunker's. May I book you?"

"Only if you promise me a sequel," a melodious voice murmurs – my commanding view of the room in the mirror as nothing compared to my heart's unfolding vision:

"How - did - you - know - it - was - me?" I pant, motioning the redhead to muzzle Willie Nelson. "How-"

"The same way you recognized me, my darling: by the joy apparent in your voice."

"No. I mean, yes. Of course. But no, how did you know I'd be here?"

"I spoke with your parents this afternoon. They told me the exciting news - Pamela's engagement-"

"Of course; and it is exciting-"

"And the sale of your business?"

"Yes ... I've been trying to call-"

"But Dorothy prevented you?"

"Yes. No ... me. It's me."

Would you turn off Willie, please!

"You?"

I don't know how ... don't think I can turn a man off!

"Yes ... me. I've been doing battle with myself; struggling to find my way, my path-"

"Alone, we can barely see our feet, much less the path they should take."

"Meaning?"

Would somebody please turn down the jukebox? or play another song?

"Meaning, 'Where two or three are gathered together in His name'-"

"Oh ... I was hoping for another-"

"Wedding?"

"No. Yes ... no, I mean-"

"Then, what?"

"Another visit. Another trip up here to help me find my way."

"But you don't need me for that. You know already, sweetheart. Listen to your heart - the heart for which I yearn to belong."

"And you do. I mean, I do ... I mean-"

"I know, darling ... but-"

I'll tell the man to turn the jukebox way down low ... And you can tell your friend there with you, he'll have to go-

"Minnie, I'll insure it. I'll take Dot.Com home right now, then call you back."

"OK.

Would somebody please turn UP the jukebox?

This world clean fails me: still I yearn...
(Melville)

XXXVI

IT ALL BEGINS THE DAY OF MY FUNERAL, MY SERVICE
looming as the aegis of all my regrets; for it's during my funeral that
Dorothy appears, as petulant as ever. Dorothy crossed over before me - her
death as instantaneous as our sudden impact with a tree. A heated argument had driven us from Pamela's party, and straight into a stubborn birch
- our impromptu reunion occasioned by my death the following day.

But it's onerously apparent Dorothy has kept up with the goings-on,
her postmortem antics in step with the latest events, Reverend Minnie
Ruth Taylor - her sweet soprano trilling like a coloratura in the anguish of
my eulogy - hardly more surprised than I am as Dorothy begins demonstrating her savvy.

Falling rose petal soft on listening ears, my sweetheart's pleasing elocution graces my pain with tenderness, prompting regard of my mother:
her expression stoic, her blue eyes sad - but growing suddenly alert as
Dorothy's magical "thought imposition" finds a voice in the reverend, old
Mother Eve's fascination with the unknown as nothing compared to the
stark fear of knowledge in my dear mother's eyes.

"Now as paradoxical as it may seem," Minnie's soprano descending to
a stressful, unnatural pitch, "profound thoughts can be more easily entertained in a comfortable setting. Why, even Thomas a Kempis could have
improved his philosophy if he had only allowed himself a few luxuries. Yes

... and suspecting this, our Melvin ... Aaah! our Melvin," her irksome bass rumbles, "our Melvin worked feverishly for conspicuous success – only to succumb to the fever.

"And as if to prove his lesson unlearned, he's succumbed twice, my dear ones. Twice born and twice dead, our Melvin. *Twice Melvin!*" Minnie shouts - Dot.Com performing under the tyranny of habit, bolstering my new beginning.

"Goodbye, whoever you are now," I beam over her hostile thoughts, "I am not vanquished, only diminished ... and fully recoverable. See ya next time!"

And just like that, I'm enjoying a specter nectar in the Galaxy Lounge, courtesy of Old Geezer and Old Faithful.

Thank the Creator, some things never change!